Education for Administrative Careers
in Government Service

Education for Administrative Careers in Government Service

Editor

STEPHEN B. SWEENEY, Ph.D.

*Director, Fels Institute of Local and State Government,
and Professor of Governmental Administration,
University of Pennsylvania*

Assistant Editor

THOMAS J. DAVY, Ph.D.

*Educational and Research Associate, Fels Institute of Local and
State Government, and Assistant Professor of Political Science,
University of Pennsylvania*

Consultant

LLOYD M. SHORT, Ph.D.

*Director, Public Administration Center, and
Professor of Political Science,
University of Minnesota*

Philadelphia
University of Pennsylvania Press

JF
1338
.A2
S9

Printed in the United States of America
American Book–Stratford Press, Inc., New York

Special Acknowledgment

This acknowledges the special contributions of the educational staff of the Fels Institute to the program herein described and to this publication. This staff is composed of Associate Professors William C. Beyer and George S. Blair, and Assistant Professors Fredrick T. Bent, James G. Coke, and Thomas J. Davy. Each member devoted a major portion of his time during 1956 and 1957 to this project. The individual and joint contributions of the staff members were unique in a number of ways. Working in close cooperation through frequent staff conferences, they formulated the plans and programs of the two workshops and the conference, did the research, and prepared the working drafts of the discussion outlines and final papers. All elements of the program, which were the primary responsibility of Drs. Bent and Davy, were subjected to extensive group review and criticism by the staff during this period of concentrated activity. Thus, the events as they unfolded and the evolving drafts of the papers were the result of a concerted staff effort. This special acknowledgment is to express the appreciation due to the members of this team for their individual and joint contributions.

STEPHEN B. SWEENEY,
Program Coordinator

Foreword

What is the best education and training for those aspiring to careers of administrative leadership in local and state government? This volume presents the results of a research-conference program conducted during 1956–1957 to find some answers to this question.

The program was a cooperative effort of the American Society for Public Administration, the International City Managers' Association, and the Fels Institute of Local and State Government, University of Pennsylvania. It was one of the activities held in observance of the seventy-fifth anniversary of the Wharton School and the twentieth anniversary of the Fels Institute. A special grant from the Samuel S. Fels Fund financed the program. Professor Lloyd M. Short, Chairman of the Political Science Department and Director of the Public Administration Center, University of Minnesota, served as general consultant. The academic staff of the Fels Institute did the research and prepared the initial drafts of the working papers.

This program was the culmination of informal discussions over a period of years among political scientists especially interested in education for public administration careers. These discussions indicated the need for a rather thorough reconsideration of the fundamental assumptions and elements of preparation for such careers. Under Professor Short's guidance, there evolved a proposal for a year-long program of research and conferences involving both administrators and educators. This proposal was enthusiastically accepted by the Fels Fund and the University of Pennsylvania. The Committee on Education and Training of the American Society for Public Administration, under the chairmanship of Luther Gulick, endorsed the proposal, and the Council of the Society agreed to cooperate. So too did the Committee on Professional Training of the Inter-

national City Managers' Association, under the chairmanship of L. P. Cookingham, City Manager of Kansas City,
Missouri.

In September 1956, Professor Short and Jeptha J. Carrell of the ICMA staff met with the Fels Institute staff
to review alternative plans for the program. Suggestions
were then submitted to a Steering Committee later that
month. The members of this Committee were: John
Lederle, University of Michigan; Roscoe C. Martin, Syracuse University; Henry Reining, Jr., University of Southern
California and then President of the American Society for
Public Administration; Wallace S. Sayre, Columbia University; Lloyd M. Short, University of Minnesota; York
Willbern, then of the University of Alabama and now of
Indiana University; and Fredrick T. Bent, Thomas J.
Davy, and Stephen B. Sweeney, of the University of Penn-
sylvania.

The Steering Committee adopted the following objectives for the program:

1. To enable educators through coordinated study and
discussion to formulate desirable emphases in educational
curricula and to identify methods appropriate for preparing pre-service students for professional careers in local and
state government administration;

2. As a basis for this study and discussion, to elicit from
local and state administrators their concepts of the position
and role of administrative officers, and of the knowledge,
skills, and attitudes they should have;

3. To suggest guide-lines for governmental policy relating to the recruitment and placement of people trained for
professional careers in local and state government;

4. Through publication of the proceedings of this program, to provide educators and administrators with a basis
for evaluating the assumptions and elements of career development programs.

The Committee agreed that the most feasible arrangement for realizing these purposes would be a program of workshops and conferences. One or more workshops composed of leading administrators in local and state government throughout the country should be conducted to formulate a comprehensive definition of the position and role of administrative officers. Substantive outlines reflecting current thinking in public administration regarding the administrator's leadership role, his major responsibilities, and the kinds of knowledge and skill he needs should be prepared by the Fels Institute staff for discussion at these workshops.

These workshops were then to be followed, the Committee agreed, by a conference of educators. This conference should explore the nature of the curriculum, teaching methods, the preparation of the specialist for general administration, the relationship of higher education and governmental employers, and perhaps other aspects of education for administrative careers. Discussions at this conference, the Committee suggested, should center on papers prepared jointly by members of the Fels Institute staff and others in the field, so that the conference might elicit as broad a representation of views as possible. The conclusions of the administrators' workshops were to be made available to the authors of the conference papers.

Finally, the Steering Committee agreed that the principal focus of both the administrators' workshops and the educators' conference should be career preparation for "administrative policy-making positions." A statement of criteria for identifying such positions follows this foreword.

On the basis of the general objectives and procedures discussed by the Steering Committee, two administrators' workshops and one educators' conference were held during 1956–1957. The first workshop, composed of city managers from all sections of the country, was held in St. Louis,

Missouri, November 24 and 25, 1956. The workshop was organized in cooperation with the International City Managers' Association and was chaired by Mr. Cookingham. The second workshop, composed primarily of a mixed group of administrators from larger local and state governmental jurisdictions, and from both staff and line activities, was held in Chicago, March 20 and 21, 1957. This workshop was chaired by Professor Short, and was organized and conducted in cooperation with the American Society for Public Administration. These workshops together involved approximately fifty principal administrators representing all sections of the country and a wide variety of administrative situations, and they consumed about twenty-five hours of intensive discussion about the position and role of the administrative policy-making officer. Part II of this volume presents the summaries of these discussions. Also included in this section is an address, "Administrative Leadership in Local and State Government: Its Meaning and Educational Implications," given by Stephen K. Bailey at the annual in-service banquet of the Fels Institute, September 13, 1956.

The conference of educators was held at the University of Pennsylvania, June 12 through 14, 1957. Professor Short was General Chairman, and the conference was attended by approximately 150 people. Part I contains the papers presented at the conference, and the discussion summary for each session prepared by each of the panel chairmen. Because of its significance to the purpose of the conference, the address, "Partnership for a Better Public Service," delivered by the Honorable George M. Leader, Governor of Pennsylvania, to the winter commencement of the University of Pennsylvania in February 1957, is also included.

This program was built upon the ideas and efforts of a large number of people, including many who were not able to participate directly in the proceedings. To all of those

who through the years have worked toward a better understanding of public administration and especially toward
higher standards of education and training for administrative careers in the public service, we express our appreciation.

We are deeply grateful to the following people for their
special contributions to the program: the members of the
Samuel S. Fels Fund, whose financial grant made the program possible; the late C. Arthur Kulp, former Dean of the
Wharton School, University of Pennsylvania, who authorized the program and gave it his full support and valuable
advice; Lloyd M. Short, who suggested the program, and
who advised on all of its aspects; the members of the Steering Committee, whose specific contribution is described
above; Orin F. Nolting, Executive Director of the International City Managers' Association, and Jeptha J. Carrell of
his staff, who helped to plan and organize the workshop for
city managers in St. Louis; Robert J. M. Matteson, Executive Director of the American Society for Public Administration, and Luther Gulick, Chairman of the ASPA's Committee on Education and Training, who gave their support
to the program; Don Bowen, Assistant Director of ASPA,
who participated in the workshops and the conference, and
who was especially helpful in organizing the workshop in
Chicago.

We would record our thanks also to Mr. Cookingham
and the city managers who participated in the St. Louis
workshop, as well as to the administrators who took part in
the Chicago workshop. Their names and affiliations are
noted in Appendix III. Their well-articulated, comprehensive statement of the administrator's position and role
should be a valuable guide to all concerned with his education and training for many years to come.

We express our deep appreciation to those who made
the educators' conference so rewarding an experience for

all concerned, especially the authors of the papers, the panel chairmen, and the panel discussants. They are listed in Appendix II. We acknowledge also the excellent staff assistance throughout the program by the Fels Institute's faculty, government service consultants and administrative and secretarial staffs. A final word of appreciation is due to Miss Margaret M. Henrich and Miss Elizabeth S. Micheals for their continual service in supplying extensive library and administrative assistance respectively throughout the project.

One of the most satisfying aspects of this program has been the remarkable teamwork among the administrators, the educators, and the professional associations. This volume clearly demonstrates, we think, the advantages of a close and continuing relationship. It is hoped that the educators' conference will be considered a precedent for periodic meetings among those concerned with preparation for careers in public administration. As one reviews the proceedings of both the workshops and the conference, it is apparent that many important aspects of administrative career preparation could only be touched upon and that further analysis and discussion of them would be highly desirable

S. B. S.

Philadelphia, Pa.
May 1, 1958

Criteria for Identifying
Administrative Policy-Making Positions

(This statement was formulated by the Fels Institute staff in consultation with Professor Short. It was sent to approximately twenty-five administrators throughout the country for their comments. The consensus of their replies was that to be classified as "administrative policy-making," a position should satisfy most of these criteria.)

An administrative policy-making officer is one who satisfies the following criteria:

1. He bears a primary responsibility in the planning of the programs and activities of his agency or jurisdiction;

2. He has an effective voice in the development of the budget of his agency or jurisdiction;

3. He exercises appointing authority or advises on appointments to activities under his direction;

4. He is responsible for administrative policies and systems that are essential to the accomplishment of the major purposes of the parent agency or jurisdiction;

5. He is responsible for the direction and general supervision of a significant amount of the manpower resource involved in the programs of the parent agency or jurisdiction. Some of his subordinates perform important discretionary duties, and others perform routine duties;

6. He is recognized by the executive officer, and the legislative body, and in small and medium-sized municipalities by the general public, as responsible for a major activity, whether it be staff, managerial, or line, and is expected to provide administrative leadership for this activity;

7. The adequacy of performance of his subordinates is as much affected by his concern for administrative matters (budget, recruitment, selection and training of personnel, organization and procedures, etc.) as by his concern for the

substantive and technical problems of the activity for which he is responsible (land use analysis in a planning agency, cost accounting system in finance department, epidemic control in health department, etc.).

Contents

plex Government; The Shortage of Qualified
Personnel; Public Attitudes toward Govern-
ment; The Community of Interest between the
Campus and the Capitol; Importance of Higher
Education at the Undergraduate Level; Gradu-
ate Education for Public Administration; Does
Public Administration Measure up to the Needs
of Our Time? Toward a Synthesis of Research,
Teaching, and Practice; Summary

SUPPLEMENT

PART II. THE POSITION AND ROLE OF THE
ADMINISTRATIVE POLICY-MAKING OFFICER

Research Program to Provide Framework for
Evaluation; Administrators Define Elements of
Positions for Which People Are Being Trained;
Career Development Requires both Pre-Service
and In-Service Preparation; Leadership Role
Discussed in Contexts of Internal and External
Relationships; Administrators Identified Four
Major Categories of Responsibilities; Adminis-
trator Has Responsibility to Work with Agen-
cies and Groups outside of His Jurisdiction;
Knowledge of Governmental Environment Es-
pecially Stressed; Six Classes of Essential Administrative Skills Identified; Differences according to Basic Variables Noted

SUPPLEMENT

APPENDIX

PART I

Education for Administrative
Policy-Making Careers

I

Introduction:
Educational Organization for Instruction
in Public Administration

LLOYD M. SHORT *
University of Minnesota

INTRODUCTION

It was in 1938–39 that George Graham made a survey of university education for public administration under the auspices of the Commitee on Public Administration of the Social Science Research Council. His excellent review of some of the specific training programs then in operation and his analysis of the problems encountered by the colleges and universities which had entered this emerging and rapidly growing field of education were very informative and challenging. In the intervening years the number of training programs has multiplied and the nature of such programs has been modified in the light of experience, new knowledge about the field, and a re-thinking of the problems involved.[1]

* *Lloyd M. Short, Ph.D., is Professor of Political Science, Chairman of the Department of Political Science and Director of the Public Administration Center, University of Minnesota.*

[1] Graham, George A., *Education for Public Administration*, Public Administration Service, Chicago, 1941. For more recent articles and surveys, see the following: Walker, Robert A., "The Universities and the Public Service," *Am. Pol. Sci. Rev.* 39:926-933 (Oct. 1945); Fesler, James W. "Undergraduate Training for the Public Service," *Am. Pol. Sci. Rev.* 41:507-517 (June, 1947); Greene, Lee S. "Regional Research and Training in Public Administration," *Pub. Adm. Rev.* 7:245-253 (Autumn, 1947); McLean, Joseph E., (ed.) *The Public Service and University Education,* Princeton University Press, 1949, esp. Part V; Graham, George A. "Trends in the Teaching of Public Administration," *Pub. Adm. Rev.* 10:69-77 (Spring, 1950); Martin,

The calling of a conference on Education and Training for Administrative Careers in Local and State Government in June, 1957, in recognition of the 20th anniversary of the Fels Institute of Local and State Government at the University of Pennsylvania, offered an appropriate occasion for an examination of the current status of education for public administration. This particular article is concerned with the institutional setting and ordering of training programs in public administration. Trends in the content of and newer approaches to the study of public administration will be examined in another article. In the preparation of this paper, the writer has had the benefit of a questionnaire survey of graduate education programs in public administration made by a staff member of the Fels Institute of Local and State Government (see appendix). He also has examined the catalogs and special bulletins of approximately 40 colleges and universities offering work in this field, and as the director of a university graduate training program in public administration he has tried to keep in touch with developments at other institutions through personal correspondence, conferences, and professional meetings. No opportunity was available, however, for visits at even a sample of institutions with established programs such as was undertaken by Graham in the study referred to above.

Roscoe C., "Political Science and Public Administration," *Am. Pol. Sci. Rev.,* 46:660-676 (Sept. 1952); *Educational Preparation for Public Administration,* Public Administration Service, Chicago, 1952; Martin, Roscoe C., "Educational Preparation for Public Administration," in *Higher Education,* Office of Education, U.S. Dept. of Health, Education and Welfare, May 1954, pp. 135-146; Waldo, Dwight, *The Study of Public Administration,* Doubleday and Co., Garden City, 1955; Cliffe, Frank B., Jr., *The Higher Teaching of Administrative Sciences in the United States,* mimeo essay prepared for the International Institute of Administrative Sciences, Am. Soc. for Pub. Adm., Chicago, 1956; Millett, John D., "A Critical Appraisal of the Study of Public Administration," *Adm. Sci. Quarterly,* Sept. 1956, pp. 171-188.

UNDERGRADUATE INSTRUCTION IN PUBLIC ADMINISTRATION

With relatively few exceptions, specialized instruction in public administration is given at the graduate level. Undergraduate instruction, when offered, tends to provide a broad, general education in the social sciences with the opportunity for some specialization in public administration, usually as a part of an undergraduate major in political science.[2] Notable exceptions to this general practice are to be found in professional schools of public administration, such as those at American University in Washington, D.C., and the University of Southern California at Los Angeles where an undergraduate major in public administration is offered and where a special effort is made to meet the needs of government employees who have entered the public service without college training and who are desirous of more specialized education. The School of Public Administration of Florida State University also offers an undergraduate major in public administration. Unless indicated otherwise, the remainder of this paper will be concerned with graduate education.

LOCATION OF RESPONSIBILITY FOR PUBLIC ADMINISTRATION TRAINING

Graduate instruction in public administration, in a substantial majority of institutions, is offered as a field of specialization in departments of political science. The School of Government and Public Administration at American University, the School of Government at George

[2] Typical, perhaps, of the role of the liberal arts college in offering instruction in public administration is that expressed by Earl Latham of Amherst College, who, in describing his courses in public administration and administrative law to an alumni meeting some years ago, expressed the view that such courses "are no more vocational than courses in economics, mathematics, or music." Amherst Alumni Council News, December, 1948, p. 45.

Washington University, the School of Public Administration at Florida State, the Harvard Graduate School of Public Administration, the Graduate School of Public Administration and Social Service at New York University, the Woodrow Wilson School of Public and International Affairs at Princeton, and the School of Public Administration at Southern California are examples of the tendency to regard professional education in this field as justifying an educational unit comparable to that in other specialized fields of learning.

In addition to these and other separate professional schools, one finds public administration offered as a department, school, institute, or curriculum in the College of Business Administration, such as at Denver, Georgetown, and Georgia, or in a combined school of business and public administration as at Cornell, Missouri, and Pennsylvania. The Maxwell School of Citizenship and Public Affairs at Syracuse is the social science division of the university and the graduate programs of public administration are the primary responsibility of the Department of Political Science in that school, but the existence of the school with its special emphasis upon preparation for public service activity seems to give it in effect the status of a professional unit. At a number of institutions such as Colorado, Michigan, and Texas, an Institute of Public Administration or Public Affairs or a special curriculum, operating as a separate educational unit or program under an interdepartmental faculty committee, has been set up to provide graduate instruction in this field.

Finally, even in those institutions in which education for public administration remains a function of the department of political science, which is a unit within the college or graduate school of liberal arts, there are interdepartmental committees which function in an advisory or integrating role, thus evidencing the recognition that preparation for a career in public administration is the responsibility of several departments. Also one finds institutes or centers within departments of political science such as those at Boston, Indiana, Minnesota, and Washington, which tend to point up the professional or specialized nature of the training program. The Southern Regional Program in Public Administration, in which the Universities of Alabama, Kentucky, and Tennessee participate, is a unique educational organization in which the departments of political science at each institution have major responsibility.

TYPES OF PROGRAM GOALS

Most of the institutions offering instruction in public administration have as their goal the preparation of the administrative generalist and the staff specialist who may find employment at any level of government—national, state, or local. A few, such as Cornell, Michigan, Minnesota, and Wayne have undertaken to train administrative officers for service in line or functional departments. Cooperative arrangements with professional schools or departments such as public health, engineering, forestry, and social work, have facilitated the education of line administrators. New York University has combined public administration and social service in a single professional school.

CONCENTRATION ACCORDING TO LEVEL OF GOVERNMENT

Location, type of institution, and special financing have influenced the decision as to whether the program will concentrate or at least put major emphasis upon the training of administrators for a particular level of government. It is natural and logical for a state university to emphasize the state and local government service. Urban universities tend to emphasize municipal administration, but of course the universities in Washington, D.C., are an exception to this and several others such as Boston, Wayne, St. Louis, and

Southern California, which are located in cities where there are large concentrations of federal employees, have developed special programs to meet the needs of such persons. Harvard, Princeton, and Yale look to Washington and the national government as the principal user of their graduates in public administration. At Columbia, where graduate study in public administration is a function of the Department of Public Law and Government within the larger Graduate Faculty of Political Science, there has always been a strong interest in municipal government and administration. Pennsylvania, with its Fels Institute of Local and State Government in the Wharton School of Commerce and Finance, has concentrated largely upon the fields of municipal management and state government administration. A number of other universities such as Iowa, Kansas, and Western Reserve stress city management. A few schools of public administration include as one of their objectives the preparation of young people for foreign and international service, but for the most part training for overseas administration is separately organized.

Most of the training programs also undertake to prepare students for service in bureaus of governmental research and quite frequently offer their students some research and field experience through closely allied bureaus of public administration. The former School of Government Management at Denver, now a part of the School of Public Administration in the College of Business Administration, was set up and financed for this particular purpose. In announcing the establishment of a Bureau of Governmental Research at the University of Missouri in 1957, it was pointed out that the new bureau would "offer valuable training to graduate students in research on practical problems of Missouri government."

NATURE OF CURRICULA

The curricula of graduate schools and programs of public administration, though evidencing considerable diversity, reveal a substantial agreement as to the core subjects which are the hallmark of specialized instruction in this field. As the questionnaire data show (see appendix), by far the largest number of institutions reporting prescribe certain courses and permit the student to elect other courses for the balance of his program at the master's degree level. Thus the curriculum tends to be individualized to meet the interests and needs of the student and the requirements of the government service into which he hopes to enter.

Admittedly, similarity in course titles does not necessarily mean similarity in course content, but an examination of bulletins and catalogs leaves one with the impression that such commonly required courses as "administrative organization and management," "Public personnel administration," and "public finance administration" are much the same wherever taught, allowing of course for the individuality of the teacher and the methods of instruction which he employs. The same can be said for courses in constitutional and administrative law which also are frequently required or elected. A course in research methodology and report writing appears to be included in the study programs with increasing frequency. The balance of individualized curricula often include courses drawn from a variety of departments and fields of study but with political science courses predominating.

Those institutions which have established professional schools of public administration, which have relatively liberal admission policies, and which undertake to serve the needs of both pre-service and post-entry students on both a full- and part-time basis, offer a much greater variety and more highly specialized courses. Part-time faculty drawn from the ranks of the specialists often are employed to give such courses. American University, New York University, and the University of Southern California are outstanding examples of this development. By way of contrast, the Harvard Graduate School of Public Administration and the Woodrow Wilson School of Public and International Affairs at Princeton place primary emphasis upon education in the basic social sciences and offer very few if any highly specialized courses in public administration *per se*.

For the most part, schools and programs of public administration build their curricula with courses given in the traditional manner and by departments wherever located throughout the college or university. Relatively few provide more than a course or two designed exclusively for the students enrolled in such schools and programs, though these few include those institutions which enroll the largest number of students. A unique program in this respect is the so-called end-on-end program at Syracuse in which the courses are not open to other graduate students and where with one or two exceptions the student pursues one course at a time intensively over a period of weeks.

FOREIGN LANGUAGE AND THESIS REQUIREMENTS

The traditional foreign language requirement for a graduate degree has been waived by a good many institutions for students in public administration who are working toward the masters degree. In its place one finds that statistics or accounting are required or may be substituted, presumably because the latter are deemed more useful tools for both practice and research. The growing emphasis upon training for overseas administration and the study of comparative public administration may lead more institutions to re-introduce foreign language at least as an alternative requirement. The thesis requirement also has disappeared from a considerable number of public administration programs at the masters level, though written reports, term papers, and case studies are required either as a part of the work in residence or as a part of an internship or field project.

LENGTH OF PROGRAMS AND TYPES OF DEGREES

Most of the specialized training programs in public administration are limited to one academic or calendar year and students who complete these programs receive a masters degree. Internships or field work may extend the required period of study from three to nine months. Exceptions to the one-year masters degree program in residence include Cornell, Harvard, Princeton, Washington, and Yale, in which two academic years are normally required. The traditional master of arts degree is the one most commonly granted, followed closely by the degree of master of public administration.

Graduate study in public administration beyond the masters degree in most institutions takes the form of the normal Ph.D. program with a major in political science and with public administration as the field of concentration and research. A few institutions, however, offer a more specialized and professional doctorate in this field. The School of Government and Public Administration at American University offers the doctorate both in public administration and in government. At Harvard, two doctoral programs are offered by the Graduate School of Public Administration, one in political economy and government leading to the traditional Ph.D. degree and the other in public administration leading to the degree of Doctor in Public Administration. The Graduate School of Public Administration and Social Service at New York University offers through the Graduate School of Arts and Science a Ph.D. with a major in public administration. The student may offer work in a number of rather highly specialized fields such as administrative theory and practice, organization and methods analysis, financial administration and fiscal policy, personnel administration, labor and social security administration, public relations, planning and housing, international and comparative public administration, law enforcement and correctional administration. The School of Public Administration at the University of Southern California offers the professional degree of Doctor of Public Administration (D.P.A.). To qualify for this degree the student must evidence a mastery of four fields including organization and management, personnel, and finance and one field of administrative application such as public health administration, public works administration, and municipal management. The Maxwell Graduate School of Citizenship and Public Affairs at Syracuse also offers a professional degree of D.P.A.

In an increasing number of institutions, a non-degree program in public administration is being offered to meet the needs of government employees in service. Certificates are awarded to students who complete satisfactorily the prescribed program of study which usually includes some required and a larger number of elective courses.

ADMISSION POLICIES

Admission to graduate work in public administration at many institutions is limited and is granted upon a competitive basis. Admission requirements commonly include superior scholastic standing in undergraduate work, a major in one of the social sciences or graduation from a professional school such as law and engineering, at least a minimum of basic work in political science, and personal qualifications considered of value for administrative work. Government work experience also is deemed desirable, especially where the educational program emphasizes the post-entry student or where the program leads to a professional doctors degree. Some universities cater to the part-time student who is a government employee and who must be served almost entirely by late afternoon and evening classes. Others admit only full-time students with perhaps an occasional exception.

Harvard has moved increasingly toward a student body made up of advanced graduate students with previous government experience and who are studying on a full-time basis. Dean Mason, in his 1955–56 report, expressed the hope, however, "that the composition of our student body will continue to include a substantial number of recent college graduates." At Pennsylvania, the Fels Institute of Local and State Government undertakes to serve two fairly distinct groups of students, namely, a pre-service group restricted in number and studying full-time, and a much larger group of post-entry people who are employed in local and other governments in the Philadelphia area and who attend late afternoon and evening classes and seminars.

It is apparent that an increasing number of students from foreign countries are being admitted for graduate study in this field, particularly in universities which have contracts with the International Cooperation Administration for technical assistance in public administration in universities abroad.

FINANCIAL ASSISTANCE TO STUDENTS

Financial assistance to students at the graduate level in the form of scholarships and fellowships, teaching and research assistantships, and paid internships is very common. This probably reflects both an effort to attract well qualified students to this still relatively new field of educational specialization and to assist worthy young people who could not undertake graduate study without such financial aid. In the earlier years, and perhaps even now to some extent, there was present also the need to encourage students even to consider careers in government service. Institutions like

Harvard, which undertake to recruit relatively mature students for advanced training who are presently employed in government and who must take leaves of absence for full-time study, must be prepared to offer relatively generous fellowships, although to some extent government agencies are legally able and willing to finance some of their employees for specialized study in public administration at colleges and universities.

INTERNSHIP REQUIREMENTS

Approximately one-half of the institutions reporting in the questionnaire survey (see appendix) require an internship or field work experience as a part of the requirements for the masters degree. A few others make this phase of the training program optional. The internship training period varies in length from three to nine months. It may precede graduate study in residence, as in the Southern Regional Training Program, it may be undertaken concurrently with resident study especially where the institution is located in a city where such opportunities are readily available, it may be served in the summer months between two years of graduate study as at Princeton, or as in most of the institutions requiring it, the internship may come after the resident study period.

Since the National Institute of Public Affairs was organized in 1934 to provide internship opportunities in the national government on an unpaid basis for college and university graduates, government agencies at all levels have evidenced an increasing willingness to provide such opportunities, frequently on a paid basis. City managers have been especially cordial to the internship or traineeship system and universities like Kansas and Pennsylvania which have emphasized preparation for careers in municipal administration in their training programs have developed close working relations with city managers in providing such field work experience for their students. The internship is designed to provide a planned work experience and a period of observation for the pre-service student.

Frequently, where the internship is required and is an integral phase of the training program, the student is obligated to submit periodic reports to his academic advisor either by mail or, as at Kansas, in person at conferences held at stated intervals at the university. A masters thesis or case study, when required, may be written during the internship training. This gives to the student an opportunity to engage in research on the job where problems and source materials are readily available and where he has the benefit of conference with and supervision by experienced public administrators.

CONCLUSIONS

This brief and somewhat sketchy survey of the institutional setting within which education for public administration is presently provided will perhaps serve to indicate the diversity of programs and approaches to the field which is the genius of the American system of higher education and which is particularly appropriate for a still new and emerging field of professional service. On the other hand, one finds a substantial similarity in the programs at many institutions, particularly at the masters degree level, although even here one must take account of differences in what is taught under the rubric of public administration.

There is a fairly clear line of demarcation between those institutions which have fully accepted the field of public administration as one worthy of professional training and have made specialized provision for it through more or less separate and autonomous educational units and programs, and those institutions which look upon public administration as one aspect of the broader field of government and politics and which offer a limited number of courses as a part of a general graduate major in political science. This line of distinction, however, is blurred by a good many variations tending in one direction or the other.

The Fels Institute of Local and State Government at the University of Pennsylvania has provided the first of what the present writer hopes will be a continuing series of conferences of educators in this field. It may be that the time has come for the formation of some sort of an association of schools, departments, and programs of public administration similar to those now serving other fields of professional education. In any event, those engaged in this area of educational endeavor would profit from a periodic exchange of ideas and practice. Close liaison should be maintained with those who are engaged in the practice of public administration. The present Committee on Education and Training of the American Society for Public Administration and the Committee on Professional Training of the International City Managers Association should be of material help in this respect.

One of the areas of greatest challenge is the development of a closer and more effective relationship between education for general administration and education for the administration of the various functions of government. Each has much to learn from the other. It has been this writer's privilege to represent the field of public administration for a number of years on the Joint Land Grant College Department of Agriculture Committee on Training for Government Service. The importance of training in administration for workers in agriculture has been recognized by department officials for a long time, but the introduction of even a single course in administration as an elective in the curricula in agriculture and related fields has been difficult to achieve.

2

Trends in the Study and Teaching of Public Administration*

WALLACE T. SAYRE **
Columbia University

When the first textbooks in public administration appeared in the United States a little more than 30 years ago (Leonard D. White's *Introduction* in 1926, and W. F. Willoughby's *Principles* in 1927), they were based upon premises and concepts about the executive branch and its administrative agencies which had been at least a half century in the making. The Civil Service Reform Movement beginning in the late 1860's and culminating in the Pendleton Act of 1883, Woodrow Wilson's essay on "Public Administration" in 1887, Goodnow's *Politics and Administration* in 1900, the work of the New York Bureau of Municipal Research and its counterparts throughout the country, the Scientific Management Movement in industry, the Reorganization Movement (including the Taft Commission studies of 1910–12, the Illinois and New York reports of 1915), the City Manager Movement beginning in 1910, the Budget and Accounting Act of 1921, the Classification Act of 1923, the New York State governmental reorganizations under Governor Smith—all these as well as other events and writings helped to provide the raw mate-

* This paper was presented as part of the discussion of "Desirable Subjects and Emphases in Pre-Service Curricula."

** Wallace S. Sayre, Ph.D., is Professor of Public Administration, Department of Public Law and Government, Columbia University.

rials for the syntheses attempted in the pioneer textbooks in public administration. These texts not only provided the first effective teaching instruments for the new field of study; they also codified the premises, the concepts and the data for the new "public administration."

THE CODIFICATION OF THE TEXTBOOKS

What were the main elements of this codification of 1926–27? They may be very briefly summarized as:

1. The politics-administration dichotomy was assumed as a self-evident truth and as a desirable goal; administration was perceived as a self-contained world of its own, with its own separate values, rules and methods.
2. Organization theory was stated in scientific management terms; that is, it was seen largely as a problem in organization technology—the necessities of hierarchy, the uses of staff agencies, a limited span of control, subdivision of work by such "scientific" principles as purpose, process, place or clientele.
3. The executive budget was emphasized as an instrument of rationality, of coordination, planning and control.
4. Personnel management was stressed as an additional element of rationality (jobs were to be described "scientifically," employees were to be selected, paid, advanced by "scientific" methods).
5. A "neutral" or "impartial" career service was required to insure competence, expertise, rationality.
6. A body of administrative law was needed to prescribe standards of due process in administrative conduct.

In these pioneer texts the responsibility of administrative agencies to popular control was a value taken-for-granted; the responsiveness of administrators and bureaucrats was not seen as a problem because everyone understood that politics and policy were separate from the agencies of administration which were concerned exclusively with the execution of assignments handed down from the realm of politics.

THE HIGH NOON OF ORTHODOXY

The events of the 1930's—depression, New Deal, the rise of Big Government—served at first to confirm the premises of the texts. The expansion of government, especially the great growth in the size, complexity and discretionary power of administrative agencies, was regarded as making all the more relevant and urgent the tools of rationality which public administration offered to the practitioners in the new and expanded agencies of the executive branch. Many of the teachers and the students of public administration themselves became practitioners.

The Report of the President's Committee on Administrative Management and its literary companion-piece, Gulick and Urwick's *Papers on the Science of Administration,* both appearing in 1937, represent the high noon of orthodoxy in public administration theory in the United States. In the Gulick and Urwick *Papers* were brought together eleven essays constituting the classic statements then available in the United States and Europe, in business and public administration, of the elements believed to be embodied in *the science* of administration. (It is perhaps worth noting that of the ten authors only Gulick wrote as a political scientist.) The Report of the President's Committee set forth in eloquent language the prescriptions of public administration made orthodox by the texts of 1926–27. The significant and impressive changes in the executive branch of the national government which were made as a result of the Report strengthened the prestige of public administration as a body of precepts.

POST-WAR DISSENT

But the high noon of orthodoxy had a brief hour of prominence. World War II interrupted the further develop-

ment of public administration research and literature, and
at the close of the War resumption took the form of dissent
and heterodoxy. Pre-war orthodoxy, it is true, was reasserted
in the reports of the two Hoover Commissions, in most of
the textbooks, and in the rash of post-war administrative
surveys at state and local government levels. There was,
however, a strong ferment of dissent in the monographic
literature, in the journals, and elsewhere. The dissent took
three main lines.

1. *The assault upon the politics-administration dichotomy.* This keystone of pre-war orthodox public administration had always been viewed with some scepticism by a
considerable number of political scientists (particularly by
those mainly concerned with political theory or with the
political process); to them, all administrative agencies and
their staffs seemed to be involved in politics. This view was
now to recruit strong support from within the public administration fraternity itself. The first textbook to appear
after the war—Marx (editor), *The Elements of Public Administration* (1946), with 14 political scientists among its
contributors—brought a new emphasis upon the involvement of administrators and administrative agencies in
policy formation, in the use of discretionary power, and in
the general political process. In 1949 Paul H. Appleby's
influential monograph, *Policy and Administration,* boldly
and persuasively described administration as "the eighth
political process." In 1950 the second post-war text—Simon,
Smithburg and Thompson, *Public Administration*—presented a systematic exposition of public administration as
a political and group process. In 1952 the first casebook in
public administration—significantly titled *Public Administration and Policy Formulation*—emphasized in each case
the political role of the administrator; and, in the introductory essay, Harold Stein wrote of "public administration as politics." These illustrations serve to reveal the

stages by which public administration as politics, as involved deeply in policy and values, was firmly established in the literature of public administration within a few years after the war. Even the most orthodox texts yielded some ground on the doctrine that politics and administration were separable.

2. *The assault upon the claims to science and to universal principles of administration.* The premises which pre-war public administration had borrowed primarily from scientific management were of course necessarily subjected to criticism by all those who were asserting that administration was a political process. These critics were soon joined by the students of the history and development of administrative theory. When, for example, Dwight Waldo published in 1948 his important study, *The Administrative State: A Study of the Political Theory of American Public Administration,* he demonstrated how value-loaded, how culture-bound, how political—in short, how "unscientific"—were the premises, the "principles," the logic, of orthodox public administration.

To these powerful critical voices there was soon added a third group: the prophets of a new science of administration. The outstanding representative of this school of thought has been Herbert Simon whose *Administrative Behavior: A Study of Decision-Making Processes in Administrative Organizations* (1947) not only attacked the orthodox "principles" of public administration as being merely "proverbs" but also presented a new administrative science based upon the argument of logical-positivism that facts must be separated from values. For Simon, the orthodox politics-administration dichotomy needs to be replaced by the new fact-value dichotomy.

The critics have successfully made their point. The claims to scientific principles and to their universal applicability have been placed on the defensive although they have not entirely disappeared from the literature of public administration. But the claims of a new science of administration have not been widely accepted.

3. *"Sociological" studies of bureaucracy.* Another stream of ideas and knowledge contributing to the post-war growth of dissent from orthodoxy has been the "sociological" study of the public bureaucracies as representing in themselves a form of political power. The primary impact of these studies has been upon the orthodox doctrines of the neutral career service. Selznick's *TVA and the Grass Roots* (1948), for example, revealed a career bureaucracy deeply involved in the political process, demonstrating that the creation and maintenance of a career bureaucracy is more a problem in values and politics than a problem of administrative science.

EMERGING REFORMULATIONS

The post-war decade of dissent and heterodoxy has not yet revealed the clear outlines of an emerging new body of comprehensive doctrine. But perhaps we can anticipate some of the major components of the reformulation now in process. The premises around which the new consensus—perhaps to become a new orthodoxy—would seem to be forming, may be stated somewhat as follows:

1. Public administration doctrine and practice is inescapably culture-bound; it is also bound to more specific values: to varying conceptions of the general public interest, to particular interest-group values, to the values of a specific administrative organization at a specific time.

2. Public administration is one of the major political processes. The exercise of discretionary power, the making of value choices, is a characteristic and increasing function of administrators and bureaucrats; they are thus importantly engaged in politics.

3. Organization theory in public administration is a problem

in politcial strategy; a choice of structure is a choice of which interest or which value will have preferred access or greater emphasis. Organization is, therefore, as Dahl and Lindblom have demonstrated in *Politics, Economics and Welfare* (1953), a determinant in bargaining.

4. Management techniques and processes have their costs as well as their benefits; each new version has a high obsolescence rate, its initial contributions to rationality declining as it becomes the vested interest of its own specialist guardians and/or other groups with preferred access.

5. Public administration is ultimately a problem in political theory; the fundamental problem in a democracy is responsiblity to popular control—and the responsibility and responsiveness of the administrative agencies and the bureaucracies to the elected officials (the chief executives, the legislators) is of central importance in a government based increasingly on the exercise of discretionary power by the agencies of administration.

3

Desirable Subjects and Emphases in Pre-Service Curricula

GEORGE S. BLAIR *
University of Pennsylvania

ROSCOE C. MARTIN *
Syracuse University

WALLACE S. SAYRE *
Columbia University

INTRODUCTION

Although there is still controversy as to the "how" of best educating graduate students for careers in the public service, there is recognized agreement that colleges and universities do have responsibility in this area. The training of students for the public service was listed as the second major objective of political science departments in response to a questionnaire from the Committee for the Advancement of Teaching of the American Political Science Association in 1950.[1] Fifteen years earlier, the Conference on Training for the Public Service concluded that

* George S. Blair, Ph.D., is Educational and Research Associate, Fels Institute of Local and State Government, and Associate Professor of Political Science, University of Pennsylvania; Roscoe C. Martin, Ph.D., is Professor of Political Science, Maxwell Graduate School of Citizenship and Public Affairs, Syracuse University; Wallace S. Sayre, Ph.D., is Professor of Public Administration, Department of Public Law and Government, Columbia University.

[1] American Political Science Association, Committee for the Advancement of Teaching, *Goals for Political Science*. New York: William Sloane Associates, 1951. Chap. IV, "Education for the Public Service," pp. 68-98.

44

"Universities and colleges have been and always will be concerned with public service because their purpose is inseparably associated with the purpose of the state. In whatever age, whether publicly or privately financed, . . . , they are quite certain to reflect in their educational policy the spirit and character of their period." [2]

The responsibility of colleges and universities in preparing future governmental leaders was well stated by the Committee of the American Political Science Association. In the Committee's words:

"In a world in which the art and science of government bear such heavy responsibilities for the good or evil of human relations, the training of future governmental leaders takes on a significance which yields to nothing in relative importance. It is to the credit of political scientists that they have long realized the necessity of this teaching function and that they have appreciated their peculiar duty for seeing that it takes place satisfactorily.[3]

In the opinion of the authors, it should be emphasized, however, that this task is by no means the responsibility of political scientists alone. Rather, this is a responsibility of virtually every department of the university.

A second point of agreement relates to the preparation of students to serve in varying capacities and roles in government service. For convenience, these capacities or roles can be divided into five categories, as follows: (1) members of political bodies and political executives. These would be persons who serve as legislators, officers of party organizations, and elected or other executives. (2) Judges and officers of courts. (3) Functional specialists, or persons who regularly perform technical duties in such fields as engineering, law, natural sciences, physical sciences, public

2 Conference on Training for the Public Service, *Training for the Public Service*. Chicago: Public Administration Service, 1935, p. 3.

3 American Political Science Association, *op. cit.*, p. 68.

health, etc. (4) Administrative specialists, or persons who regularly perform technical duties in particular segments of administrative work such as procedures analysis, budget administration, personnel management, accounting, etc. (5) Administrative generalists or administrative policy-making officers. These are the persons who can be expected with experience to serve as top management leaders, heads of operating divisions of an administrative agency, or as general aides to such top administrators.

SCOPE OF THIS PAPER

If interpreted broadly, pre-service education includes the preparation of students for careers in the five above-mentioned categories of opportunities in the government service. Since the preparation should be different for some of the categories, it seems desirable and necessary at the outset to define and establish reasonable limits for this paper. Therefore, the following aspects of the over-all problem of education for the public service are excluded from this discussion:

1. Undergraduate education for the public service. There seems to be general agreement that the undergraduate education program should be one of broad or liberal education. However, the establishment of a desirable core of courses for undergraduates planning to enter the public service will be discussed briefly in terms of the core equipping such students with essential background for their graduate education.

2. Graduate education beyond the master's degree. The Master's degree is becoming a common springboard into governmental service at all three levels of government. In commenting on the Ph.D. degree for government service, the Training Committee of the American Political Science Association stated, "Except where needed as a union card

for entry into certain restricted categories of research posts, the (Ph.D.) degree would seem to offer little of actual value to the potential public servant when specialized training is considered.[4]

3. Education for persons desiring to enter the service as members of political bodies, as political executives, or as judges or officers of courts. For the third group (judges and court officers), the law schools have a primary responsibility; for the others, there is no consensus as yet upon which to build.

4. Education of the "functionally trained specialists." Another Conference paper is devoted specifically to the problem of the preparation of these graduates. However, it seems appropriate at this point in this paper to emphasize the importance of getting some administrative content into such professional programs as the education of lawyers, engineers, public health people, etc.

Thus, through the process of elimination, this paper is to discuss curricula emphases in university and college programs of pre-service education at the Master's level for administrative generalists and for administrative specialists who hope to become generalists at some later point in their career. The term "administrative generalist" will be used interchangeably with the term "administrative policy-making officer" throughout this paper.

It is recognized that this category of positions is not normally attainable by a person immediately upon his entrance into government service, with the exception of those who enter as city managers of small cities or as assistant managers. The more common practice is to enter as functional or administrative specialists and to move into the category of administrative policy-making officers at a later date. For instance, an engineer in a state highway depart-

4 *Ibid.*, p. 95.

ment may become the commissioner of highways and thus move from a functional specialty into an administrative policy-making position. Similarly, a budget analyst in a municipality may become the finance director of that city, moving from a position of administrative specialty into an administrative policy-making position.

The educational preparation of functionally trained specialists is excluded from further consideration in this paper. Moreover, it seems justifiable for several reasons to discuss the two remaining categories—administrative generalist and administrative specialist—together. First, as noted above, the number of opportunities for graduate students to enter the public service in generalist positions is still limited. Second, a goodly number of students who prepare to be generalists wind up as specialists and vice versa. Third, in all probability the desirable content of the program for these two categories is not nearly as different as it is often supposed to be.

EDUCATIONAL PREPARATION: ORGANIZATION AND SETTING

A common statement in the literature concerning education for the public service is that there are as many concepts of how best to train for the public service as there are schools preparing graduates for such careers. While this is an overstatement of considerable proportions, there are many conditioning factors which influence and shape the programs in this field. It seems desirable to acknowledge the existence of these factors and to recognize the conditioning influence which they exercise in a general way rather than as they affect desirable program and curricula emphases. Such factors have not been and cannot be ignored in measuring any existing program against the standards or models proposed in this paper.

Among the many conditioning factors which should be acknowledged are:

1. Time limitations. Master degree programs generally extend from one to two years in duration. The limited time period is a very important factor in the subsequent discussion of desirable emphases. Since there is not enough time to include all the courses of value in the curriculum for master's students, choices must be made so that those courses which will best equip the graduate are included in the program.

2. Organizational arrangements. In approaching the problem of developing graduate educational programs in public administration, colleges and universities have chosen to utilize existing facilities rather than establish or create new ones. In essence, this has meant that schools of higher education have continued to place chief reliance upon departments of political science for the preparation of students for careers in the public service. However, this emphasis is but one of several in the purposes and curricula of political science departments and, thus, there is often no clear-cut group of courses which must be taken to satisfy requirements for a general master's degree in political science. A second typical feature of existing public administration programs is the wide use made of course offerings in other departments.

   No university or college program for pre-service education is set up as a "staff college" with complete freedom from general university or college degree requirements or considerations. Programs offered through special departments, institutes, or schools are often determined in part by higher university hierarchies through the establishment of degree prerequisites or requirements. Thus, the nature of the educational program is affected by the organizational setting in which the program is placed.

3. Varied background of students. This factor has both advantages and disadvantages for the pre-service program; moreover, both serve as further conditioning elements which influence the program and its content. If the students are too homogeneous in background, the program

may be missing its larger mission by serving as a "grist mill" for turning out a single type of graduate best prepared to serve in a single type of operation or agency. Similarly, if the students are too heterogeneous in background, the program may suffer in part through a failure or inability to determine at what level and with what emphases it should operate.

4. Objectives of the program. The wide diversity of opinion on the "how" of educating prospective administrative generalists emanates in part from a diversity of opinion concerning the objectives of such programs. The program is appreciably affected by the presence or absence of a clear statement of its objectives in educating students for careers in the public service. A special institute primarily interested in preparing students for careers as city managers will probably offer an appreciably different program than will a general department of political science which, as an incidental or secondary function, prepares students for service at the local, state, national and international level. The objectives of the specialized institute are narrower in scope and, thus, can probably be realized more concretely than can those of a broader program.

5. Available faculty. The experience of the faculty members, their technical competence, their areas of interest, and even their personality are influencing or conditioning factors on the scope and content of the program.

6. Location of the school. Physical location of the college or university is another factor which may affect its program and the objectives of that program. A school located in a large metropolitan center may give considerable attention and emphasis to metropolitan problems. A school located in the state capitol city may concentrate on state government and problems. A school located in a small municipality may not be able to make field experience a concurrent emphasis in its program of study.

7. Financial support. A college or university program financed by state legislative appropriations will in all prob-

ability find it "convenient" and even "tactical" to emphasize state and local government in its program. A special
institute which receives its support from a private fund or
contributors will be influenced in the development of its
program by the interests of its supporters.

There are a number of other conditioning factors which
affect and are affected by the institutional circumstances of
particular programs now offered in our colleges and universities. However, the seven factors listed above are the
more common influences conditioning the environment in
which graduate programs in public administration are
offered; they represent the major influences which shape
any particular program in the field.

THE PRODUCT OF THE EDUCATIONAL PROGRAM

Since the educational product under discussion has been
limited by definition to the administrative generalist, immediate or future, it can be assumed that the educational aim
is to provide graduates with essential knowledge and abilities to enable them to serve effectively in administrative
policy-making positions. In short, the aim is to equip
graduates to fill the void singled out by the late William A.
Jump, who wrote,

". . . our greatest need in public administration was for
people who had an interest in and were capable of grasping
the economic, social, policy, and other broad implications of
public programs and who at the same time were willing and
able to master some of the precise details of administration
without which not much could be accomplished. It was
possible to find 'policy people.' It was possible to find so-
called 'administrative people.' But to find people who combined the two types of qualifications was another matter.
They were then, and they are now, rarely in evidence." [5]

[5] William A. Jump, "The Professors and the Practitioners," Book Review,
7 *Public Administration Review* 212, Summer, 1947.

However, universities and colleges must accept the fact that many of their graduates who prepare for the public service will not make it a life career. This is true whether the educational product is the administrative generalist, the administrative specialist, or the functional specialist. There is some reason to believe that the percentage of administrative generalists who move in and out of the public service is higher than the percentage of staff specialists who do so. The broader role envisioned for himself by the generalist may cause him to seek the broader experience of a career in both public and private endeavors. The administrative staff specialist, on the other hand, with a narrower view of his role, may be more willing to make the public service his life-long career. The factor of career mobility is, in reality, one more of the conditioning factors discussed above which affect the organization and setting of graduate programs.

Concerning the graduates who will make their career in the public service, it seems logical to conclude that the educational program has a dual responsibility. First, it should relate in part to preparing graduates for the exercise of leadership functions and for the assumption of responsibilities as they rise on the rungs of the career ladder. Second, it should relate in part to equipping graduates with the basic knowledges and skills necessary to enable them to begin and develop in the career service. The leadership role, responsibilities, knowledges and skills of administrative policy-making officers as defined in the Workshops preceding this conference [6] are used as the frame of reference throughout this paper in the development of desirable curricula emphases.

[6] See Part II.

THEORETICAL—PRACTICAL EDUCATION

The statement of the purpose of this paper makes it unnecessary to present for a new airing the controversy of a broad versus a specialized education for students aspiring for careers in the public service. By limiting the paper to the problem of educating administrative generalists, the controversy can be narrowed to such questions as how much should be broad, how broad is broad, and what does a broad education mean? An attempt will be made to answer each of these questions—in the reverse order of their listing —as a point of reference for discussion.

What Does a Broad Education Mean? If we accept educating the administrative generalist and administrative specialist for their roles as administrative policy-making officers as our challenge, then the generalist as defined above by William A. Jump is the acceptable end-product of such educational programs. Jump's generalist was the man who could grasp the "economic, social, policy, and other broad implications of public programs" while being also prepared "to master some of the precise details of administration." This description stresses both abilities and knowledges for such persons, and both are basic and essential.

The acceptance of this type of end-product as the desirable goal, however, has not made the task of defining a broad education much simpler. There is no single type of administrative policy-making officer. It was the conclusion of the state and local government officials participating in the two pre-conference workshops that there was a rather common set of abilities required of such officers. Their conclusions regarding the leadership role and responsibilities can be translated into the following set of abilities:

a. To define objectives and to plan and organize for their effectuation

b. To see a problem as a whole with the initiative to tackle it and with the judgment to evolve a workable solution.

c. To analyze and synthesize many disciplines in meeting and carrying out public purposes.

d. To sense both internal and the external limitations on administrative policy actions.

e. To write clearly and to read comprehensibly.

f. To develop, promote and maintain necessary interrelationships and to establish and maintain devices for control and coordination.

Similarly, a broad education for administrative policy-making officers can be defined in terms of the basic knowledges which workshop participants concluded were essential for such officers. The categories of knowledges which they recommended encompassed:

a. The economic, social and political environment.

b. The administrative process.

c. Human relations.

d. General technical services.

e. Governmental services.

Whether viewed in terms of required abilities, essential knowledges, or both, a broad education for administrative policy-making officers is one which gives the graduate student (a) a breadth of viewpoint, (b) an appreciation of government's role in modern society, (c) an understanding and proper sense of the internal and external limitations on administrative action, and (d) a capacity for leadership.

How Broad Is Broad? It must be recognized as a practical matter that college or university education can never equip the graduate as a finished product for administrative policy-making positions. The end purpose of equipping the graduate for the positions he will grow into must be tempered by his preparation to do the jobs he will be called upon to do along the paths of the career ladder. The importance of this dual responsibility of education has been vividly expressed by one writer as follows:

"We are bound to see more and greater emphasis upon specialization. This poses a familiar dilemma. The tremendous rewards for specialization encourage narrow training; and for certain purposes of science, business, and government, this is useful. But a world of ever-ramifying specialists soon cries out for generalists. Someone must be able to see beyond his immediate job and be able to cope with the larger relationships.

"With this in mind, the most forward-looking of our colleges and universities are making active efforts to ensure that every specialist will build his specialty on a base of general education so that he will have some flexibility and breath as a background for specializing. What the future is going to demand is specialists who are capable of functioning as generalists." [7]

An education is broad if it gives the student diverse knowledge in the liberal arts, social sciences, humanities, natural sciences, etc. This, however, is the role of a student's total education—not exclusively, not even primarily, of his graduate education. Graduate education for a public service career is broad if it fortifies, strengthens, or gives the student preparation in the five categories of essential knowledges listed above. This means a graduate preparation combining broad and specialized education, for the graduate must be equipped to work effectively in the positions he will first hold as well as be provided with the breadth necessary for effective service in the positions he will grow into as he rises in his career service.

How Much of the Education Should Be Broad? This question, of course, cannot be answered with any degree of

[7] John W. Gardner, "The Great Hunt for Educated Talent," 214 *Harper's Magazine* 51, January, 1957.

definiteness. The graduate must be equipped with both knowledges and skills if he is to make a career for himself in the public service. The distinction between knowledge and skill advanced in the pre-conference workshops seems acceptable, i.e., that one is *educated* to knowledge and one is *trained* to skills. At the risk of semantic difficulties, it seems desirable, therefore, to equate education with the acquisition of knowledge while training is associated with the acquisition of skills. It is recognized that neither operates without considerable influence and conditioning by and upon the other, but this represents a convenient division for purposes of discussion. If this division is accepted, then graduate programs for administrative generalists should aim to provide their potential generalists with some competence in one or more specialties within the framework of a program which is general or broad in orientation. This competence is essential if the graduate is to survive in the career service and if he is to fill his first position effectively.

There are several devices by which this competence in a specialty or specialities can be woven into the program without disrupting its broad aims. One method involves the effective choice of electives by the student in a specialty area. If there is a thesis requirement, this, too, represents an area in which, through selection of a thesis topic, the student can gain competence in personnel, finance, budgeting, reporting, or some other specialization of his choice. If the program has concurrent or pre- or post-academic field experience, this, also, provides an excellent device for enabling the student to develop a specialty. Other convenient devices or techniques include special reports by the student in specialty areas, problem solving, role playing, case study, etc.

The degree to which the student can be given both broad and specialized training and education has a direct relationship to the organizational pattern of the program. If the graduate education is offered in a general department of political science, as one of the major emphases of that department, the program will likely be broad or general. Generally, programs offered in such a department are more flexible and have a minimum of required courses, making them more adaptable to the particular needs of the student. Such programs, however, seldom offer the student electives in courses in which he can gain a particular specialty except through concentration on a thesis topic area or special reports.

If the graduate education is offered in a special department, school, or institute of public administration, the program will more likely reflect a combination of broad and specialized education and training. This is in part warranted because of the narrower objectives of this type of organizational setting and because of the recognized need for this type of course for the effective development of the student. A study of the comparative curricula of the two types of programs reveals that this relationship actually exists in practice, at least in a large number of schools now offering graduate instruction in the department of political science or through a more specialized organization.

A DESIRABLE UNDERGRADUATE CORE

A discussion of a desirable core of courses in graduate education for administrative policy-making officers must be preceded by some recognition of undergraduate preparation. While it is generally agreed that colleges and universities can best serve the cause of public administration by *not* offering a narrowly vocational undergraduate curriculum in public administration, it is also recognized that there are some courses which undergraduates aspiring for careers in the public service should complete at this level. This common core in the otherwise varied backgrounds of graduate students is desirable because of the limited time spent in graduate preparation at the master's level.

Writing a decade ago, Fesler stated:

"Students planning to enter the public service need more than any other group a breadth of viewpoint, an appreciation of government's role in modern society, and a capacity for leadership that cannot be gained if the multiplication of required public administration courses precludes broad ranging over the fields of the social sciences and the humanities." [8]

However, he went on to propose a hard core of seven courses for undergraduate training for public administration, as follows: political science, economics, American history, public administration, statistics, English composition and psychology. Other courses which Fesler believed merited consideration for inclusion among required courses included sociology, anthropology, public speaking, public policy and political parties and public opinion. He felt that government accounting seemed of too specialized a value to merit rating as a required course for all students.[9]

A second list of desirable "requirements" for persons in the public service was compiled by George A. Graham in his systematic and extensive study of education and training for the public service.[10] Replies to a questionnaire from Graham concerning courses that persons in the public service believed should be required resulted in the following order of courses: public administration, economics, statistics, political science, public finance and fiscal administration, personnel administration, constitutional and administrative law, accounting, English and psychology.[11] A

[8] James W. Fesler, "Undergraduate Training for the Public Service," XLI *American Political Science Review* 510, June, 1947.

[9] *Ibid.*, p. 511.

[10] George A. Graham, *Education for Public Administration*. Chicago: Public Administration Service, 1941.

[11] *Ibid.*, p. 323.

question concerning courses of instruction found most useful by persons in managerial work resulted in this listing in order: economics, public administration, statistics, political science, English, accounting, public finance and fiscal administration, personnel administration, history and law.[12]

Combining the Fesler and Graham studies with the results of workshop deliberations, the need for a basic core of undergraduate courses is well substantiated. This core of seven course areas includes political science, economics, public administration, American history, statistics, English composition and accounting.[13] Whether or not some or all of these core areas are prerequisites for entrance into the graduate program or degree prerequisites for the master's degree will depend, in large part, on the institutional setting of the particular program. Undergraduate students, in most cases, will enter graduate programs with some course work in the areas of political science, American history and English composition. Public administration can be assumed to be an integral part of the graduate program for the student. Thus, the decision really concerns course work in economics, accounting and statistics. In many programs offering a master's degree in public administration, these three courses are required as prerequisites for entrance or as degree prerequisites in the program. In a majority of the programs offering a general master's degree in political science, these course areas appear not to be required:

[12] *Ibid.*, p. 320.

[13] The authors recognize that the listing of these seven subject-matter areas as "courses" is somewhat ambiguous, since the question arises as to what specific courses in these areas are implied. In each area, the basic, principles or introductory course is the specific course intended rather than more specialized courses. This statement should not be interpreted to imply that additional or more specialized courses would not be desirable, particularly in the fields of political science and economics.

PATTERN OF THE GRADUATE PROGRAM

The controversy of broad versus specialized education carries over to the internal composition of the training program. There are basically three alternative patterns of curriculum organization, and each pattern has its supporters in the literature of public administration as well as in practice. These alternatives are: the required curriculum, the core program plus electives, and the complete elective system.

The required curriculum is a common pattern in some programs which have definite program objectives and which aim to prepare graduates for service at a particular governmental level. In addition to the required program in residence, there are usually degree prerequisites which must be satisfied and these also are uniform for all graduates.

The core program plus electives is the most common pattern of graduate education both in special schools and departments and institutes of public administration and in programs offered in general political science departments. An examination of college catalogues indicates the required or recommended core to vary from some six hours to about twenty-seven hours for public administration majors. The total degree requirement in hours varies from twenty-four to sixty-two or more. Thus, students are required to take some prescribed courses but have a considerable degree of flexibility or choice of electives.

Some schools still retain a program of complete electives depending on the background and preparation of the individual student. These programs, most commonly, are those which are offered in general political science departments leading to a master of arts degree.

Considering the three alternative patterns, that of a basic core plus electives seems to be the one most desirable for graduate education. This pattern is advanced even for special schools, departments or institutes which may have a definite set of objectives and which educate for a particular service level. For these programs, the required core can be larger, but if the requirement is absolute, the result is a failure to recognize the differences in the undergraduate preparations of the students. For instance, if public planning is a required course, the course is thereby limited in its appeal to a student who did considerable work in this area as an undergraduate.

As a generalization, it is recommended that programs of graduate education for the public service establish a basic core which is supplemented by electives selected by the student to complement his special interests or to make up for deficiencies in his undergraduate preparation.

MAKE-UP OF THE DESIRED CORE

Upon examining the recommended core of courses for graduates aspiring for careers as administrative policy-making officers, two concepts become apparent. First, the core discipline running through the program is public administration; and second, the individual course areas represent "slices" or segments of the parent area. Some of the course areas represent vertical slices of the subject matter of the field, while other areas more nearly represent horizontal segments or divisions.

Concerning the parent discipline of the program—public administration—a number of excellent definitions have been framed by writers and practitioners in the field. One of the better and more complete definitions is as follows:

"Public administration concerns government; more specifically it concerns the action side of government. . . . (It) has to do primarily with the executive branch of the government, and it centers on the collective activities of the men and women who transact the everyday affairs of government. Its principal focus is men at work. It occurs at every level and in every agency of government where there are tasks to be done and staffs to do them." [14]

The particular course areas recommended below relate to the setting or framework within which the executive branch operates and to significant aspects of the administrative process. It is emphasized that the titles which follow represent course areas and not specific courses. Course titles are deceptive in that they are likely to imply either more or less than is actually offered. The descriptions which follow the recommended areas are, therefore, more significant than the titles. Each of the five areas recommended is proposed as a one-term or one-semester course. Thus, this core of courses is advanced as constituting one-half of the ordinary requirements of work toward the master's degree, leaving the student a choice of electives from which to round out his program and his personal development.

The Environment of Public Administration. Although this course will be the first direct educational contact for some students with the field of public administration, it should not be designed as an introductory course. Rather the course is proposed as one which concentrates on the political and social setting within which the administrative process is carried on. The external limitations, controls, and pressures affecting the administrative agency would be the center of inquiry.

The course would consider administration in terms of its constitutional setting, its relationship to the judicial and legislative branches, and its control and direction by elective and political executive. Similarly the external relationships of administration and administrative agencies to

[14] Roscoe C. Martin, "Educational Preparation for Public Administration," X *Higher Education* 135, May, 1954.

political parties, pressure groups and clientele groups would be explored, as would the internal relationships of agencies within government to other governmental agencies. The important problem areas of direction and control of bureaucracy, the accountability of bureaucracy, internal and external communications and public relations would also be treated.

The content of this course area relates directly to the economic, social and political environment and to the administrative process as well. This body of material is designed to provide the student with basic understanding and to equip him for the exercise of the essential abilities.

Organizational Theory and Management Concepts. This somewhat awkward title is used to suggest a course area that is more than theory yet stops short of a "how to" course. The practical aspects of the course are directly related to the theoretical content and serve more as illustrative examples than as a "manual of arms." Essentially the course integrates the various theories of or approaches to organization and relates organizational theory to the rising problems of technological extension.

Thus, the course is concerned primarily with approaches in organizational theory. These approaches may be identified as (1) organization as a technological problem in scientific management; (2) organization as a social process emphasizing human relations, informal organization, face-to-face relationships, etc.; (3) organization as the anatomy of decision-making, explored by an analysis of formal and informal decision-making patterns; and (4) organization as the concept of an entity which can and should be held accountable for something and responsible to someone. Such management functions as leadership, coordination, direction, control, planning and reporting would be explored within an organizational context.

The content of this course area relates specifically to the administrative process and to human relations but less directly to the economic, social and political environment. Again the material covered provides basic understanding of the needed abilities and a sense of or feel for their effective exercise.

Public Finance and Public Budgeting. While this course area may seem to be combining two "separates," the combination is deliberate. The basic purposes of this course area are to give the student information relating to the development and administration of revenue and expenditure systems and the allocation of public resources for the provision of services to citizens. The two purposes are closely related—or should be—in the thinking of administrative policy-making officers.

The portion of the course area dealing more specifically with aspects of public finance would relate to the structure of revenue systems, the pattern of expenditures and fiscal planning. Public budgeting would be presented as a major management process through which revenues are allocated to service programs. This would include an analysis of the budget-making process through a study of organization, procedures, and influences—both governmental and non-governmental—on the allocation of resources.

A course area so presented would contribute to the student's knowledge of the technical process of budgeting as a major management tool, the administrative process, and the economic environment. The course area would add appreciably to the effective exercise of a number of the basic abilities of administrative generalists.

Personnel Management. The underlying assumption of this course area is that personnel management in a democratic society must be viewed in the over-all context of public policy development and execution. Although personnel management is a basic administrative tool or process, its more important role is to help make democracy work by enabling line agencies to fulfill their substantive functions in providing services to citizens. Thus, personnel management should be considered within the governmental context as a process to advance the social and political aspects of government.

After establishing such a frame of reference for personnel management in the public service, the development of governmental personnel administration would be traced from its beginning period of emphasis on systems, controls and tenure to the present emphasis upon its role as a positive instrument of administration. The distinguishing characteristics of the public service should be emphasized through exploration of the problem of giving direction to and exercising control over the bureaucracy within a framework of administrative responsibility. The problems of a rigid bureaucracy, recruitment, training, security, loyalty, etc., would be studied. Thus, the course would cover personnel management in its setting, by analyzing its major issues and by considering its methods of accomplishing its purposes—but always in the larger context of its place in the operations of government.

A course so constructed would relate directly to advancing knowledge of an important management process. Knowledge of human relations would similarly be advanced since much of personnel management is human relations in action. As in the case of other course core areas, this course would contribute to effective performance of several of the prerequisite abilities noted above.

Research and Communication Laboratory. The growing tendency to recognize research as a logical basis for aiding in decision making and the increased need for research findings as a guide for action in many areas necessitate consideration of the place of research in graduate preparation for the public service. In many programs, research training is primarily limited to the preparation of a master's thesis, while in other programs the formal thesis requirement has been replaced by a seminar in administrative writing and reporting. The title of this course area is purposely broad so it can encompass both types of practice.

The use of "communication" in the course area title permits training or exercise in both oral and written communications. Although experience in oral and written expression is one purpose of every course, this area is important enough for administrative policy-making officers to warrant special consideration. It can receive such emphasis in a laboratory, workshop, or seminar which stresses communication as well as training in research technique. In this course area, special consideration would be given to the materials, principles, and techniques of research in government by exploration of the major sources of data for research in this field.

Such a course would contribute directly to the acquisition of knowledge and ability in the field of the important technical process of research while contributing indirectly to all the categories of knowledge recommended for administrative policy-making officers. Similarly, the course area would contribute to the development of the basic communication abilities of such officers.

Other Course Areas. The above listing of five course areas reflects the recommended core for programs preparing their graduates for careers in the public sevice. This course core is advanced as constituting one-half the graduate's preparation at the master's level, leaving the other half for electives. There are many additional course areas which have much to offer the student; he should be guided in his selection of these areas by considerations of his special interests and weaknesses or shortcomings in his total education. Among the many courses which could be recommended as desirable electives are administrative law, political theory, public planning, public policy development, political parties and interest groups, the American constitutional system, urban sociology, cultural anthropology, economic systems and theories, etc.

It should be noted that the recommended electives exclude training in specific technique courses such as governmental accounting, statistics, public purchasing, tax administration, etc. The recommended curriculum is advanced for prospective administrative generalists, and such graduate students should concentrate on principles rather than techniques. Techniques vary from jurisdiction to jurisdiction, but principles remain more constant. The graduate student on the job can more easily pick up the techniques if he has the theoretical framework into which these fit than he can fit particular techniques into a theoretical framework.

For the graduate student who will begin his career as an administrative policy-making officer, e.g., as manager of a small community or as an assistant manager, it is desirable that he be given substantive knowledge in the field of local government organization and services. This course area, which might be entitled *Governmental Policy and Services,* would consider governmental organization and powers as well as the major functional areas of government, i.e., public health, safety, welfare, utilities, streets, education and recreation. There is good reason for including a substantive course or courses relating to the line activities of government, at least as electives, in the programs of all prospective administrative policy-making officers.

There appears to be considerable merit to the requirement of a formal field experience or internship period, planned and supervised jointly by the educational institution and the sponsoring governmental agency, as an integral part of graduate program preparing students for administrative careers in the public service. The case for and against this proposal is the subject of another paper. It may be noted, however, that the conditioning factors which influence the educational program of an institution in terms of course requirements exert an even stronger influence on the decision for or against an internship program. Allowance, therefore, must be made for institutional circumstances, including the location of the institution, its financial resources, the governmental climate in which it operates, etc.

SUMMARY

Vocational training versus broad or general education is a major issue in many fields of higher education; the issue is particularly acute in the area of preparation of future administrative generalists. There is unanimity of opinion, however, that the educational product of graduate programs must be a man of breadth and vision.

There is abundant evidence of the need for competent men in the public service at all governmental levels. In discussing this need, President Harry S. Truman stated at the Princeton Bicentennial Conference on University Education and the Public Service:

> "If our national policies are to succeed, they must be administered by officials with broad experience, mature outlook, and sound judgment. There is, however, a critical shortage of such men—men who possess the capacity to deal with great affairs of state.
>
> "The government has recruited from our academic institutions many members of its professional staff—geologists, physicists, lawyers, economists and others with specialized

training. . . . But we have been much less effective in obtaining persons with broad understanding and an aptitude for management. We need men who can turn a group of specialists into a working team and who can combine imagination and practicability with a sound public program. . . . Men trained for this kind of administrative and political leadership are rare indeed. . . . (The Universities) should develop in their students the capacity for seeing and meeting social problems as a whole and for relating special knowledge to broad issues. They should study the needs of government, and encourage men and women with exceptional interests and aptitudes along the necessary lines to enter the government service." [15]

Desirable Subjects and Emphases in
Pre-Service Curricula
Panel Discussion

Chairman: STEPHEN K. BAILEY, Professor of Public Affairs, Princeton University

Panel:　　HAROLD F. ALDERFER, Executive Deputy Secretary, Department of Public Instruction, Harrisburg, Pennsylvania; formerly Professor of Political Science and Executive Secretary, Institute of Local Government, Pennsylvania State University

ROSCOE C. MARTIN, Professor of Political Science, Maxwell Graduate School of Citizenship and Public Affairs, Syracuse University

[15] Harry S. Truman, *New York Times* (June 18, 1947), p. 20, as cited in American Political Science Association, *op. cit.*, p. 80.

RICHARD H. McCLEERY, Instructor in Political Science, Michigan State University

NORMAN D. PALMER, Professor of Political Science, University of Pennsylvania

WALLACE S. SAYRE, Professor of Public Administration, Department of Public Law and Government, Columbia University

GEORGE A. WARP, Associate Professor of Political Science and Associate Director of the Public Administration Center, University of Minnesota

The past two days have seen a stimulating mixture of systematic thinking and evanescent insight. We have had both astronomy and star dust. If in this time we have not been able to throw a cosmic intellectual net completely around our subject, it is perhaps because a conference title such as ours is in truth boundless. *Education and Training for the Public Service* is a reasonably short and direct title but it has only two unemotive and reasonably circumscribed words: "and" and "for." It could plausibly be argued that child psychologists or even geneticists could meet meaningfully on this topic, for we know that the felicity of institutional life depends in large measure upon the quality and abilities of the humans in charge—and who knows where quality and abilities begin? It is a humbling, but sobering, thought that a chemical formula fed to expectant mothers or an additive to kindergarten milk may some day do more to produce administrative leaders in our society than all the graduate schools of Public Administration and Public and International Affairs combined! Even now, perhaps the most important service our professional schools in this field can perform is to identify and attract able, personable, and bright young people into the public sector of our society—no matter what we teach them.

This particular conference, however, starts from where these esoteric speculations leave off. The double-barrelled panel I was asked to chair has been particularly concerned with the question of what we should teach men and women who have already determined upon administrative careers in state and local government but who have not yet entered the public service. The assigned topic for the panel was *Desirable Subjects and Emphases in Pre-Service Curricula.*

My job as a summarizer is not an easy one. Two sessions of astronomy and star dust—no matter how stimulating— can get in one's eyes. And not all the star dust came from the same galaxies. Furthermore, there is the problem of accurate reporting, not on the part of the excellent staff of Fels Center upon whose notes I have heavily relied, but on my part. Non-verbatim notes are bound to be cryptic. I worked over one set for about forty minutes this morning before I realized I was looking at my score card to last night's ball game.

Our first panel session on Wednesday afternoon began with an outline by Professor Martin of a paper prepared by George Blair of the Institute staff, and Professors Martin and Sayre. Although granting that administrative generalists were only one out of many identifiable breeds of workers in the vineyards of state and local government, Professor Martin stressed that the paper addressed itself particularly to the issue of desirable education and training for this breed of administrative policy-making official.

The assumed aim of educational programs for future administrative generalists was defined in the following language: "To provide graduates with an interest in and ability for grasping the economic, social, and other broad implications of public programs while equipping them with a willingness and ability to master some of the precise details of administration without which not much could be accomplished"—the goal then of "a Jack of all trades and master of *one*," or if "trades" has an invidious connotation, "a 'philosopher' who knows at least one skill."

How to build an educational program to do this, especially if administrative leadership encompasses more than intellectual breadth and useful skills, but some x quality—some personal factor—what Wilson once called the capacity to "give sight to the blind hopes and aspirations of the people."

A desirable core for graduate education was proposed—granted always the modifications that disparate circumstances of place and people impose upon any educational formula; and granted further the degrees of permissiveness in course choice which various educational philosophies allow.

Accepting, however, a part-table-d'hote-part-a-la carte educational menu, what should the basic required core curriculum be for those desiring to enter state and local government with the ultimate goal of top administrative posts in mind?

Professor Martin stressed:

1. the environment of public administration (the institutional and cultural setting)
2. organization theory and management concepts (internal *environment;* not O and M)
3. public finance and public budgeting
4. personnel management
5. research and communications laboratory
    a. research as a means for increasing rationality in decision-making
    b. exercise in oral and written expression. Some mention was made of the possible substitution of this research and communications activity for a thesis requirement.

This, then, is the recommended core. Other course areas were suggested as desirable electives: administrative law, political theory, public planning, policy development, American constitutional law, urban sociology, economic systems and theories, etc.

For the small community administrator-to-be, a special course called Government Policy and Services might be desirable—a course which would study major functional areas of local government.

Finally, the report stressed the merits of formal field experience or internships—although left this to another panel specifically charged with discussing this topic.

Here, then, was the basic framework of our discussion for two sessions. In quick summary:

A 50-50 mixture of core courses and electives designed to give students some sense of the milieu of administration and some of the most important related skills and techniques involved in the effective exercise of administrative responsibilities—all this within the context of educational breadth, even at the possible sacrifice of precise technical knowledge.

The discussion immediately following Professor Martin's presentation seemed to be concerned with three kinds of issues:

1. Semantic and logical issues. Whether words like "knowledge" and "skill," "generalists" and "specialists," "research" and "communications," "procedure" and "process" were being properly or clearly used in the paper or in the discussion; or, in the cases of certain word pairs, were the pairs in fact logically separable;
2. Issues relating to emphases within the recommended curriculum. For example, how much time should be allotted to techniques such as research; should a thesis be required; and if so, in connection with what kinds of student ex-

perience; could the entire job be done in one year, or even two—and so on;

3. Philosophical issues. Whether in fact the core curriculum as outlined was not still far too narrow and technical in its conception; whether the vast worlds of human behavior, politics, and human value systems generally did not need more explicit attention; whether the great relevancies of our age were in fact getting the attention they deserved in the suggested curriculum; whether we were not in danger of falling into the teacher's college trap of reifying process at the sacrifice of substance.

In the second session of the panel, Wally Sayre's brilliant summary of the development of Public Administration as a field, took most of the heart out of the seeming controversies of the first session; even if it added some fresh ones. As one of the co-authors of the first paper, Professor Sayre made it quite clear that new wine had been poured into old semantic bottles. Words like "administration," or "organization," or even "budgeting" do not have the connotations today that they once had. Strange phrases have replaced familiar ones: "Administration is one of the major *political* processes"; "Public Administration is culture bound and its myths are not fixed and universal"; "Public Administration is a problem in political strategy"; "Administrative virtue is stable; administrative sin is dynamic" (my rough translation of Sayre's law); "The real problems of Public Administration are problems in political theory —the responsibility of the bureaucracy to popular control." This, if you will, is the new Public Administration and the old words used in the report of the preceding day must be re-examined because they no longer mean what they once did.

It is, in short, this new world of administrative arts and sciences that must be subsumed when traditional words are used in curriculum building.

But some of the discussants were still uneasy. If administration is culture-bound, isn't our first job to know a great deal about our culture? In a society marked by occupational mobility (although I, for one, feel that dangerous rigidities are beginning to form in the ease of job transfer), should we not extend our training to include generalists in the church and in business? For all of our good talk—including our new talk—are too many of us still setting up trade schools designed to the transient whims of the job market—and in the process, are we not corrupting educational standards and important traditional values? Are we considering sufficiently our new role in the world and the international demands that will be made on American specialists and generalists in state and local government? Can the egg-head approach and the bread-and-butter approach really be reconciled?

These are not rhetorical questions; these are *real* questions—and as Roscoe Martin implied in his final rejoinder, the most important thing is not that we construct dogma, but that we continue to question whenever we get comfortable about what we are doing. Implicit also in Professor Martin's summary is the humbling theme that we are all just putterers in the garden. We cannot make the flowers grow. It is what St. Francis called our Brother the Sun and our Sister Water, what theologians call grace, that make the seeds actually burgeon.

But surely this does not excuse us from attempting to cultivate the garden with wisdom and skill.

Stephen K. Bailey

4

Teaching Methods—Course Instruction

FREDRICK T. BENT *
University of Pennsylvania

JOSEPH E. MC LEAN *
Trenton, New Jersey

INTRODUCTION

As an area of inquiry the subject of course instruction is almost as old as language itself. Although of particular interest to students of education, the search for the "best" way of presenting material to students has plagued instructors in all fields of knowledge. Despite the ink spilled, no "scientific principles" have been yet devised since unfortunately the results of experiments on methods of course instruction have been indecisive. Consequently, teachers have been forced to rely upon their own judgment in deciding which teaching method is most applicable for the material they are presenting. Although no single key to this puzzle has been found, baffled but determined educators continue their quest. In a paper of this length nothing can be added to what has already been written by people who have spent a lifetime studying and evaluating various teaching techniques. What will be attempted is a sketch of some basic educational assumptions and a suggestion of

* *Fredrick T. Bent, Ph.D., is Educational and Research Associate, Fels Institute of Local and State Government, and Assistant Professor of Political Science, University of Pennsylvania; Joseph E. McLean, Ph.D., is presently Commissioner of Conservation and Economic Development for New Jersey, and was formerly Professor of Politics at the Woodrow Wilson School of Public and International Affairs, Princeton University.*

76

which categories of teaching method are most applicable to the various courses commonly offered in a public administration curriculum.

CATEGORIES OF TEACHING METHODS

Putting methods of course instruction into categories may be arbitrary and unrealistic, particularly since the categories themselves have different meanings for different persons. Moreover, few teachers would use one method to the exclusion of all others. Nevertheless, for ease of identification (and discussion) four categories of teaching methods will be briefly described in the rest of this paper.

1. *The lecture.* This has sometimes been called "the method of authoritative exposition" by professional educators. In this situation the student is usually passive and the lecturer is perhaps more content-oriented than student-oriented.

2. *Discussion-Seminar.* This method is characterized by active student verbal participation within the classroom environment. It is ordinarily student rather than teacher-oriented.

3. *Problem solving method of inquiry.* This includes the techniques of laboratory experimentation and role-playing in which the student actively alters physical conditions to the extent possible in a contrived situation of vicarious experience.

4. *The case method.* This method can range from complete presentation by the teacher of all phases of the case to a type of presentation that permits active student discussion or role-playing.

Before proceeding with our exposition, one assurance needs to be made: these methods are not mutually exclusive. The lecture need not preclude discussion. Depending upon the size of the class, a course that is essentially lecture can also use case studies as supplemental reading. The case method may include lectures and discussion and can be an integral part of problem solving. Of course, if these inter-relationships are carried too far no categorization would be justified and focused discussion on any one method would be hampered. With these limitations in mind, we believe that the categories can be defended and their relative merits studied in terms of the public administration curriculum.

ASSUMPTIONS FOR A DISCUSSION OF TEACHING METHODS

Three basic assumptions underlie the thinking in this paper. The first is that any discussion of methodology should not obscure the fact that teaching is essentially an art, and as such, cannot be circumscribed by rigid laws governing its expression. Thorough knowledge of methodology does not guarantee good teaching any more than knowledge of harmony theory makes a good composer. Methodology assumes that "other things are equal," something a teacher cannot assume since each class is unique. Gilbert Highet in his recent book *The Art of Teaching* lists three essentials to good teaching: know the subject, like the subject, and like and know the students.[1] Methodology by itself is no substitute for these fundamental requirements of effective teaching.

The second assumption is that no one teaching method is equally applicable to all courses or to all phases of a single course. Certain subjects, especially those that are one or two semesters in length, may lend themselves to a flexible adaptation of several or perhaps all of the four teaching methods. The introductory course in public administration, for example, ordinarily covers such a wide array of subjects and topics that the instructor may find it prudent to use different teaching techniques for different phases of the course if only to keep the students from getting bored. In

[1] Gilbert Highet, *The Art of Teaching*. New York: Vintage Books, 1954, pp. 12-25.

others, the subject matter dealt with, the objectives sought, or the number of students, may limit method alternatives. Thus, the lecture method may be imperative if the class is over sixty, whereas the course content of statistics and accounting justifies reliance upon problem solving. Courses in human relations, on the other hand, normally call for active student participation.

The third assumption is that every institution is subject to a series of variables that influence the selection of any one teaching technique regardless of the "proven" superiority of one method over another. The following list is only suggestive and the factors probably do not apply with equal force to all departments. Nevertheless, generalizations about the usefulness of any one teaching method should be qualified to the extent that these variables do exist and are recognized.

1. *The aim of the course.* Course objectives will inevitably influence teaching methods. Thus, a survey course probably will not be taught in the same way as a course in techniques emphasizing skill.

2. *The established curriculum.* The period of time over which instruction is offered affects the choice of method. Thus, a curriculum in which several courses are taken in the same semester might provide for greater teaching flexibility than courses organized on a "bloc" system.[2] Similarly, the length of time of each classroom period is a qualifying factor.

3. *Physical facilities and budget.* The availability of written material, official documents, or library facilities may limit the use of a particular method. The number and experience of instructors and other professional assistance are also significant.

4. *The strategic location of the institution.* The oppor-

[2] In the bloc system the student concentrates exclusively on one subject for a period ranging from several weeks to several months.

tunity for observing diverse governmental operations and the availability or accessibility of practitioners as guest lecturers vary widely.

5. *The type of student.* The homogeneity of class membership in terms of career objectives is a variable factor. Some students may be interested in striving for positions with general administrative responsibilities whereas others may be interested in particular functional or operational aspects of public administration.

6. *The influence of teacher personality and preference.* A teacher must be "comfortable" in whichever method of instruction is used; his style should not be unnecessarily cramped.

7. *Student reactions.* Students as well as teachers need to respond positively to the method used. Prior educational experience may so condition a student's reaction that teaching innovations may be received with indifference.

The above points are self-explanatory. However, a few words should be injected here with respect to the statement that the teacher should use those teaching techniques which suit his personality and taste. Although we accept the premise that the primary agent is the student, and not the teacher, nevertheless, no technique should be recommended unless the teacher gets some satisfaction from its use. Some may obtain this from the lecture, others in the give and take of a discussion. Individual preference in the choice of methods is almost as important as the selection of the courses that he would like to teach. No teacher can be fully effective unless there is some reasonable accommodation to his interests and skills.

In view of these variables and the assumption that however ingeniously devised, no one teaching method is preferable in all courses in public administration, this paper will not propose any one method as "the best." This note of caution is predicated upon the absence of extensive experimentation testing the value of any one teaching method over another. Although it is true that some testing has been done, "controversy over the implications of these experiments still continues partly because some of the results have seemed contradictory or too scattered and impressionistic to be conclusive, partly because devotees of one approach or another are so completely convinced of its peculiar merits."[3] This observation is even more relevant in public administration since few efforts have been made to appraise the various methods currently being used or proposed, and advocates have justified their enthusiasm for certain techniques on hypotheses, plausible but as yet unverified.

The balance of the paper discusses in summary fashion the pros and cons of the four categories of teaching methods as they apply to the teaching of public administration. Without making any authoritative generalizations, the authors are willing to suggest which teaching methods, in their opinion, can be used for specific areas of knowledge.

THE LECTURE

Historically, the lecture is the earliest method of formal instruction. The lecture system developed in medieval universities because there were few books. Often only the teacher possessed a book and he read from it to the class, as we learn from the fact that "lecture" is derived from the Latin *legere*. Old and venerable as it is, the lecture method has had to undergo drastic modifications, but it is still the most commonly used teaching method. Nevertheless, as psychologists and educators have delved deeper into the psychology of learning, it has come under constant criticism.

In over-simplified terms, the lecture system may be either

[3] Philip E. Jacob, *Changing Values in College*. New Haven: The Edward W. Hazen Foundation, 1956, p. 88.

"pure" or modified. In the former, the lecturer does all the work, the students listen. In the latter, there may be more than one lecturer and students are encouraged to ask questions and discuss propositions. It requires only a little perspicacity to criticize adversely the pure lecture system and teachers have been quick to level two basic objections to its use. In the first place, it is essentially subject-matter oriented rather than student-oriented. This means that the instructor is primarily concerned with *what* he is saying (that is, with course content) and less with whether the material is being understood by the class. The material is so well organized that it can be comprehended easily by an alert class and any deviations from the prepared script interrupts the orderly train of thought. That this is a realistic assumption is highly debatable. The second objection to the pure lecture method is that it fosters verbalism. The students listen passively, take notes, memorize and forget the material in about that order. Unless the students relate what they have heard to what they already have experienced, the effect of the lecture is negligible. However, these two criticisms are less applicable to the modified lecture system. Although the lecture is still the central feature of the session, it is now audience-oriented thereby permitting the lecturer to adjust his mastery of the subject to the reception level of the class.

Teachers of public administration have been more specific in their criticisms of the lecture. Public Administration, they assert, is a unique discipline and the traditional teaching methods are consequently inappropriate. Public Administration stresses the application of knowledge to concrete human activities in an institutional setting. Much of the essence of administrative life cannot be explained from the podium. The lecturer is unable to make clear the role of human relations in administration. Internal struggles for power cannot be described adequately in the classroom, nor can the prestige rivalries, which so often characterize actual administration.

Even for advanced graduate students, the lecture provides an unrealistic and incomplete picture of administrative activities. Topics such as budgeting, procurement, personnel, and other management procedures are presented serially, whereas in practice no one of these subjects can be considered outside the context of others. Thus, the administrative process is artificially segmentized. Furthermore, the lecture is seldom able to provide a forum where beginning students can relate their personal experiences to typical administrative situations. For the most part, even graduate students have had little or no experience in a public administrator's office. Lacking even a modicum of on-the-job experience, the student cannot understand and appreciate a lecture which is based on practical experience. On the other hand, when the lecture expounds theories the student feels that this type of presentation may not help him in his initial assignment.

Despite these objections, the lecture cannot be written off as archaic and totally inappropriate. Educators are generally agreed that so far as the teaching of elementary subject matter is concerned the lecture method is as good as any other. Therefore, in those subjects where it is desirable to furnish the student a general knowledge, the lecture may be used to advantage. In the two workshops held prior to this conference, local and state administrators emphasized the importance of knowledge of the social, political and economic environment that conditions administrative practice. There are untold numbers of courses, which although essentially elementary in character, could be recommended to the student. These include, basic economic theory, economic institutions, public utility regulation, sociology, human ecology, social psychology, American history, political theory, political parties, and metropolitan government. No doubt methods other than the lecture could be profitably used even in these fields. However, in view of the limited time available, the level of knowledge required, and the economy of large classes, the most efficient method of instruction appears to be the lecture.

The lecture system can also be employed profitably in other areas of knowledge which are more related to administration. For example, familiarity with the basic concepts underlying specific public activities such as health, education, welfare, public works, transportation and law enforcement, *et cetera* would be of value to the student. A limited number of well-prepared lectures probably will supply the student with the necessary terminology to get along with people working in these areas. The device of using practitioners as guest lecturers has often been used successfully particularly when time has been provided for questions and discussion.

A strong case can be made for teaching the basic course in public administration by means of the "modified lecture." A vast amount of material needs to be covered in a brief period of time. In most cases, this is the student's first exposure to administration and the course is therefore designed to set the stage for the more technical and complex subjects to follow. It can also provide the student with a frame of reference or rationale for the study of administration. Rather than being technical, the presentation could be theoretical with emphasis on the external forces that influence administrative behavior. Since the introductory course is not likely to be of the "how to do" variety, the disadvantages of the lecture method are less apparent.

In varying degrees the lecture system is found in all methods of teaching with the possible exception of those few courses which are nondirective and exclusively student-oriented. Nearly every college teacher is obliged to know how to use this method and he might as well learn to use it effectively. There is nothing inherently inflexible about the lecture method. The modified lecture can permit active student participation; material need not be presented seriatim; and a skillful teacher can communicate the nuances of administration quite effectively. The disadvantage of this approach is that the success of the lecture depends almost entirely upon a skill or art too rarely found.

DISCUSSION-SEMINAR

The critics of the lecture system have consistently proposed the discussion-seminar method as the most desirable substitute. It makes provision for the active participation of students—hence more learning. Further, it is flexible in that it enables the instructor to stress more clearly the key points of a topic. And, it is popular with learners because they feel they are contributing and learning at the same time. In contrast to the lecture system (particularly the "pure" lecture) the discussion-seminar is characterized by active student participation with the teacher playing a more passive (or at least different) role. In a recent symposium on educational methods it was asserted that "sustained discussion with an imaginative teacher and a powerful reading program has an openness that the lecture cannot have as an avenue of discovery for the student and an instrument of perception for the teacher." [4]

However impressive the theoretical values of the discussion method, the few controlled experiments which have been conducted in recent years have failed to substantiate the educational advantages claimed for it. Several years ago at the University of Michigan an experiment was made to compare the impact of the recitation, discussion, and tutorial methods on students' values, beliefs and attitudes in the field of psychology. It was found that there were no

[4] Quoted in Jacob, *op. cit.*, p. 92.

significant differences in the amount of factual material re-
tained, in the skill of formulating conclusions and evaluating them, and in the development of attitudes toward individual differences. Earlier studies made at the University
of Minnesota and Purdue were equally inconclusive. True
enough, the more able students appeared to do better in
smaller rather than larger classes, and the reverse seemed
true for the less able. Even these observations, however,
were subject to qualification since much depended upon
the ability of the teacher as a lecturer or discussion leader.[5]

Although these experiments were made in the field of
psychology and not public administration, involved undergraduate rather than graduate students, and were perhaps
concerned with values which are more important in psychology than in public administration, they should give
pause to those who uncritically accept the superior claims
of the discussion method. In 1940 a leading educator wrote
that "one cannot, however, actually prove the value or discussion in small groups over lectures in large groups until
one has some objective measure of all the types of progress
that one wants students to make." [6] It would seem that such
an objective measurement is currently lacking in public
administration.

Despite the absence of evidence that the discussion technique is superior to the lecture, the generally accepted advantages of the discussion-seminar method, briefly noted
above, provide ample justification for its inclusion in the
battery of methods available to teachers in public administration. If the classes are small enough (since large classes
per se prohibit its effective use), the discussion method
would appear to be most useful where the course content is
controversial enough to stimulate group discussion and

[5] Luella Cole, *The Background for College Teaching*. New York: Farrar
and Rinehart, 1940, Ch. 14.
[6] *Ibid.*, p. 331.

learning. While it is true that under the direction of a skillful teacher much of public administration can be made controversial, parts of most courses are essentially "informational" in character and need not be the object of extended class discussion so long as students can ask questions. Too often it is assumed that because a class is small in numbers the lecture is inappropriate irrespective of what the subject happens to be. The criterion for determining the teaching method to be used should not be the size of the class alone; the subject or topic that is being presented is also significant.

There are, of course, important areas of study where the course content is such that the discussion-seminar method should be used. Questions involving administrative theories and values and contentions issues in administrative practice and procedure lend themselves to discussion. It is also useful where there is need to acquire skill in oral and written presentation. The latter would include the writing of administrative memoranda, administrative research reports, public relations brochures, seminar reports on practical administrative problems, and many others. The emphasis here is upon the practical effort by each member of the class. The subsequent discussion and criticism by the class of the written or oral presentation should have substantial value.

Brief mention should be made of the tutorial system which flourishes at Oxford and Cambridge but has not generally taken root in the United States. Gilbert Highet has written that "This system is the most difficult, the least common, and the most thorough way to teach." [7] It is also the most demanding of the student and the instructor. Unfortunately, it is the most expensive too. The tutorial system is closely related in methodology to the discussion-seminar where students prepare seminar reports which are

[7] Highet, *op. cit.,* p. 108.

studied and criticized both by the class and the instructor. Thesis supervision is also tutorial in method. Another relative of the tutorial is the preceptorial method, which accents very small informal group discussions led by able, imaginative faculty members. However, despite their recognized merit as a method of instruction few departments of public administration can afford the luxury of offering tutorials because of their high per student cost.

It must be reiterated, however, that the success or failure of all methods of instruction depends upon the quality of the individual instructor. Too often the lecture method is criticized for reasons not peculiar to it but which apply with equal force to the discussion-seminar. A haphazardly conducted discussion is as fruitless as an ill-prepared lecture. The assumption that students respond to discussion sessions better than to the lecture overlooks the fact that students, accustomed to the lecture method, may be slow (or unable) to adjust to a method that requires more initiative on their part

PROBLEM-SOLVING METHOD OF INQUIRY

Problem solving through the use of assigned projects has long been a technique used in colleges and universities. Although there are many variations, the common practice is to assign a project to a group of students who do their own research and then report back to the class. The major observable difference between this type of report and the typical seminar report is that the former is usually an analysis of a particular problem rather than one directed toward a more general area of inquiry. This is not a sharp distinction, however, and problem solving in practice may differ only in degree and not in kind from seminar reporting.

The significant drawback to any seminar paper is that the "doing" is essentially of a detached variety and the student is not personally involved in the situation upon which he is reporting. Rather than participating he is observing, and although he may thereby acquire skill in oral or written presentation of the topic, he is nevertheless a reporter, not a participant. A second disadvantage of any written report is that it has, perforce, a terminal point and the presentation of the paper arbitrarily stops the action so far as the student is concerned. Like all human activity, administration is dynamic and continuous so that unless the student "stays with the situation" he is apt to form highly unrealistic impressions about the administrative activity he has described.

For these reasons two techniques have been proposed, which within the limitations of the classroom, help to overcome these shortcomings. The first, role-playing, provides a series of diverse administrative situations with students playing assigned parts. Each administrative situation commonly lasts for a two or three hour period. The second, a more complicated variation, involves the student more completely in an administrative environment by assigning him the role of a public official in a hypothetical government agency for an extended period perhaps as long as two semesters.

Role-playing to improve the skill and develop the art of administration is something like using scrimmage to improve football. It originated in psychotherapy with the aim of giving patients freedom to express themselves and to work out their relations with others. It has been defined as the "presentation of a spontaneously acted playlet by a few members of the group acting in assigned roles." [8] In public administration these "playlets" are less spontaneous than planned and are designed to give students practice in analyzing practical administrative situations in the hope of obtaining positive transfer value. The fact that they are

[8] Claude E. Buxton, *Improving Undergraduate Instruction in Psychology.* New York: Carnegie Foundation, 1952, p. 212.

simulated encourages experimentation with different procedures that seem promising.

Role-playing has been strongly advocated because it avoids the dangers of verbalism without experience and because it overcomes many of the difficulties of teaching a subject which is better adapted to "practice" than to mere classroom discussion or lecture. Examples where role-playing can be used include such exercises as reporting to council, conducting a public hearing, presiding at public meetings, participating in staff discussions about changes in administrative procedures, and many others. While role-playing assumes basic knowledge in administrative subjects, it provides an opportunity for the student to relate this information to administrative problems, and in the process, react to and adjust to the practical objections and points of view of those affected by an administrative policy or decision.

In those institutions where role-playing has been used it has been considered a supplementary teaching device and has seldom integrated with subjects concurrently studied in other classes. Since it is a comparatively new method, many teachers are skeptical of its usefulness, despite its ready acceptance in psychotherapy. The number of students who can participate in any one situation is limited—with the rest of the class spectators. It requires special preparation of realistic administrative situations, and it is subject to the charge that if used too frequently it will lose realism and become obviously artificial. Practical difficulties of scheduling, if not insuperable, also may restrict its extensive use at any one time.

It is helpful, however, in developing those skills where conventional teaching methods do not penetrate. The staging of contrived administrative problems which the student is forced to analyze may help to provide experience in "sizing up" situations and people (what we have called "situational analysis"). He may become more sensitive to the importance of administrative relationships. Practice in negotiation and conference techniques can be arranged. Role-playing may also provide the student with the opportunity to practice the application of various administrative techniques to concrete situations.

The success of role-playing in accomplishing these objectives varies with the skill in which the situations are contrived and how ingeniously they are related to other courses in the curriculum. The experience to date would indicate that the ambitious objectives of role-playing can seldom be achieved fully because the situations themselves are of short duration so that the students are unable to see the full implications of their action. Also if the situations are too frequently altered they become increasingly artificial. There is also the possibility that the student-actor will be tempted to respond with a characterization that attempts to fulfill the "good" standards for behavior. To date, no attempt has been made to compare the achievements using this method with those using conventional teaching methods, if only because the objectives which might be set forth are so different, particularly in comparison with the typical lecture class which is oriented toward information and controlled largely by the instructor.

The basic defect of artificiality and incompleteness of presentation in role-playing has been in part corrected by what Robert Connery has described as the "laboratory experiment." [9] Briefly, a class in political science was given the assignment to administer a hypothetical state labor relations statute. Students organized the administrative agency and were assigned key posts within it. Since the project extended over an entire academic year, the students became increasingly familiar with their positions, and with the

[9] Robert H. Connery, "A Laboratory Method for Teaching Public Administration," 42 *American Political Science Review* (February, 1948), pp. 68-74.

policy implications of administrative decisions. Over the course of the year power struggles with other student-officials became frequent and revealing and there apparently was a growing awareness that the administrative process is a highly interrelated one. The student observes, perhaps for the first time, the fact that the personnel officer cannot perform his work until the line departments furnish him data on their requirements, that the budget office cannot act until the personnel man does, and so on around the circle.

Unfortunately, the laboratory method has not been extensively employed and, therefore, a fair evaluation is difficult to make. Connery feels, however, that it has three major advantages. In the first place, although it is an adaptation of the case method, it has the added incentive of a realistic and critical examination of cases. Secondly, it applies the basic principles of learning by "doing" under a controlled situation. Finally, it is easily adapted to the intellectual level and the maturity of the students, as well as to the availability of library facilities.

As a teaching method it is subject to the same limitations we have alluded to in our comments on role-playing. In addition, it apparently places greater emphasis on maturity and some familiarity with administrative subjects. It also presumes a considerable supply of government documents and reports which may not always be readily available. A recent publication by the Citizenship Clearing House while admitting that learning by seeing and doing are necessary adjuncts to book learning, adds this warning. "Education by exclusively seeing and doing is probably no more feasible than education exclusively by unregulated discussion. Learning by experience is frequently called 'learning the hard way' and it is a long way too." [10]

[10] Thomas H. Reed and Doris D. Reed, *Preparing College Men and Women for Politics.* New York: The Citizenship Clearing House, 1952, p. 46.

THE CASE METHOD

Perhaps no one teaching method has been the subject of more contentious debate in recent years than has the case method of teaching.[11] Although fairly recently introduced in the field of public administration, it has been the principal teaching method used in the Harvard Business School for over twenty years. Its strongest advocates assert that the case approach to learning is not a technique but a philosophy of education that relegates other teaching techniques to the level of McGuffey's reader. Some skeptics of the case method are no less dogmatic in their adverse judgments.

As disclosed in our remarks on the other teaching techniques used in public administration, it is clear that the case method as a technique of teaching can be used in connection with discussion-seminars and the problem-solving method of inquiry (but hardly with the pure lecture system). For example, it could be used in seminars to present students with problems of a relatively concrete nature. In addition, it could also be used in connection with role-playing with students actually participating in a situation described by the case. To this extent we might say that role-playing is a first cousin of the case method of instruction. The difference between the methods lies in the participation of the individual student. In the role-playing situation the learner's role is predetermined: but in the

---

[11] See J. A. Culbertson, "The Case for Cases in the Study of Administration," 42 *Educational Administration and Supervision* (November, 1956); George A. Graham, "Trends in Teaching of Public Administration," 10 *Public Administration Review* (Spring, 1950); C. G. Sergeant and G. E. Flower, "Case Method in Education for Administration, An Addendum," 78 *School and Society* (August, 1953); Herman Somers, "The Case Study Program: Where Do We Go From Here?", 15 *Public Administration Review* (Spring, 1955); William Anderson and John Gaus, *Research in Public Administration*. Chicago: Public Administration Service, Ch. 3, 1945; Malcolm McNair and Anita C. Hersum, *Case Method at Harvard Business School*. New York: McGraw-Hill, 1954.

typical case study, the role of the discussant may shift in the course of the discussion.

Nevertheless, both are adaptable to teaching aimed at altering attitudes and behaviors. They are similar in that problems are typically centered around an open-ended discussion of a problem situation for which there is no single "right" solution. But the dramatized situation (that is role-playing) is limited to a short span of time and the primary contact groups. The undramatized case narrative can consist of a series of events over both time and space involving some persons not interacting directly. It may, therefore, be used to develop insights into complex administrative decision-making as well as human relationships.

Definitions of what is meant by a "case" are almost as numerous as the cases themselves. There may be general agreement that a case is a written record of human experience centered on an administrative problem faced by a person or a group of persons. The problem may vary from the simplest kind involving an individual reacting in a situation to a complex administrative issue affecting the destinies of many individuals and several administrative units or institutions. Recently published public administration cases have been characterized by their great length (some running to over 200 pages), their common concern for background and historical information, and their emphasis on the social, political, psychological, and economic factors that affect decision-making and the processes of administration.

The case method emphasizes the importance of looking at a specific concrete situation as it exists and plotting a course of action in the light of the facts of the situation rather than merely in light of rules and principles. Students are not given general theses or hypotheses to criticize; rather they are given the facts out of which decisions have to be reached and from which they can realistically draw conclusions.

Proponents of the case method assert that it is particularly adaptable to public administration, not only because it accords with modern learning theories, but more specifically because the case situations are typical and recurrent and thus immediately relevant to neophytes who lack practical experience in their chosen career. A few examples may illustrate this point more clearly. The case method assumes that learning must start with the concrete rather than with the abstract in what may be called "action-oriented situations." Thus, after posing a typical administrative problem, the student can be asked not only what he would do were he in a position of responsibility, but how he would do it.

The assumption is usually made that the material presented in the case approximate reality as closely as possible. Administrative principles isolated from their real environment have been re-set more naturally so that administrative theories or concepts are discussed within a specific context of an administrative situation. The cases confront the student with the necessity of making decisions in a whole series of action sequences in which external factors and internal power struggles severely condition the utility of doctrinaire solutions. In the Summer issue of the 1952 *Public Administration Review,* Egbert Wengert wrote: ". . . mainly the cases constitute a contribution to the education of students by freeing them from a host of conceptions that have often been part of our traditional view of public administration. . . ." [12] In part, the widespread acceptance of the case method reflects the feeling that the "facts" and "principles" so often set forth in textbooks

[12] Egbert Wengert, "For the Teacher of Public Administration" (Book Review), 12 *Public Administration Review* (Summer, 1952), p. 197.

"were not as firmly established as they were presented to be." [13]

These avowed advantages of the case method as a technique of instruction lend powerful support to those who advocate its extensive use in the public administration curriculum. Nevertheless, a few cautionary comments should be made. In the first place, the case may come between the participant and the situation reported on. Some of the reality may be sapped away in the impersonal printed document since even a skillful writer may be unable to bring out important aspects of personal character or situations without expanding the case to unmanageable lengths. Since all of the details cannot be described, it is the writer who arbitrarily decides and interprets what is pertinent.

This may or may not be serious. To the extent that the author does present a "complete" picture, much of the information needed for analysis and decision-making has already been incorporated into the case by the case-writer. On the other hand, in the "live" administrative situation, deciding what information is required and getting it (if indeed it is available with an appropriate expenditure of effort) is one of the important tasks of the administrator. Thus, the complete presentation may leave little to the ingenuity of the reader who is presented with a tightly-written package. On the other hand, it is doubtful whether the printed word can impress upon the student the importance of administrative minutiae—the importance of the daily supervision of details and the checking up on results. In short, the case may leave the student with a feeling of finality when such is seldom true.

The case method is, of course, inadequate in terms of conveying systematically broad economic, social and political knowledge. However successful a particular case may

[13] Dwight Waldo, *The Study of Public Administration*. Garden City: Doubleday and Company, 1956, p. 35.

be in describing the internal and external environment surrounding a particular administrative situation, it is considerably less appropriate for conveying a comprehensive picture of the typical milieu in which administration takes place. Apart from failing to supply this broad background which it has been generally agreed that administrators should have, it is equally inappropriate as a vehicle for teaching vocational techniques such as auditing or accounting where technical proficiency is desired.

Irrespective of the quality of the cases themselves, they are the core of a relatively new technique of teaching; hence, the ability of the students to adjust may be crucial. Accustomed to the security of definitive texts and obsessed with the idea of coming out with principles that will take care of all exigencies, the case method may seemingly confuse rather than clarify. From the point of view of the instructor this may be realistic teaching. However, unless the student is equally convinced of its utility, the effectiveness of the case method is markedly reduced.

The question of which areas of study in the public administration curriculum the case method is suited for is a difficult one to answer. In terms of subject matter content the cases have been concerned largely with the decision-making aspects of administration. Although a substantial number of cases involve local and state government administration, they have not emphasized many of the technical problems involving the use of professional skills such as budget making and position classification. In addition, the number of cases dealing with the regulatory process and planning and urban renewal is limited.

In terms of the suggested core program which was outlined in an earlier paper, the case method would appear to be appropriate in certain phases of "the Environment of Public Administration," "Organization Theory and Management Concepts," and in "Public Finance and Public

Budgeting." In these three areas the case method might be useful in making concrete the theoretical concepts brought out in the lecture. The existence of conflicting "principles" in public administration can be made more explicit through case study; interrelationships in the administrative process are more easily understood through concrete examples; the importance of human relations in administration is best appreciated through practical examples; and the danger of applying pat formulas to a given set of facts can be most forcibly revealed through case analysis.

These are all important contributions to the study of public administration. Without question the case method has added a new dimension to the student's view of his future position in government. The case method, however, needs the support of other teaching methods that supply what it cannot: systematic presentation of the theories that underly the use of administrative techniques and procedures.

CONCLUSION

The limited research conducted on the effectiveness of the various teaching methods precludes generalizations about which method should be used for any one course area. Moreover, even if tentative conclusions could be drawn, the variables listed above would suggest that caution be exercised before any one method is replaced by another. If the dichotomy of knowledge—skills is accepted, it would seem that the latter can best be acquired through those techniques emphasizing the "doing," that is the problem-solving method of inquiry. In those institutions that include in their curriculum field work and internship assignments as a part of degree requirements, this emphasis may be less necessary.

Above all, the selection of any one teaching technique must be left largely to the discretion of the teacher. Although matters of course scheduling, budget, and physical facilities are no doubt often controlling, the planning of the course to meet the requirements of the class is his singular responsibility. The selection of the technique to be used is the art of teaching in the highest sense. But every teacher profits in the development of his own style by hearing the opinions of others.

Teaching Methods — Course Instruction

Panel Discussion

Chairman: JOHN M. GAUS, Professor of Government, Harvard University

Panel: EDWIN A. BOK, Staff Director, Inter-University Case Program, New York City

        RICHARD T. FROST, Instructor, Woodrow Wilson School of Public and International Affairs, Princeton University

        GERALD J. GRADY, Assistant Professor of Government, University of Maine

        PHILIP E. JACOB, Professor of Political Science, University of Pennsylvania

        JOSEPH E. McLEAN, Commissioner of Conservation and Economic Development, State of New Jersey; formerly Professor of Politics, Woodrow Wilson School of Public and International Affairs, Princeton University

        DONALD W. SMITHBURG, Associate Professor of Political Science, Illinois Institute of Technology

1. The basic document before the Workshop and the presentation by Mr. McLean emphasized the assumption underlying most educational methods and devices in modern education: they should be employed to stimulate active participation in learning by the student. The methods described and appraised were: the lecture, the discussion seminar, problem solving inquiries, and presentation of data in case form. To these there were added in discussion the individual conference of teacher or consultant and student and the employment of consultants drawn from public administration and related activities.

2. The report further emphasized the view that there is "no one best way" in teaching methods. The use of each is contingent upon personalities of teacher and student, the phases of courses and programs, the nature, resources, location and objectives of the institution, and similar variables of time and place. It further emphasized the strategic role of the teacher. The discussion as well as the document suggested that the encouragement of his development should be given attention along with the emphasis on student-orientation. These cautions against focus upon any one device were supported by the view that research on relative values of different methods is limited and inconclusive. Discussion revealed differences of opinion, for example, as to how much we know as to student attitudes, and the impact of teacher or method or content upon individual student development. This general situation may not be like the special situation in the relatively new schools of public administration, but even in them we just don't know about these attitudes and relations that are important for the evaluation of our teaching methods.

3. It is apparent that the schools of public administration in their relatively brief history have borrowed practices from other fields, rather than invented new methods.

In the borrowing, however (as with the case method, internships and the seminar), adaptation to new conditions and
objectives offers new experience in teaching methods that
needs, first of all, recording, then comparison and evaluation. The recording now is urgent when many of the pio-
neers are still living. Something of this recording and appraisal is being done consciously for the use of cases.

4. Such recording and appraisal go somewhat against the
grain of traditional college and university faculty attitudes.
These reflect suspicion of methods emphasis, and approval
of emphasis on command of content knowledge and on research. This is reflected in status and salary standards. Some
discussants urged that an emphasis on teacher qualities and
methods, and the relation of the public administration
work to the entire resources of an institution, be given in
the development of our programs of education in public
administration.

5. Here, as at every point in the discussions, the interdependence of methods of instruction with the topics considered by the other workshops was present. What are the
objectives and proper emphases in schools of public administration? What must be left to in-service education? What
can we learn from, and should be left to, substantive professional schools for particular public services, such as education, health, defense, city planning, and social work? Or
professional schools, many of whose graduates form a large
and important part of the public service, such as forestry,
law, medicine and engineering? Beyond all this, what re-
flection of the setting of public administration within
American government generally, the American economy,
society and culture should appear in our methods? Of the
international setting?

6. Clearly we teachers in a relatively new field have immediately urgent need to record methods and experiences

we view as significant and in company perhaps with colleagues in related substantive fields, and in our professional
societies, to practice what we preach as to the importance
of operations and methods!

John M. Gaus

5

Teaching Methods—Field Experience

THOMAS J. DAVY *
University of Pennsylvania

YORK WILLBERN *
University of Alabama

INTRODUCTION

Few people would question the importance of the principle of "learning by doing" in an applied field like public administration. Other professions and crafts observe this principle primarily through an apprenticeship arrangement of some kind. In medicine, nursing, law to some extent, social work, education, and other professions, a period of guided field experience during or following academic work is considered necessary to qualify for practice. In some professions it is required for certification.

Such is not the case in public administration. Apprenticeship for the administrative generalist or administrative specialist is not a general professional requirement, but rather depends upon the policies of individual employers and schools. The questionnaire survey made for this conference found that of the 45 schools offering a master's degree in public administration, 23 of them expect some form of field experience. Of the 18 schools that specifically re-

* *Thomas J. Davy, Ph.D., is Educational and Research Associate, Fels Institute of Local and State Government, and Assistant Professor of Political Science, University of Pennsylvania; York Willbern, Ph.D., is Professor of Political Science and Director of the Bureau of Public Administration, University of Alabama.*

quire an internship, six give academic credit for the work.
This ranges from five hours to 16 hours of credit.

There are several explanations for the fact that apprenticeship is not a requirement for professional status in
public administration considered as a general discipline.
There is less technical homogeneity in the field than there
is in the professions mentioned above. Perhaps because of
this fact, the nature of professional organization in public
administration is quite different from that in these other
fields; associations based upon the common elements of the
administrative process have relatively less authority over
their members and less control over standards than do organizations based upon a greater degree of technical homogeneity. There is no certification procedure. In fact, many
scholars and practitioners in the field have serious misgivings regarding the desirability of certification, even if such
a procedure might be possible. The fact that public administration in many schools has grown up as part of a social science or political science department with a general
education rather than a vocational orientation would also
appear to be a factor.

Yet, regardless of the parentage of public administration
and the nature of its professional organization, the value
that other applied disciplines attach to the principle of
"learning by doing" and to apprenticeship as a device for
applying it would appear relevant to preparation for administrative careers in government.

PURPOSE AND SCOPE

The purpose of this discussion is to consider field experience as a teaching method in preparing people for administrative careers, and to explore those aspects of field experience that can make it most effective from this point of view.
Depending upon the aims and attitudes of a person, all

work experience can contribute to his development. To obtain more effective administrative leaders, the types of experience appropriate for each stage of their development should be considered. However, this discussion refers only to the kind of experience appropriate during the initial period of their careers for people who prepare especially for public administration. It is assumed that experience during this initial period is at least somewhat related to academic study and is planned and organized with the person's ultimate career objectives in mind. The term "internship" is used to identify this particular kind of initial field experience. The paper covers the following points: the nature and purposes of internship in public administration; the factors to be taken into account in determining the responsibility that the college or university may assume for the internship; the special advantages and problems of pre-academic, concurrent, and post-academic internships; the problems of arranging an effective internship; the kinds of student work assignments that may be appropriate; faculty guidance and supervision of interns; compensation of interns; and integration of internship with the academic program.

Though the question of the school's responsibility for the internship is discussed at some length later in the paper, it is to be noted here that the discussion is oriented throughout toward initial field experience for which the school assumes some responsibility. Many of the observations would also seem pertinent to internships sponsored exclusively by governmental employers. Since the predominant theme of this conference is the preparation of people for administrative policy-making positions, this discussion concentrates on internships for students aiming to achieve such positions eventually. However, many schools also prepare administrative specialists, for whom an apprenticeship would be an equally valuable experience; many of the points in this paper would also apply to internships for them.

It is unfortunate that the time and resources available for this conference did not permit a detailed survey of the internship policies and procedures of all schools requiring some form of field experience. Such a survey would undoubtedly have uncovered a variety of policies and procedures that other schools contemplating the adoption of the internship as a teaching method would find useful. Although some information was obtained about other programs, the authors have had to draw most of their points and illustrations from the experience of the programs with which they have been associated: the Southern Regional Training Program of the Universities of Alabama, Kentucky, and Tennessee, and the Master of Governmental Administration Program of the Fels Institute of Local and State Government, University of Pennsylvania. Both these programs have had many years of experience with the internship.

It is perhaps appropriate at this point to emphasize that the authors are not proposing that the higher administrative positions in the public service be restricted to graduates of public administration programs. Assuming that such a proposition were possible, the formation of an administrative elite that well might result from such a policy would violate the basic values that this conference is aiming to strengthen. We are proposing only that men and women who have selected public administration as their vocation, who have invested in special preparation for it, and who appear to possess qualifications for success in it, be accorded the optimum opportunity to develop their potential for eventual administrative leadership to the fullest extent. Whether they make the grade will depend, of course, upon their effectiveness in competition with everyone else who may be considered for positions at each level on which they serve.

NATURE AND PURPOSES OF INTERNSHIP

The internship has both intellectual and practical purposes. The practical purpose of the internship is to afford the intern the opportunity to form at least some of the attitudes, sensitivities, habits, and skills needed for eventual administrative leadership. These have been identified in rather complete detail by the administrators' workshops preceding this conference. For this reason, and also because the practical aspects are the ones most often emphasized in discussions of apprenticeship, they need not be further elaborated here. Some educators and employers also believe that the initial period of field experience should qualify the intern technically in one or more management specializations, such as finance, personnel, public relations, planning, etc.

The intellectual purposes of the internship are similar to those of case analysis, role-playing, problem-solving, and other methods of demonstration, interpretation, and application. However, the internship has some special advantages in that field experience is direct not vicarious, and responsibility is actual not simulated.

Intellectually, the internship is an opportunity for the student to make especially vivid and meaningful for himself the administrative generalizations he studies in his courses. The prospective administrator should understand such concepts as organization, coordination, administrative values, decision-making, leadership, and others in concrete as well as abstract terms. If he is stimulated either during or following academic study to relate the conditions and problems he has personally observed in specific administrative situations to the theories of which they are manifestations, he will better understand these theories. He can more easily recognize the many variable factors encompassed in such theories, and therefore appreciate the variations often necessary in interpreting and applying them. The internship is also an opportunity for the student to formulate his own hypotheses regarding the administrative phenomena he observes. These processes of deduction and induction are important to the effectiveness of the internship as a teaching method.

Another intellectual purpose of the internship is the acquisition of specific knowledge of governmental functions and operations considered desirable for administrative leaders and not usually obtainable in formal courses. If the public administration course program includes courses in governmental policies and services at all, the subject matter can usually be treated only in rather general terms. For each function or functional area, such as police administration or economic regulation, a general course in governmental services will typically cover the economic, social, and political trends that have shaped its development and present status, general legal and organizational patterns that commonly prevail in its administration, its broad social and administrative purposes, and perhaps the principal types of operational problems and procedural systems encountered in its administration. It is both necessary and proper that an educational program should deal with subject matter on this level of generalization.

Yet the administrative policy-making officer also needs specific knowledge of governmental functions. For in almost every administrative situation, he is called upon, either by law, or custom, or necessity, to make substantive as well as administrative decisions. He must also communicate with subordinates who are specialists; such communication often involves substantive questions requiring some technical knowledge, and knowledge of problems, conditions, and people peculiar to the functional area which the specialist represents.

A city manager, for example, should know not only administrative principles and the general characteristics of local governmental functions; to provide the leadership and make the decisions required of him, he must also have a rather intimate acquaintance with the organization of each of the functions under his direction, the major administrative and technical problems peculiar to each function, the working relationships that exist between staff and line agencies, and many other specific matters of this kind. It is true that administrators, especially in larger organizations, will often approximate the ideal of the true generalist. Yet there are times when they too must deal with specific service and technical problems. The reason may be incompetence of a principal subordinate who for some reason cannot be dismissed, or an emergency, or a politically sensitive situation, or other reasons. Then too, service problems—deficiency in police protection, inadequate hospital facilities, location of an incinerator—are usually of greatest concern to the public and to legislative bodies, and they expect the principal administrator to be conversant with them.

The more diversified the administrator's operational knowledge, the better equipped he is to handle the variety of problems he is called upon to deal with day-by-day. Depending upon the nature of a person's experience, this kind of knowledge will accumulate in greater or less degree throughout his professional life as he may serve in various administrative situations. For the aspiring administrator, the internship is an especially advantageous opportunity for acquiring in a directed and conscious way some of the specific operational knowledge that the administrative policy-making officer needs.

The extent to which these purposes can be achieved during the internship depends upon a great many factors. The abilities and attitudes of the intern and of the sponsoring administrator are fundamental. Whether or not the experience is obtained prior to, during, or after course study, and the length of the internship period are important determinants of the quality and intensity of the experience. The relationship of the intern to the sponsoring administrator and the organization, the administrative maturity of the organization, and the intern's work assignments largely determine the quality of the guidance and the nature of the challenge that the intern receives. These and other factors should be considered carefully when planning the internship program.

RESPONSIBILITY FOR THE INTERNSHIP

As indicated previously, there is little question regarding the value of internship for vocational preparation. But the degree of responsibility that colleges and universities should accept for assuring that their public administration students aspiring to administrative careers obtain this type of experience is another question.

Ideally, the internship should be the responsibility of governmental employers; it is their special interest to see that the quality of administrative leadership is continually improved. Yet schools with public administration programs, especially on the graduate level, share this interest with employers. It would seem to follow that those associated with public administration programs should accept some degree of responsibility for providing their students with adequate internship experience.

This responsibility can be discharged in several ways. The school can devote some effort to promoting the values of the internship among governmental employers, and to assisting them in establishing sound internship programs. It can also urge its students to seek this kind of experience in the initial stage of their careers. It can require an internship of its students, and it can grant degree credit for the work. It can go so far as to set conditions for the internship, make arrangements for the student with the employer, and even subsidize the student during the period of the internship.

The basic questions are whether the internship should be an integral part of the academic program, and if so, what the balance should be between course work and guided practical experience. Certainly there are no conclusive answers to these questions. They are matters of educational judgment, and what may be appropriate for some schools and some areas of the country may not be appropriate for others.

In deciding these questions, one of the factors that a school may consider is the degree of responsibility for internships that governmental employers are willing to assume. If a high value is placed upon the internship for administrative career preparation, somebody has to take the initiative. The increasing number of governmental internship programs in recent years indicates that employers are becoming more aware of the values of and need for such programs. Several states and large cities have rather broadgauged programs. A number of smaller municipalities, most of them under the council-manager form of government, have sound internship, or administrative assistantship, arrangements. Viewing the local and state governmental scene as a whole, however, the progress in this regard is rather discouraging. Generally, governmental employers have not yet recognized the importance of this kind of initial experience in the preparation for higher administrative positions.

In most jurisdictions the public administration graduate can obtain employment only in rather narrowly defined positions and can develop professionally only through relatively restricted lines of promotion. The graduate who develops his career in this way tends to lose the broad perspective desirable for higher administrative responsibility that he has acquired during his academic study. He concentrates on technical problems and the acquisition of technical knowledge and skills. He may have little opportunity to become proficient in leadership skills. His duties and work environment for many years after leaving school condition him to acquire the outlook and interests of the specialist rather than the generalist. In such a situation, his experience tends to nullify the effects of his academic preparation. To the extent that this may occur, the school's public administration program fails to achieve its purpose.

Will the number of governmental internship programs increase appreciably in the future? This is of course a matter of conjecture. Legislators and politically elected and appointed executives are sometimes inclined to make a short-term rather than long-term approach to their responsibilities. Their perspective is influenced by their term of office. They seek politically acceptable results before the next election, and therefore center attention and resources on those activities that may produce short-term results. An employer with this approach would tend to recruit specifically qualified people who can contribute directly to program accomplishment. He would be reluctant to invest in enterprises whose benefits may accrue slowly, even though such benefits to the agency may in the long run far exceed the costs and may also help to improve the entire public service.

Yet the internship implies a rather long-range approach by employers and a rather mature attitude toward career service and in-service staff development. It implies also a willingness on their part to invest in the improvement of the public service generally, since interns often do not remain in the jurisdictions or agencies in which they serve.

Some influences are at work tending to counteract this tendency toward a short-range view of policies and programs among governmental employers. Professional associations, leagues of municipalities, and similar organizations can often be quite effective in this regard. The International City Managers' Association and the American Public Health Association, to cite but two examples, have long promoted a broad policy of employee development among their clientele. Some educational institutions have had similar success in broadening the horizons of employers in their areas. The example of businesses, federal government agencies, state governments, and municipalities with successful employee development programs may sometimes influence other employers to emulate them. Underlying all such influences is the fact that as specialization increases, the general educational system is less able to provide people with specific knowledge and skills; if governmental employers are to satisfy public demand for more and better governmental services, they must accept more responsibility for qualifying their employees. If a jurisdiction's leadership has some degree of political security, and if its bureaucracy is professionally motivated and enjoys the respect and confidence of the public and those in political authority, such influences can often be quite persuasive. Conditions and influences like these appear to have been present in some degree in most jurisdictions and agencies that have established well-conceived internship programs.

It seems reasonable to expect that governmental internship programs, or similar arrangements for providing aspiring administrators with broad initial experience, will grow in number, though how rapidly is difficult to say. It may be that this development will occur at different rates in different parts of the country. Evidence would seem to indicate, for example, that local governmental employers in the western half of the country are generally more inclined to accept in-service training, internship, and similar concepts than those in the East, perhaps because they are less inhibited by tradition. There are, of course, significant exceptions to this observation.

Concerning the degree of responsibility that a college or university should assume for the internship, the writers submit the following suggestions:

1. Every school preparing students for administrative careers should consider the internship a vital element of adequate career preparation. It should cooperate with other schools and with professional organizations in efforts to persuade governmental employers to establish internships, or similar arrangements. It should assist employers in its area, when it can, to plan and organize satisfactory internships.

2. The school should prevail upon its public administration students aiming toward governmental careers, especially those on the graduate level, to obtain internship experience. Counseling may be enough. Or the school may find it advisable to make the internship a requirement for a certificate or degree, and even to grant degree credit for it.

3. If its students cannot obtain satisfactory internships through their own efforts, then the school should probably assume some responsibility for arranging them and perhaps for subsidizing them, if it can.

The rest of this discussion is oriented toward the internship for which the school assumes a major responsibility. This orientation appears best for the purposes of this conference. It does not mean that the writers believe the academically arranged internship is necessarily best for every school.

SPECIAL ASPECTS OF PRE-ACADEMIC, CONCURRENT, AND POST-ACADEMIC INTERNSHIPS

Internships sponsored by public administration programs throughout the country are of three basic types, distinguished according to their relationship to the course of study: pre-academic, concurrent, and post-academic. There are two types of concurrent internship: the block type, which is served during the summer months or a quarter between academic terms; and the continuous type, in which a part of each day or one or two days each week are devoted to field experience throughout the academic year. The internship of the Southern Regional Program is pre-academic; the Fels Institute program includes both the continuous concurrent and post-academic types; the University of Washington has a concurrent internship of the block type; the University of Kansas and several other schools have post-academic programs only. Obviously these types of internship are not mutually exclusive: a program could include all three types, or various combinations of them.

The purposes and values of internship discussed in this paper can be achieved by all three types, and most of the points suggested for making the internship an effective teaching method apply to the three. However, each of the principal types has peculiar advantages and difficulties which should be noted.

Perhaps the most significant advantage of both pre-academic and concurrent internships is that they make the classroom assignments much more meaningful. They help the students to participate creatively in the formulation of hypotheses and generalizations concerning administration. Generally persons who tend to think deductively will consider that field work experience represents an application of principles learned in the classroom, and will therefore prefer a post-academic type of program. Those who have more doubts as to principles, and feel that students can be helped to build up their own hypotheses and generalizations will want at least some of the field experience to precede or be co-terminous with course study. However, this point should not be over-emphasized. If the student's experience is planned carefully, the inductive and deductive approaches will be possible in all types of internships. The ideal program is probably one that combines either pre-academic or concurrent and post-academic experience. Such a combination would tend to maximize the student's opportunity to achieve the purposes of an internship.

The pre-academic and concurrent programs also tend to make students more aware of the areas of governmental activity for which their previous preparation is particularly weak. Thereby, the student is better able to make effective choices of whatever electives are available in the course program. They also help the student to select the area of public service in which he would prefer to concentrate his study and further experience.

There are certain difficulties to be anticipated in the pre-academic internship. If the students do not have sufficient background in political science and public administration, it may be less of a learning experience than that obtained during or after course study. One purpose of field experience is to help the student overcome his weaknesses and increase his strengths. Since the school is less able to judge the abilities and needs of students prior to direct contact and observation, it is sometimes hindered in fully realizing this purpose. Another purpose more difficult to realize in the pre-academic program is the placement of students with peculiar personal characteristics in agencies that can best enable them to overcome personal weaknesses and to increase strengths. Compensation of interns may also be a problem in the pre-academic program. A student serving a post-academic internship may be employed eventually by the sponsoring agency; the pre-academic intern must leave after the prescribed period of service to complete his education.

Certain conditions appear necessary for the establishment of a concurrent internship of the continuous type.

For this experience to be most effective, it is desirable that the student receive experience in a variety of administrative situations, under the supervision of a number of principal administrative officers. Therefore, the school probably has to be located in an area within easy travel distance of a number of governmental jurisdictions or agencies in a metropolitan area, or a good-sized city, or within easy access of the state capital.

The in-course program provides some special advantages. Direct personal contact can be maintained between the faculty and supervising administrators, and the faculty advisors can give personal and continual guidance to the students. Work assignments can often be closely related to emphases of the course program, and can thus serve as a basis for interpreting administrative theories and concepts, as they are being studied, in terms of comparative administrative environments. They can also be "custom-tailored" to each student's career interests, if he knows them, and to his professional needs. Another advantage worth noting is the fact that through effective supervision of a student's work and through consultation with the supervising administrator, the public administration faculty can spread its competence over several important problem areas, and thus contribute to administrative improvements within the jurisdictions and agencies to which students are assigned.

Organization of an in-course program involves many questions. How much of the student's time should be allocated to such experience *vis a vis* course work? How should field work be scheduled, on a daily basis or on a block basis of some kind? Should daily field work be scheduled for morning or afternoon hours? How many assignments should a student have during the academic year and what is the optimum allocation of time to each assignment? Many other questions of this nature must be considered. Generalizations on these points are highly tentative, since policy with regard to them will depend to a large extent upon the educational purposes and policies, location, and other factors peculiar to each school.

As an illustration of how these questions are handled by a specific school, the program of the Fels Institute of Local and State Government at the University of Pennsylvania may be cited. The students spend fifteen hours a week, usually 9:00 A.M. to noon, Monday through Friday, on field assignments throughout the academic year. They are assigned to higher level administrators in the Philadelphia City government, the suburban governments, and in agencies of the New Jersey and Pennsylvania State governments located in the metropolitan region. The Institute has experimented with various periods of assignment over the years, and has found that four assignments of approximately eight weeks each usually permit the student to make useful contributions and at the same time achieve optimum academic benefit. The student's assignments are varied so that he may serve in large and small agencies, central city and suburban jurisdictions, line and staff functions, etc., and thus have the opportunity to observe a variety of administrative environments. The student is responsible in each of his four assignments for producing a formal report on a project of value to each sponsor. The faculty advisors assist the students and the agencies in these projects, and challenge the students to relate their experience to their courses.

An arrangement like this is possible only if the public administration faculty can completely control the scheduling of the students' courses so that a block of time will be available for this type of in-course experience. For most institutions, it would be difficult, if not impossible, to control the student's program to this extent.

The post-academic internship provides special opportunities for realizing the purposes of academically-related field experience. The interns have completed their course of study and have acquired some of the basic general knowledge, skills, and attitudes needed by the administrator. If they have also had pre-academic or concurrent field experience, they have some practical knowledge of administration. By the end of the course program, many students have fairly definite ideas about their specific career objectives and at least some idea of how they hope to achieve them. They therefore tend to approach the internship with a professional attitude. For these reasons, the intern can usually contribute significantly to the sponsor's major administrative needs, and thereby justify a close and continuing relationship to him.

What is the most appropriate time interval for a post-academic internship? There are primarily two points to consider: (1) the appropriate interval for the initial stage of development for administrative policy-making positions; (2) the effect of extended internship periods on the problem of recruiting for the public administration program.

Leonard White in his study of a government career service for the Federal level stated: "Instead of six months, we need a probationary period of not less than full five years, for training and testing the young administrator." [1] By probationary period White has in mind the initial stage of career development. Perhaps the larger the governmental jurisdiction, and consequently the more diversified the administrative operations, the longer this initial, or "administrative apprenticeship," stage should be.

We would suggest that an administrative apprenticeship period of five years, extending from the start of graduate study to a position of substantial and independent administrative responsibility, is not an unreasonable idea.

The academically-related internship could be only part of this period. If the internship is a requirement for the master's degree, then it probably cannot exceed a year. A

[1] Leonard White, *Government Career Service,* 1935, p. 49.

one-year internship would in most cases mean a two-year master's program. Probably a longer period would place public administration in a poor competitive position in recruiting students for graduate study.

Existing post-academic internships appear to vary from three months to a year in length. We recommend that the public administration faculty strongly urge its graduate students and the agencies with whom they are placed to consider the academically related period as only part of the administrative apprenticeship, and to seek an additional period of internship-type experience, either as an intern or general assistant to a principal administrative officer. Sometimes the school can, when arranging the internship with the sponsor, prevail upon him to keep the student on an "extended internship status" after he completes the academically arranged internship period.

ARRANGING THE INTERNSHIP

In arranging internships the selection of the sponsoring administrator and location, the types of work assignments given the student, the manner in which he is to be guided and supervised, and the financial arrangements between the employer and the student are important. If the school establishes general standards and procedures regarding these matters, it will be more likely that the student will obtain optimum benefit from his experience.

It is important that administrators who sponsor and supervise students (1) be on the administrative policy-making level, (2) be willing to accept the conditions for internship specified by the school, and (3) be generally recognized as highly competent administrators. The agency should be of sufficient size and diversity to afford the student the opportunity to achieve the major purposes of the internship suggested previously. The internship arrangements should be acceptable to the student as the most suitable one available for his career objectives.

The school may adopt conditions for an adequate internship for the guidance of students and sponsors. Such conditions may include the following:

1. If the internship is an integral part of the academic program, the student's major work assignments, and any important changes in them, should be jointly agreed upon by the sponsor and the school.

2. The student should work directly under the supervision of an administrative policy-making officer; if for some reason this officer cannot be the sponsor himself for the entire internship period, the sponsor should arrange to have the student serve under his direct supervision for at least part of the period.

3. The student should be assigned responsible work that will enable him to contribute significantly to major administrative needs of the agency.

4. The intern should be located in the sponsor's office, or, if this is not possible, at least close enough that he can be directly influenced by the environment of that office.

5. The intern should attend meetings of the agency's governing body, senior staff meetings, special board meetings, and the like, when it is convenient for the sponsor to have him do so.

6. The sponsor should counter-sign student work reports, memoranda, or similar documents required by the school.

7. The sponsor should be requested to submit to the school periodic evaluations of the student.

8. The sponsor should abide by the school's policies with respect to compensation of the student services.

Such conditions are intended to assure the student optimum opportunity for beneficial career experience. However, the student has an obligation to justify his sponsor's investment. If his work falls short of the sponsor's standards over a period of time, or if he violates what must necessarily be a confidential relationship with the sponsor, it would be unreasonable to expect the sponsor to abide by such conditions.

Arrangements for academically required internships should probably be negotiated by the school with the sponsor. It is inadvisable to permit the student discretion in modifying the school's internship arrangement, any more than he would be permitted to modify the standards and requirements of the course program. This does not mean that the school dictates to the student his internship location and arrangement. It is essential at this stage of his career that the student be convinced his internship is the best available for equipping him to achieve his career objectives. A means of helping him focus his thinking is to have him prepare a memorandum covering such points as: (1) his career objectives and tentative plan for achieving them; (2) the geographical or functional area in which he may wish to work; (3) the particular aspects of his own competence that he believes need strengthening; (4) several locations which he thinks might meet the school's criteria and in which he could enthusiastically serve. The school can then evaluate these locations as to their relative suitability for the student and their adequacy in terms of its internship criteria, and select the preferable alternative.

It has been suggested that the school establish minimum internship conditions and exercise some initiative in arranging it. It is sometimes argued that this can be done only if the school subsidizes the student; if the sponsor pays the intern, then the school can have only a very limited role in arranging and supervising the internship.

However, the respective interests of the school and the sponsor in the internship stem not merely from a financial arrangement, but rather from mutual advantage and professional interest. The school offers the sponsor several advantages even when it does not subsidize the student: a specially selected and trained person, who can usually contribute to the sponsor's operation, and who, in the case of the post-academic internship, may become a valuable addition to his staff; the best thinking of its faculty—who have first-hand knowledge of internship programs in many agencies—regarding a sound internship arrangement; the advice of the faculty and the resources of the school, available through the student, during the internship.

Mutual professional interest is an equally important consideration. The school's objective is to provide the best opportunity for an adequate administrative apprenticeship. Administrators who accept interns presumably have some interest in strengthening their profession and share this objective with the school. The school and the sponsor both expect the intern's work to be a worthwhile contribution to the agency's needs. Mutual advantage and interest, then, are the basis of the school-sponsor relationship, rather than a particular financial arrangement. As a practical matter, however, there is no question that a school which subsidizes interns is in a better position to prescribe internship conditions than one which does not. Joint sponsorship of internships is probably most feasible for local and state government. Whether such an arrangement is practical at the federal level is open to question.

THE INTERN'S WORK ASSIGNMENTS

Since the intern seeks a broad, practical perspective of government administration and a basis for comparative analysis of administrative operations, he should serve in a variety of situations irrespective of the size of the agency. In the pre-academic and post-academic internships, such variety is obtained by service in a number of operational areas within one jurisdiction or agency. In the in-course program, such variety can be obtained in a number of agencies.

The size of the jurisdiction is an important factor in structuring the internship. If the intern tried to cover all the major functions in a large city or in state government, he could only do a superficial job at most. In such situations, it is usually advisable for the intern to concentrate his efforts. Leonard White suggests that the basis of concentration should be the "functional area of specialization." [2] By this he means a group of departments or programs with fundamentally the same major social goal. For example, in state government the intern may work on assignments in agencies or programs concerned with public welfare: public assistance, mental health, vocational rehabilitation, probation and parole, etc. Such an arrangement helps the student understand the inter-relationships of programs serving essentially the same governmental purpose and thus helps to qualify him better for eventual administrative leadership. The length of the internship period influences the extent to which assignments can be diversified; too much diversity in too short a period produces a shallow experience.

To orient the intern to the agency and to have him acquire specific operational knowledge, some schools and sponsors have him work for varying periods in the major functional divisions of the agency. In a city government, for example, he may work for a month or so in the police department, another period in the health department, another period in the finance office, and so on. This arrangement has many advantages. It also has one serious shortcoming: it removes the intern for extended periods from direct association with the chief administrator and his environment.

The Fels Institute tries to achieve the advantages of this arrangement and avoid its shortcomings by having its students prepare weekly memoranda during the first half of

[2] Leonard D. White, *op. cit.*, 1935, p. 28.

their post-academic internship, each of which deals with a major operational aspect of the agency. The intern prepares the memoranda on his own time, but the Institute asks the sponsor to assign the student for a day or so each week from his office to the particular unit on which he is writing, so that he can obtain the necessary information. Most of the sponsors discuss the memoranda with the student and evaluate his conclusions and recommendations. Many sponsors value the memoranda for the fresh perspective and useful suggestions they often contain.

Some people believe that the intern should spend some of his time on routine work in the agency. Undoubtedly such experience contributes to the student's sense of realism and helps him keep his feet on the ground. But from the point of view of the internship's major purposes, routine work should probably be kept to a minimum. In most agencies production emergencies occur over a period of time, in which everyone from the chief to the clerks is expected to help; such situations will often provide the intern with some experience in routine work. Most of his time should be devoted to work of value and significance to his sponsor that enables him to develop insight into the problems of the administrative policy-making levels.

The intern's major work assignments should be scheduled carefully. It is usually more beneficial for him to work on a number of assignments than to concentrate his effort on one. He may, for example, be assigned projects in finance, personnel, public relations, production and procedures analysis, etc. He should also have assignments in the line areas of the jurisdictions' work. Often staff and line aspects can be combined in a project. The Fels Institute has found that in a six months period an intern can usually produce a significant contribution in from three to five major administrative areas; the larger the jurisdiction, usually the smaller the number of major work projects that the student can handle effectively. Sometimes sponsors find checklists of possible memoranda and project assignments submitted by the school especially helpful in scheduling the intern's work. Care should be taken, however, that such checklists do not inhibit the sponsor from assigning interns to the administrative problems that are most important to him.

FACULTY GUIDANCE AND SUPERVISION OF INTERNS

Supervision of the interns has an important bearing on the benefits they receive from their service. Indoctrination to the purposes and conditions of field experience and orientation to the jurisdictions or agencies in which interns serve are important. Care in this regard is especially necessary in the pre-academic type of program, since the students usually have minimal background in public administration, and the school has usually had a limited opportunity to become acquainted with the students. The orientation conference is a useful device. Reports prepared by interns previously serving in a location, and other background materials, may be made available to the students. In concurrent and post-academic internships, individual faculty counseling is especially valuable.

In the pre-academic and post-academic programs, communication between the school and the student poses some difficulties. Ideally the faculty advisor should make personal visitations periodically to each student. When the students are dispersed over a wide geographical area, however, this is difficult and expensive. In all types of programs the interns should be required to submit periodic work reports summarizing what they have done and learned, in addition to whatever substantive memoranda and reports may be required. In the Southern Regional Training Program, the faculty supervisor selects excerpts from each intern's periodic reports and distributes them to all the interns.

The sponsor's evaluation of the student is valuable to the school for advising the student regarding his further career development. Such evaluations may be requested at intervals during the internship; there should be a comprehensive evaluation upon completion of the student's service.

It should be noted that if care is taken in selecting the sponsor and in arranging the internship with him, the school's problems of supervision during the internship are greatly simplified. Its main concern then becomes one of assuring that the intern achieves maximum intellectual benefit from his experience. Close association with the sponsor and the intern's work responsibilities will in most cases adequately take care of the practical purposes of the internship.

COMPENSATION OF INTERNS

Though existing policies of various schools imply differences of opinion on the question of compensation during the internship, the authors believe that the sponsor's compensation of the student may influence materially the nature of the experience and therefore is a matter of concern to the school. Governmental jurisdictions pay interns varying amounts. If there is no restriction on compensation, the student's incentive in preferring a location may become the compensation rather than the value of the location to his career development. If jurisdictions compete for interns, the selection process may assume the nature of an auction; this well may have an undesirable effect upon the intern's professional values.

The question of intern compensation is most pertinent to the post-academic type of internship. In the pre-academic program and the in-course program of the block type, compensation, if given, is usually nominal and is intended to defray the student's basic expenses.

In the post-academic program, the internship should probably be a shared cost of either the school and/or the student and the sponsor, since all three parties benefit from the arrangement. It is advisable for the school to specify a maximum combined (school and/or student-sponsor) compensation allowable during the internship period in order to eliminate compensation as a competitive factor in selecting locations. The fact that family situations of the students often differ may be taken into account in formulating policy on allowable compensation. Such policy should also recognize that sometimes there are outstanding administrators in excellent administrative situations who want an intern, but who cannot pay him. Such an internship may be so desirable that the school will find it advisable to underwrite it. It is not unusual for students to serve without compensation in such situations, even when it means undertaking an appreciable personal debt. Though advocates of the "hair shirt" approach to professional training may feel that on the whole this is good for the student, we believe that the work he does rather than the rent he pays should be his internship challenge, and that as much as possible the responsibility of compensating the intern should reflect the mutual benefits of the parties to the arrangement.

INTEGRATION OF FIELD EXPERIENCE WITH THE COURSE PROGRAM

Implied throughout this paper is the assumption that the program of professional training for public administrators should be a highly integrated one: every part should be vital to eventual administrative leadership; every part should complement every other part. The administrators' workshops preceding this conference stressed that one of the important qualifications of an administrative officer is the ability to relate his specific day-to-day problems to the broader administrative and social problems and trends of which they are manifestations. The student, therefore, should be conditioned to do this during his period of study.

Integration enriches both field work and course study. The emphasis in recent years on the case method of teaching public administration is based partly on the assumption that illustrative situations through which administrative intangibles can be identified and analyzed are essential for adequate presentation of the subject. Provided the student is assisted in analyzing the significance of his experience, there is probably no substitute for direct participation in a meaningful administrative situation. Conversely, the intern's work projects should be more valuable to his sponsor and himself if he relates them to the theories and concepts studied in his courses.

Integration is achieved primarily by relating work assignments to course emphases and by faculty counseling of the students during the internship period. The alternative subjects on the checklists for the intern's administrative memoranda and project studies that may be submitted by the school for the sponsor's consideration can be based directly upon course emphases.

Scheduled faculty consultations with each student also help make his field experience more meaningful to him. In the concurrent field work program faculty-student conferences can be frequent and at regular times. In such conferences not only should the student be advised regarding the specific problems of his assignment; he should also be challenged to analyze the broader administrative aspects of both his assignment and his situation.

Seminars are also used for this purpose. It is highly profitable for the students as a group to analyze their field experiences under faculty guidance. In the Southern Regional

Training Program a substantial portion of one of the first seminars deals with analysis of experiences and observations of the students during their pre-academic field experience. The University of Kansas (post-academic internship) has a very interesting arrangement. Its interns are enrolled in the "Seminar for Apprentices" and return to the campus for a three-day session every six weeks during the nine-months internship period. Each meeting considers a special topic on which each student submits a written and oral report regarding its aspects in his location. Problems encountered on the internship are also discussed. Usually sponsoring administrators participate in the seminar.

Field work offers interesting possibilities for the use of the case method. If the assignments are related to course emphases, illustrative situations are usually available in the major subject areas for fruitful class discussion. As subjects are taken up in class, the students who have been involved in situations related to the points under consideration (assuming the pre-academic or concurrent type of program) can present the problems they encountered for general discussion and analysis. Internship reports can be useful for background study and class discussion; post-academic materials are especially valuable in this regard. The instructor, if he participates in field work counseling and seminar discussions, and especially if he consults with sponsoring administrators, can provide the students with additional insights into many of the problems discussed. To use field experience effectively for class analysis, the students should be trained early in their course work in the techniques of problem identification and analysis.

One other aspect of course-field work integration, the thesis, bears special notice. Some schools have their students write the master's thesis during the internship. This arrangement may often produce more valuable theses than those written solely during residence study, since it often permits a greater degree of original research. However, there is a danger that so much time will be devoted to the thesis that some of the other, and perhaps more important, values of the internship may be neglected. It is also possible that some students may not complete the work for the degree, since students and sponsors are naturally inclined to concentrate on day-to-day problems as they arise. Such an arrangement also complicates faculty supervision of thesis preparation.

Some educators feel that the usual thesis requirement for the master's degree should be modified for public administration majors. They question whether the investment in thesis preparation returns commensurate value for professional career preparation. A better arrangement might be for the school to accept a report or reports concerning the student's field studies for the thesis requirement. Such an arrangement allows the student to devote more time to research and writing of the type that he will find most valuable as an administrator. It also enables him to obtain deeper knowledge of a number of important areas of administration, rather than of only one such area.

It is to be noted that the opinions of educators on this suggestion are divided. Many believe that the value for the prospective administrator of the intellectual discipline involved in preparing a major thesis supersedes other values that may be substituted for it. Most graduate public administration programs with internships appear to require a thesis in addition to field studies, though often the thesis is based upon a field study.

SUMMARY

"Learning by doing" is an important teaching principle in an applied field like public administration. The internship is perhaps the most effective method for applying this principle. His internship should enable the student to acquire some of the operational knowledge, sensitivities, attitudes, skills, and habits required by administrative policy-making officers, and to contribute significantly to his sponsor's major administrative needs. It should also challenge him to formulate his own hypotheses regarding the administrative phenomena he observes in the field, and to analyze field adaptations of the theories and generalizations he studies in his courses.

The internship should be the responsibility of governmental employers primarily. While governmental internships can be expected to increase, it is probably advisable for most schools with graduate public administration programs to accept some responsibility for internships for their students, since the internship is such a vital element in administrative career preparation. Depending upon the educational policies of the school and the internship opportunities available to its students, such responsibility may range from mere promotion of the internship concept among governmental employers to arrangement of the internships and subvention of the students.

The advantages and difficulties peculiar to each of the major types of internship should be taken into account in planning the academically-related field experience program. The internship should be considered only part of the apprenticeship stage in the preparation of administrative policy-making officers. As a rule of thumb, this stage might be five years from the beginning of graduate work to appointment to specific positions.

If the internship is an integral part of the academic program, careful consideration should be given to the conditions to be met by sponsors and students, to the procedures of arranging the internship, to the types of work assignments given the student, to the way the faculty guides and supervises interns during the period, and to policies governing sponsors' compensation of interns. Such matters have an important bearing on the quality of the intern's experience.

It is well to integrate as much as possible the internship with the academic program. Such integration helps the student to realize the intellectual purposes of the internship. Field studies by interns are often useful materials for case analysis in the classroom. Adaptation of the usual thesis requirement to make the thesis a more valuable contribution to the student's career preparation may be considered; it may be desirable to accept field reports for the thesis requirement.

Teaching Methods—Field Experience

Panel Discussion

Chairman: GEORGE A. SHIPMAN, Professor of Public Administration and Director of the Institute of Public Affairs, University of Washington

Panel: GARY P. BRAZIER, Assistant Professor of Political Science, Western Reserve University

LYNTON K. CALDWELL, Professor of Government, Indiana University

ROBERT J. MOWITZ, Associate Professor of Political Science, Wayne State University

YORK WILLBERN, Professor of Political Science and Director of the Bureau of Public Administration, University of Alabama

Is experience in professional practice an essential part of professional education? In one way or another, all professional education encounters this question. It must be decided whether to develop the student for his professional role wholly through instruction within the educational institution, or whether the program is to be some blend of instruction and junior professional experience. In public administration, participation in practice can be generally termed "field experience," and the internship is often used as the formal vehicle.

In the conference session, field experience as a teaching method was regarded as required and specially arranged service in a governmental agency, or in an activity closely related to the governmental process. The period of service and the work assignments were assumed to be planned and administered as an integral part of the educational program.

The conference noted that, of the eighty-nine institutions responding to the conference questionnaire, only nineteen reported requirements for field experience as a prerequisite to the degree. Where this experience is required, institutions differ in the relationships of field experience to formal instruction. The range covers pre-academic, concurrent and post-academic arrangements. The conference discussion disclosed no strong conviction as to the desirability of one type over another; the choice could reasonably depend upon the feasibilities existing in the local context. The group was more concerned with weighing the desirability of field experience *per se,* in terms of the advantages sought and the difficulties encountered.

In summary, the conference recognized these potential advantages to be gained by field experience:

1. Field experience can serve to project institution-centered or academic instruction into the reality of operating experience. Academic instruction, in setting forth the de-

sirable and the undesirable, the effective and the ineffective, tends to emphasize contrasts for purposes of class communication. The student may develop an oversimplified and even artiflcial understanding of these contrasts. In the world of practice, he learns that extremes are seldom encountered; there are subtle gradations, shadings from effective to ineffective. He finds that the task is one of optimizing opportunities to do a job as effectively as possible under all the circumstances.

2. Field experience can give unity to academic instruction. Courses and programs can be structured in many ways. There is probably no ideal, no one best design of instruction. In practice, all approaches tend to become facets of an integrated whole, the effort to develop a professionally effective person. In this connection, field experience aims at emphasizing the essential unity of professional practice, and problem and "issue centering" of administrative work. After all, administration seems to be a stream of experience, moving from situation to situation. Each situation represents some combination of all the considerations that have come to the student in the course of his instruction.

3. Field experience seeks to develop early in the experience of the individual student a sense of relationship between the specifics of junior work activity and the broad policy mission of the agency or activity. This many of us regard as of critical importance. It is a perspective that is essential if the man is to grow toward top leadership responsibility, and not to become lost in the routines of early work experience. In this respect, a continuing problem in this field was pointed out: the junior man inevitably enters the public service in a position with numerous routine aspects. There is a real risk of his accumulating serious, and sometimes crippling, frustrations, in a period of working at a pedestrian level with routine concerns after education aimed toward preparing him for the ultimate assumption of top leadership responsibility. Hopefully, field experience as part of his instructional activity builds

into him the perspectives he needs to sustain him in the early routine of his professional life.

4. Field experience enables the student to develop poise, self-confidence, and self-identification in a work context. It gives him an opportunity to measure himself, his personal qualities and characteristics, against requirements of work performance, and to become sensitive to the personal adjustments he may need to make to become effective on the job.

5. Finally, field experience gives the student the opportunity to collect field data upon which a thesis, project report, or other evidence of analysis work and competence can be based. Such evidence is basic to his degree requirements.

Efforts to provide useful field experience in these terms encounter a number of difficulties. These also can be summarized briefly:

1. From the institution's standpoint, the placement needs a willing and cooperative sponsor in an agency having sufficient substance and diversity to give the student a meaningful experience. These considerations have two sides. The sponsorship must be official to give sanction to the rather special status of the student. At the same time, sponsorship must be direct and personal. A person in a position of administrative leadership must be ready to assume the responsibility for seeing to it that a work program is developed for the student, that the student has access to the information and understanding he needs, and that he is accepted as a full participant in the agency's activities. Ideally, the setting should be one in which work production interacts with significant decision-making, and policy considerations pervade routine performance. The agency should have a sense of its unresolved problems to which systematic analysis is applicable, so that the student can participate in administrative analysis. In many areas, such placements do not come easily.

Where they are available, sensitive and patient negotiation is invariably required to pave the way and to elicit the agency's active collaboration in the student's development.

2. Fitting the student into the work context can present major difficulties. An intern can be regarded as a specially favored person by others on the job. He can be isolated from the insights and understandings essential to a useful experience. Special financial treatment can complicate his relationships, especially if the permanent staff regards him as an expensive non-contributor to the group effort.

3. The educational institution and the operating agency inevitably have rather different objectives. The institution is concerned primarily with a degree of integration of field experience and course work, and with a strong emphasis upon the educational impacts of the work assignments. The agency necessarily has to be concerned with the justification of an additional special or part-time person. Particularly where the intern is compensated by the agency, the expectation is that he will earn his way; he is not being subsidized. In addition, the agency may be inclined to view the internship as a special channel for recruitment and to look upon the arrangement as desirable or not, depending upon whether the student joins the staff on a permanent basis. Such differences in primary interest and emphasis are probably unavoidable. Whether they make relatively little difference, or destroy the educational value of the placement, is always a matter of concern.

The group fully recognized the presence and the importance of such difficulties. The central question was whether they are to be regarded as so serious and so nearly insuperable as to leave the internship with little practical value, or whether they are seen as barriers that can be surmounted by careful and intelligent efforts upon the part of the academic staff. Those who felt that their internship programs had been successful expressed the conviction that the risk of difficulty could be greatly reduced by a clear-cut structuring of the internship plan, careful selection of the cooperating agency, and fairly detailed planning of the individual intern's program.

Throughout the discussion of the advantages sought and the difficulties encountered, the fundamental issue remained in the center of attention. Is field experience a necessary and desirable part of professional education? It developed that a matter of definition was involved. Some members of the group appeared to regard the internship as little more than work experience, often, they feared, of a far too routine nature to be valuable in the student's development. These members preferred to apply the students' time to research and writing designed to develop and demonstrate competence in those areas. Members of the conference who supported the internships most strongly, however, emphasized that an internship should be designed to provide a clinical setting for rigorous training in analysis work. From their standpoints, field experience is analysis experience. Its strength is that analysis skills are developed in the action setting rather than in the university library or classroom.

There appeared to be general agreement that every student should be thoroughly trained in analysis work. There was probably less agreement that the action setting was the most desirable one for this phase of instruction. Points of view seemed to differ with the practices and experiences of individual institutions. Immediately related was the question of the responsibility of the administrative agency for the development of junior administrative people. At least implicit in this question was the attitude that the educational institution should assume primary responsibility for those aspects of professional development adapted to the institutions' role and capacities, while the agency should undertake those needing the setting of administrative operations. Again questions of definition arose. However, it seemed to be agreed that in time larger responsibilities on the part of the administrative agency would be feasible. In the case of the Federal establishment a gradual development of this kind may be under way; in most state and local agencies it is still remote.

This line of discussion led to the larger question of whether professional development should be viewed as planned in-service career development, with agency and university conducted activities interrelated over a much longer period of time than had hitherto been regarded as applicable to qualifications for a graduate professional degree. This possibility was recognized as having far-reaching implications, considerably beyond the scope of field experience as posed for the conference discussion. Time did not permit its exploration.

Altogether, there seemed to be general agreement that educational development for professional careers in public administration needed the combined contributions of both the educational and the administrative sides. This was the real objective of field experience. It was suggested that the need was not simply for formal combination of institutional resources, but for interrelation of the contributing roles of academic people and of practitioners. There were, of course, differences of opinion upon how these academic and practitioner roles can be most effectively interrelated, but these differences were healthy and potentially productive ones. There was accord that professional education for public administration needs imagination and experimentation to meet the challenge of its public responsibilities.

George A. Shipman

6

Equipping the Professionally-Trained Functional Specialist for General Administrative Responsibility

JAMES G. COKE *
University of Pennsylvania

JOHN W. LEDERLE *
University of Michigan

GENERALISTS VERSUS SPECIALISTS

The Setting of the Problem. During the past twenty-five years in the United States, the subject of recruiting and training the administrative generalist has increasingly occupied the attention of teachers and practitioners of public administration. Undoubtedly there have been a number of factors to which this emphasis can be attributed. One of the earlier factors was the example of the British administrative class, the members of which not only possessed no specialty when they entered government service, but also were completely untutored in any formal academic discipline called "public administration."

Another factor in the new emphasis on the generalist was

* *James G. Coke, Ph.D., is Educational and Research Associate, Fels Institute of Local and State Government, and Assistant Professor of Political Science, University of Pennsylvania; John W. Lederle, Ph.D., is Professor of Political Science and Director of the Bureau of Public Administration, University of Michigan.*

the growing recognition that administration was, at least in part, a universally applicable skill. The burgeoning administrative theory of the 1930's made this explicit: good administrators could perform well in many organizational units, no matter what the subject matter. An individual might not be able to play the Marxian role of farmer in the morning, fisherman in the afternoon, and critic at night. But, if he were a skillful administrator, he would be equally acceptable to a Department of Agriculture, a Fish and Game Commission, or a Board of Motion Picture Censors.

A third impetus toward acceptance of the generalist arose out of attempts to make the American public service more attractive as a career. If governmental employment were to achieve the prestige of private employment, the public service had to become a respected career. And if it were a career, it was almost axiomatic that its personnel practices had to produce generalists for upper-level positions. The concept of the generalist was implicit in the concept of a career service.[1]

The British example, the universality of administrative technique, and the idea of a career service formed an imposing battery of arguments for the wider use of public servants who were specifically trained as generalists. But perhaps one reason why such persons have not been more widely used is that each of the arguments could be countered by a converse proposition that rendered it less cogent. British personnel administration was seen to have more points of similarity with U. S. practice than dissimilarity. Moreover, there were those who argued that the adminis-

[1] For example, see early works on the career service like Leonard D. White, *Government Career Service*. Chicago: The University of Chicago Press, 1935, and *Better Government Personnel*, Report of the Commission of Inquiry on Public Service Personnel. New York: McGraw-Hill Book Company, Inc., 1935.

trator, in any event, has to administer *something*.[2] Besides, the American public service still has a long way to go before it becomes a career service. Its prestige still remains low among college graduates, who would seem to be the best source of generalist talent.[3]

In spite of the spirited advocacy of the generalist, and in spite of a limited acceptance of the generalist concept in a few fields, such as city management, government agencies continue to employ increasing numbers of functional specialists: engineers, foresters, social workers, lawyers, accountants, architects, economists, nuclear physicists, doctors, and almost every other specialty in which educational institutions offer instruction. It is the specialist who receives initial preferment, and it is the specialist who is likely to advance to positions of administrative responsibility.

In terms of sheer numbers, the employment of specialists by government is impressive. Of every one hundred engineers in the United States, seven are hired by the Federal government, and sixteen by local and state governments. Government at all levels employs 43 percent of the nation's biologists, 27 percent of the mathematicians, and 25 percent of the physicists.[4]

Functional specialists can expect to rise in the administrative hierarchy. The U. S. Forest Service recruits foresters and accountants, and expects its administrators to come up through the ranks as foresters. The Forest Service has not used the JMA registers. In the Washington offices of the Navy Department, over half of all the civilian senior man-

[2] Lewis Meriam, *Public Service and Special Training*. Chicago: The University of Chicago Press, 1936, p. 2.

[3] Morris Janowitz and Deil Wright, "The Prestige of Public Employment: 1929 and 1954," 16 *Public Administration Review* 15 (Winter, 1956).

[4] National Science Foundation, *Trends in the Employment and Training of Scientists and Engineers*. Washington: U.S. Government Printing Office, May, 1956.

agement positions are occupied by engineers and scientists. In addition, a study of the Navy Department in 1953 showed that the senior engineers, who numbered 1,350, spent between 60 and 80 percent of their time on management duties.[5]

If we turn to the field of public health, we also find there that functional specialists fill many management positions. In 1951, there were 581 physicians working full-time in state or territorial health departments. Fifty-two of these occupied the position of health officer. Of 1,645 full-time physicians in local health departments, 1,003 were health officers.[6] The Yale Public Health Personnel Research Project discovered that in its sample of 875 public health workers, "none of the physicians, nurses, laboratory personnel, or sanitary inspectors and only 2 to 3 percent of the sanitarians and engineers had had major education in general administration."[7]

Private enterprise, it might be added, does not materially differ from government in the recruitment and promotion of specialists. A survey conducted in 1949, for example, showed that fifty of the 150 largest business corporations were headed by engineers.[8] In fact, the predominance of the specialist and a growing concern for the development of generalist talent (usually called "executives" by business writers) characterize both the public and the private sectors of the economy. And in private employment, no less than

[5] James C. Stephens and Gilbert Chester Jacobus, "The Engineer Manager: Training the Technician for Executive Responsibilities," 30 *Personnel* 374 (March, 1954).

[6] Leonard S. Rosenfeld and Marion E. Altenderfer, "Physicians in Public Health," 70 *Public Health Reports* 384 (April, 1955).

[7] Edward M. Cohart, William R. Willard, and Frances Kord, "Education of Public Health Workers," 70 *Public Health Reports* 1019 (October, 1955), p. 1024. The term "major education" includes "minors" or "majors" at the graduate and undergraduate level.

[8] A study by Dr. Earl B. Norris, reported in Stephens and Jacobus, *op. cit.*, p. 375.

in government service, the liberal arts graduate gets equally short shrift.[9]

What appears to be of greatest significance for purposes of this paper is that the potential contribution of the generalist was recognized *at the very time* when intense specialization was beginning to characterize the public service. The rapid proliferation of functional specialists in government after 1930 and the tendency among writers on administration to apotheosize the generalist were concomitants. These writers seemed to reflect a growing concern about the possibility of a fragmented bureaucracy, in which sheer size and diversity would make it increasingly difficult for the few top policy-making officials to formulate and carry out a consistent policy.

In short, many observers feared for the public interest in a bureaucratic world of guild identification and pressure group alliances. They sought to institutionalize a measure of protection for the public interest. Obviously one means of achieving this end would be to open top-level positions to a group of public servants who could see the organization whole, who could allocate scarce resources according to some over-all set of priorities, and who would not become so thoroughly identified with either program or clientele that they would resist coordination with others.

The Purpose of the Paper. This ideal is certainly not new. It is at least as old as Socrates' philosopher-kings. The nature of the public service which Andrew Jackson voiced made every man his own generalist. And the politicians against whom the nineteenth century civil service reformers made common cause were, in a different, inverted fashion, generalists, though, it must be admitted, generalists with a vengeance.

[9] See, for example, William H. Whyte, Jr., *The Organization Man.* New York: Simon and Schuster, 1956, especially Chapters 7 and 8, and pp. 103-104.

The ideal is still valid. However, modern conditions make it unlikely that much progress will be made by exclusively aiming pre-service education at the production of generalists. The specialist himself must be got at in some way, for tomorrow's managerial class will contain a very high proportion of today's specialists. The importance of the specialist in government is likely to be enhanced by both the character of the educational system and the nature of public personnel practices.

The emphasis in United States educational institutions is strongly upon the vocational, private-enterprise aspects of the world outside, and such an emphasis will produce specialists in greater numbers. As Albert Lepawsky has written, "Our main problem is that upon this classical structure of our knowledge we have chosen to erect a system of professional education which intrenches medicine but not government, engineering but not public management, law but not politics, divine but not public affairs, business administration but not public administration." [10]

Likewise, many public personnel practices give the specialist a running start. Among them may be listed the limited opportunities for in-service training, narrow career ladders, position classification methods, and the common requirement that examinations be practical in character.

Because of these considerations, it is the purpose of this paper to approach the problem of upper-level management from the perspective of the specialist, rather than the generalist. As a practical matter, the generalizing ability that Brooks Adams revered must be stimulated in the specialist, if that ability is to become a major hallmark of bureaucracy at all.

The paper will proceed in three stages. First, the functional specialist has characteristics that both foster and in-

<hr/>

[10] Albert Lepawsky, "The University and the Public Service," 2 *Journal of Legal Education* 253 (Spring, 1950), p. 261.

hibit the effectiveness of his performance as an administrative policy-making officer. These characteristics will be identified in general terms. Second, an attempt will be made to assess the specialist's needs for administrative skills at the various steps in his career development. Third, the role of educational institutions in meeting these needs at the appropriate stage of the specialist's career will be discussed.

It should be noted here that, in one sense, the problem of equipping the specialist for general administration is even more pressing today than it was a generation ago. This is because management is becoming within itself a more self-conscious and specialized activity; less and less is it concerned with technics. As David Riesman aptly observes, the man who becomes truly successful in his craft is forced to leave it.[11]

Thus, there is even more reason for educators in administration to be concerned with the expert who may be tapped for the top.

THE CHARACTERISTICS OF THE FUNCTIONAL SPECIALIST IN THE ADMINISTRATIVE PROCESS

The functional specialist has a number of very important strengths. Many of the strong points that make him a good specialist also strengthen his potential capacity for effective performance in administrative policy-making positions.

Perhaps the most important of these strengths is his knowledge and competence in a particular subject-matter. The greater this skill, the more he possesses a firm foundation for exercising the program-related responsibilities of high-level posts in agencies that deal with this subject-matter.

Furthermore, the functional specialist tends to be ac-

[11] David Riesman, with Nathan Glazer and Reuel Denney, *The Lonely Crowd*, Garden City, New York: Doubleday & Company, Inc., 1956, p. 154.

cepted within his field of competence by other members of the organization, simply by virtue of his prior training and experience. He has what has been called "functional status"; [12] if he makes a recommendation based upon his expert knowledge, the presumption is that he is right.

Another important strength of the functional specialist, particularly in large, complex governmental units, is his acute sensitivity to the motivations and aspirations of the technically-oriented organization of which he is a member. Therefore, he can be a spirited advocate of the professional point-of-view. In very large organizations, this may be a highly desirable form of creative conflict. The frontiers of public service may well be implicit in the newest techniques of a particular specialty.

Finally, mention might be made of a strength that does not belong to all functional specialties, but rather to those whose practitioners find their major employment opportunities in government. For many of these, such as city planners and foresters, the values inculcated by the pre-entry professional education strongly reinforce the organizational objectives of the agencies in which the students will work. Where this occurs, the functional specialist at the top has an easier job of communicating with the other members of the agency he commands. He can more easily achieve homogeneity. Needless to say, the homogeneity of the professional group may be purchased at the price of conflict with coordinate organizational units.

The functional specialist is prone to display certain weaknesses, some of which are the obverse of his greatest strengths. In the first place, his very competence in a particular subject-matter may lead him to think primarily in narrowly technical terms, in which he is apt to feel more comfortable and assured. If this habit continues as he as-

[12] Herbert A. Simon, Donald W. Smithburg, and Victor A. Thompson, *Public Administration.* New York: Alfred A. Knopf, 1950, p. 190.

sumes greater administrative responsibility, then program policy will in fact be neglected. At the higher levels of the hierarchy, technical matters play a significant role in policy formation to the extent to which their relevance is judged by considerations that transcend technique. Top-level policy problems are the economic, social, and political implications of technical facts.[13]

A second weakness, which is almost unavoidable, is that specialization creates difficulties in communicating with others. Communication with experts in remotely-related fields is especially difficult. Faced with this undeniably strong handicap, the specialist may fail to understand fully the communications from specialties not his own. If he so fails, his capability as an administrator suffers, for "it is this relating of 'different' things to the totality of things in application to a whole people that is the essence of that synthesis which is public administration." [14]

Another potential weakness of the functional specialist is that he is likely to confuse techniques with objectives. He may fail to appreciate the fact that the accepted technical statements of his speciality are often unconsciously used to mask implicit value judgments. In referring to the field of city planning, Norman Williams has described well this myopia of technique: "It is remarkable how often, in a highly technical planning discussion, differing uses of various planning devices can be most realistically viewed as rather sophisticated expressions of different social forces. . . . When one of these situations arises, normally there is no such thing as avoiding the issue, or making a decision on the 'technical' and 'non-controversial' problems only, or finding a safe and dignified refuge in accumulating end-

[13] *Ibid.*, p. 350.

[14] Paul Appleby, "An American View of the British Experience," in Joseph E. McLean (ed.), *The Public Service and University Education*. Princeton, New Jersey: Princeton University Press, 1949, p. 186.

less piles of unassimilated information and hoping that somehow it will speak for itself." [15]

Just as the functional specialist may perform valuable service in advocating the technical point-of-view, it is also true that, as an administrator, he sometimes maintains such a strong identification with his specialty that he overvalues its importance in the achievement of governmental objectives. Of course, this is only a somewhat specialized definition of the Sin of Pride, to which, presumably, even generalists may at times succumb.

This weakness might also be called resistance to over-all direction and control in the public interest. However, it is unnecessary in this instance to define "public interest," or even to posit its existence. The weakness simply stems from the fact that only rarely does any single governmental agency comprehend all of the resources needed to accomplish the social objective to which its program contributes.

Finally, the functional specialist who belongs to a well-established profession is subject to the possibility of conflict between his professional loyalties and the needs of the public service. This conflict may take a variety of forms, such as stratification of the public service and irresistible pressures by special interests.[16]

THE NEEDS OF THE FUNCTIONAL SPECIALIST FOR ADMINISTRATIVE SKILLS

The important job for those who are concerned with the specialist's capacity for general administration is to exploit his strengths and to overcome his weaknesses. But when can this best be accomplished, and by what means? Perhaps we can shed some light on these questions if we consider briefly the course of the specialist's career.

[15] Norman Williams, Jr., "Planning Law and Democratic Living," 20 *Law and Contemporary Problems* 317 (Spring, 1955), pp. 319-320.

[16] York Willbern, "Professionalism in the Public Service: Too Little or Too Much?" 14 *Public Administration Review* 13 (Winter, 1954).

From the standpoint of the opportunity to impart administrative training, we may distinguish two major phases in the career of the specialist. First, he is a student, receiving formal, pre-service education in his specialty. Second, after the completion of a specialized curriculum, he is employed by a governmental agency in work related to his specialty. In the consideration of the nature of administrative training, graduation from the professional school acts as something of a Great Divide.

If after entry into the public service the specialist rises in the hierarchy, we may conveniently divide his career into three general stages, each with its own peculiar demands for administrative skills.

1. The first stage is the entrance level position, which requires the application and extension of the specialist skills that he absorbed in the academic environment.

2. In intermediate positions—the second stage—technical work continues, but it is combined with elementary work planning and supervisory duties. In some jobs, a more important requirement is the effective use of certain "management tool" skills, such as accounting, reporting, financial planning, and production analysis. If these staff and management services happen to be highly centralized, however, supervision and work planning are the most important requirements.

3. At top-level positions, the craft skill becomes even less significant, except for its use as a basis for the symbolic display of a professional vocabulary. The management tool skills also become relatively unimportant. At this last stage, inter-personal skills assume overwhelming importance. These skills comprehend the whole complex process of understanding, evaluation, and action in all sorts of group relationships, both inside and outside the agency. Administrative leadership and planning within the context of a specific program responsibility are an important part of the

top-level job, as well as the managerial activity commonly called "getting things done through others."

Without attempting to delineate the characteristics of a profession, we might note at this point that there are a number of specialties in the public service that have been given only limited attention in academic, pre-service professional education. Examples are fire-fighting and police work. Up to now, educators have had little opportunity indeed to impart a pre-entry administrative orientation to these numerically significant groups.

THE ROLE OF EDUCATIONAL INSTITUTIONS

In light of the career progression of the professionally-trained functional specialist, there appear to be two major questions to be answered in discussing the impact of formal education for administrative skills. These questions raise issues of the timing and content of the educational program:

1. *When* should the specialist be equipped for general administration?
2. With *what* should he be equipped, and by what methods? Is there a type of training that is most appropriate at each stage of his development—a training that fulfills emerging needs at the proper time?

In considering these crucial questions, we might set our thinking in the light of a central assumption, from which the remainder of this paper proceeds. This is the assumption that the development of the specialist in his capacity to discharge general administrative responsibility is primarily *self-development*. The specialist himself must be aware of his own needs.

If this assumption is valid, it contains at least two important implications that bear upon the role of educational institutions. In the first place, the principal motivation for acquiring administrative skills is likely to result from the *in-service experience* of the functional specialist. Motivation of this type is eminently strong, for it is a product of day-to-day pressures for successful performance on the job. Motivation that stems from these needs is a firm foundation for efficient self-development.[17]

Secondly, the concept of self-development calls for particular attention to the characteristics of the individual specialist. While recognizing that there are certain common objectives in all efforts to develop general administrative skills, we must still take into account the fact that varying circumstances make a single pattern of administrative training inadequate. Each specialist occupies a position that demands a particular configuration of skills, and he has certain promotional opportunities open to him. He possesses certain individual traits that strengthen or weaken his capacity for general administration, and he has the characteristics of his profession. All of these circumstances condition the type of administrative training that encourages effective administrative performance.

It might be suggested here that there is a need for research that would be designed to investigate the administrative strengths and weaknesses of the various professional specialties. Specifically, these studies might cover such matters as (1) the values which professional education attempts to impart to pre-service students, (2) the relationship of these values to the achievement of the program objectives of government agencies, (3) the characteristics of the organizational units that are the major employers of the various professions and specialties, and (4) the nature of the career ladders open to specialists.

---

[17] The Yale Public Health Personnel Research Project asked graduates of accredited schools of public health to discuss their pre-service education. It is interesting to note that the two most frequent criticisms were (1) not enough instruction in the practical aspects of community organization and public relations, and (2) a lack of adequate courses in administration. Cohart, Willard, and Kord, *op. cit.*, p. 1022.

A growing body of research materials of this kind would fulfill several needs. It might perform the tactical service of pointing out to many professional schools that substantial numbers of their graduates enter the public service and that many assume there positions of administrative responsibility. Moreover, it would be shown that in some professions there is a considerable movement back and forth between public and private employment. Therefore, data of this kind should point up the need for academic preparation for the demands of public employment.

In addition, research along these lines could provide a more rational basis for judging the validity of the content and teaching methods of those courses in administration that are offered to functional specialists.

Equipping the Functional Specialist-in-Training. It must be admitted that many of the conditions that accompany professional education are inimical to giving effective training in general administration. In the first place, the professional school is almost invariably organized apart from the faculty that is directly concerned with administrative education and training. This pattern of academic organization cuts down effective communication. It means that teachers of public administration usually have only a superficial acquaintance with the professional specialties, and the professional schools, conversely, are not always aware of the need for general administrative training.

A second impediment is that professional curricula are not set up in such a way that they allot much time for education in fields that *seem* peripheral to the specialty. In medical, engineering, and law schools, for example, electives are scarce, and only a very few course hours can be allotted to fields of study that are not directly related to the techniques of the specialty. In part, this state of affairs exists because of the emphasis upon private enterprise and private employment that underlies much professional education. Professional schools do not always demonstrate that they are sensitive to the nature and needs of government, and to the characteristics that distinguish public from private employment.

Influenced by the traditions of his newly-adopted profession, the separate organization of his school, and the nature of its curriculum, the specialist-in-training necessarily concentrates his attention upon acquiring the tools of the technical field. Therefore, he is apt to view courses in administration as a marginal activity, and as a secondary demand upon his time. He has not yet had the experience required to be able to see how administrative activity will fit into the pattern of his future professional career. In short, motivation for administrative self-development is not likely to be high among the students in a professional school.

As a final impediment, we may note that, in most professional schools, it is difficult to predict who will be employed in the public service. And, even if it were possible to pick out the students whose careers are to be in government, it would be more difficult still to predict who would eventually become top administrators.

Because of the conditioning factors discussed above, the outlook is not bright for imparting significant pre-service administrative education. One cannot expect to accomplish more than limited objectives in the courses in administration that are offered to functional specialists-in-training.

However, this is not to say that these limited objectives are not important, and cannot be of significance for the improvement of the public service. The non-real classroom situation must not be undersold. The student can acquire some sensitivity to administration without actually administering, although he can probably learn faster on the job.

Professional schools frequently offer specialized courses in administration, such as library administration, but we suggest here that all professional schools offer their students some formal instruction in public administration that is not tied so specifically to the organization and management of a particular program. While recognizing the validity of Robert Walker's assertion that "imposing a 'course' in government or administration on a purely technical education is [not] the proper solution," [18] we feel that well-oriented courses may be part of the proper solution, for all their inherent limitations. Because the time that can be devoted to such instruction will be quite limited, careful attention should be paid to both course content and teaching methods.

For all functional specialties, the first and primary objective of course offerings in administration should be to foster an understanding of the role of government in modern society. Professional pre-service education would appear to be an appropriate place to give the specialist-to-be a foundation of insight into the characteristics of the governmental process. By "process" we do not mean management processes, like accounting, personnel, or O & M. The acquisition of these skills can come later. We do mean that emphasis should be given to what government does, and how the governmental environment affects the administration of programs. A heavy interlarding of history may well be appropriate.

In short, the specialist-in-training should be made aware of what Appleby calls the "governmental attitude." [19] Stress should be placed upon the pervasive political character of government, its public accountability, the complexity of its objectives, and the obligation upon public administra-

[18] Robert A. Walker, "The Universities and the Public Service," 39 *American Political Science Review* 926 (October, 1945), p. 932.

[19] Paul Appleby, *Big Democracy*. New York: Alfred A. Knopf, 1945, p. 3 ff.

tors for uniform, consistent, and open action. A clear understanding of the ends, rather than the means, of political activity is essential.

Course content that attempts to go beyond these rather general objectives should be quite closely related to the particular characteristics of each functional specialty. It is there that the type of research mentioned above is needed. Preferably, this should be cooperative research between teachers of public administration and the faculty members of professional schools.

How could such research be of assistance in setting up courses in administration? We would expect it to point out the administrative strengths and weaknesses of each specialty, so that these characteristics could be taken into account in course building. Some highly tentative illustrations may be appropriate at this point.

Qualified observers have made a generalization that engineers who become administrators try to manage human activities as they formerly dealt with physical processes.[20] If research corroborates this generalization, then courses offered to engineers might well emphasize the human relations aspects of administration.

Again, it has been noted that public administration in the United States tends to be legalistic because lawyers, who as a professional group are influential in administrative decision-making, have all been trained to hold high respect for settled legal procedures. If this is in fact the case, the administrative courses offered in law schools should be program-oriented. Another factor supporting this conclusion is that in government agencies lawyers are generally organized in process units. Thus organization itself may reinforce a tendency to identify with techniques and procedures, rather than with the achievement of substantive governmental objectives.

[20] Stephens and Jacobus, *op. cit.*, p. 376.

Whether in these illustrations the premises are true and the conclusions valid is, of course, the subject of legitimate debate. Nevertheless, the illustrations show how research could fructify the educational process.

In concluding this section, we may observe that the general lack of motivation among specialists-in-training places a severe handicap upon introducing effective administrative training at the pre-service level. The problem of overcoming this handicap is extraordinarily difficult to solve, for it raises interconnected issues of the content, organization, and sponsorship of the public administration curriculum.

On the one hand, it would seem desirable to relate course emphases, instructional materials, and teaching methods to the characteristics of the specialty and to the experience of the student. This would be one way of attaining the maximum impact upon the functional specialist-in-training.

However, this does not mean that courses in administration should be exclusively within the domain of each professional school and its faculty. While the specialized courses in library administration, public health administration, public welfare administration, etc., are indeed valuable, the specialist-in-training should also be apprised of the facets of administration that transcend the problems of a single program or specialized organizational unit.

Therefore, the most desirable situation would be a strong cooperative relationship between the professional school and the school or department of public administration. There are a number of devices that can promote joint influence. One such device is the extensive use of interdisciplinary seminars, where both teachers and students can bring a number of viewpoints to bear upon a problem of common concern. Another method is to have the school of public administration offer courses within the professional school curriculum. A third device is to set up degrees that can be obtained by taking work in both schools.

Equipping the Functional Specialist After Entry into Government Service. Because of the unfavorable conditions surrounding pre-service professional education, a large part of the job of training functional specialists for general administrative responsibility must be accomplished in post-entry programs. At this point the government employer assumes substantial and continuing responsibility for the development of generalists. Governments cannot expect educational institutions either to provide full-blown administrators or to bear the full financial burden of post-entry administrative training.

In order to realize fully the advantages that educational institutions can offer, we should first set the governmental house in order. We should pay attention to those personnel policies and procedures that foster a generalist attitude among our functional specialists. We should adopt recruitment, selection, and promotion policies that encourage the specialist who has the capacity for general administrative responsibility. We should set up broader career ladders, encourage easy transfers from one unit to another, and develop ample opportunities for in-service training.[21] We should consider the establishment of internship programs for the specialist, as well as the generalist. Such programs should not encourage narrow specialization. Rather, they should be designed to extend the specialist's horizons. For example, the City of Philadelphia now requires interns appointed by the operating departments to participate in

[21] Government agencies appear to be assuming more and more responsibility in sponsoring administrative in-service training for their functional specialists. By way of brief illustration, we might mention the USDA institutes on administrative management, the Forest Service classes in administration for field personnel, and the special after-hours courses in management subjects sponsored jointly by George Washington University and the Navy Department for the latter's engineers.

seminars sponsored by the Office of the Managing Director.

At this point, the problem of self-motivation must again be taken into account. Governmental agencies should have policies and programs that help the functional specialist recognize his need for additional administrative preparation and that help him obtain it. Each jurisdiction should consciously formulate and adopt an "executive development" policy. Self-motivation receives a powerful stimulus if an agency expects its functional specialists to be more than mere technicians.

Within the framework of appropriate public personnel policies, an atmosphere can be developed for fruitful cooperation with educational institutions in the creation of in-service educational programs for functional specialists. While the respective roles of higher education and government is the subject of another paper in this volume, we might mention here a few areas where cooperation would be beneficial.

As a basis for developing in-service programs, public employers and educators should cooperate in analyzing the administrative needs of each level in the hierarchy. These needs can then be interpreted in terms of in-service educational emphases.

After this is accomplished, educational institutions can furnish course materials and instructional personnel for basic in-service preparation in management methods and general administration. They can also profitably offer refresher courses in technical fields; this is important because of the relationship of technological change to the organization of governmental programs.

CONCLUSIONS

Robert Walker wrote in 1945, "In brief, education for the public service is to a large extent a matter of reaching the technicians and specialists who find a major outlet for their skills in government jobs. Formal training in public administration has barely touched this group in the past. . . ." [22]

We believe that the crux of the matter still lies in the preparation of functional specialists to assume adequately the administrative duties to which the most talented will be called. In the foreseeable future, it seems unlikely that the emphasis upon the specialist will be materially reduced.

Because of the problem of motivation for self-development in administrative skills, the pre-eminence of the specialist places educational institutions at a considerable disadvantage if they attempt to impart administrative training. The dilemma is simply that the specialist-in-training rarely appreciates his need for administrative skills. When his in-service experience does make him aware of his need for these skills, he is then largely beyond the influence of formal education.

We have mentioned some devices that may help to overcome this difficulty: inter-disciplinary seminars, cooperative research in the characteristics of each functional specialty, degrees obtained by work in both the professional school and the department of public administration, and course work for specialists that is related to the experience and needs of the student and that stresses the role of government in the society. And there is promise in some of the developments of the last decade: new instructional techniques, such as the case method, and changing attitudes here and there in some professional schools.[23]

[22] Walker, *op. cit.,* p. 932.

[23] At Cornell, for example, engineering students are now required to take from ten to 27 credit hours in liberal arts. Electrical engineering students can be credited with up to 36 hours, which is equivalent to almost a full year's work. Undoubtedly, part of this liberality in electives can be attributed to the adoption of a five-year engineering curriculum.

While the emphasis here is upon the "well-rounded" engineer, not upon

Moreover, there has recently been a recognition of the need for "generalists-with-a-specialty." [24] This phrase implies that a broad outlook may not be enough by itself; in a complex society like ours, breadth should be reconciled with the capacity for making contributions to a particular field through the application of special knowledge. This idea is largely coincident with the emphasis in this paper on producing specialists who at the same time possess general administrative skills.

In spite of these newer trends, the functional specialist will not be adequately equipped for general administrative responsibility until there evolves a closer three-way partnership among professional schools, faculties of general public administration, and governmental employers. When this occurs, it is more likely that the gap between specialists and generalists can be bridged. Then it will be possible to pursue administrative training in an efficient manner, imparting to specialists the administrative attitudes and skills which they need at each stage of their career development.

---

administrative training *per se*, it is at least a recognition of the advantages of education in other than strictly technical skills.

In this connection, one might also cite the well-known program of the Yale Law School.

[24] The phrase is used and explained in a perceptive article by Harvey S. Perloff, "Education of City Planners: Past, Present, and Future," 22 *Journal of the American Institute of Planners* 186 (Fall, 1956).

Equipping the Professionally-
Trained Functional Specialist for
General Administrative Responsibility
Panel Discussion

Chairman: JAMES C. CHARLESWORTH, Professor of
Political Science, University of Pennsylvania

Panel: JOHN W. LEDERLE, Professor of Political
Science and Director of the Bureau of Public
Administration, University of Michigan

HAROLD G. REUSCHLEIN, Dean of the
Law School, Villanova University

RUTH E. SMALLEY, Professor of Social Casework and Vice-Dean, The School of Social
Work, University of Pennsylvania

WILLIAM L. C. WHEATON, Professor of City
Planning and Director of the Institute for
Urban Studies, University of Pennsylvania

ROBERT F. WILCOX, Professor of Political
Science, San Diego State College

The problem of how to equip the professionally trained
functional specialist for administration is to a considerable
extent peripheral or incidental to the main purposes of
the conference, which have stressed the preparation of the
administrative generalist. Since our previous discussions

have revealed differences of opinion on methods for preparing administrative generalists, it would be presumptuous to proceed other than cautiously when moving out from this main responsibility to assist in the education of functional specialists. We should also humbly recognize that public administration itself may be as loaded with implicit values as the other specialties toward which we direct our criticisms.

The problem of administrative preparation of the functional specialist, although incidental and peripheral, nevertheless demands a portion of our time and attention. The plain fact is that we are faced with a *fait accompli* in that the public service is filled with specialists, that their relative importance will increase, not decrease, and that these specialists frequently rise to positions of an administrative generalist character for which they have no educational qualifications. *Our problem is how to domesticate the specialist within the governmental environment.* Our main role as teachers of administration may well be, not that of training the generalist as such, but that of supplementing the education of the specialist.

We should not be overly hopeful of quick results. We face serious obstacles in any attempt to contribute to the pre-service education of functional specialists. Most professional schools place emphasis on a full pattern of required courses and leave little room for training in matters not directly related to the craft. Moreover, even if the professional school educators wished to broaden curricular opportunities, they frequently find themselves imprisoned by professional licensing provisions which require full time attention to so-called bread-and-butter courses.

A further dampening influence in a large university with associated professional schools is the tendency toward extreme compartmentalization of the various disciplines. Often aggravated by salary differentials and uneven finan-

cial support of physical plant and research, contact between professional school faculties and teachers of administration is quite limited. Moreover, the specialist-in-training is not likely to appreciate the values of instruction in
matters that seem unrelated to his craft. With inadequate
knowledge of the very real possibility of a subsequent public service career, with its frequent demand for administrative training, professional school students bring to the subject little academic motivation.

Despite an adverse climate and the many difficulties, we
nevertheless feel that it is highly desirable to expose functional specialists to a broad course in public administration. We would begin rather modestly with an elective
course. Its objectives would include development by the
professional student of an awareness of public policy issues.
While recognizing those points at which "government is
different," it would be emphasized that administration is
an activity of universal application, and further that it is
not necessarily an extension of craft skills. In view of the
private enterprise bias of many professional schools, stress
would be placed upon the governmental process and the
"governmental attitude." The complexity of governmental
objectives, the political character of democratic government and administration, the peculiar nature of official
accountability to assure even handed and honest administration would receive special attention.

The discussions brought out one point that needs special mention here. It is not an objective of the proposed
course to produce a new functional specialty in administration. There is no intention to concentrate narrowly on
techniques of administration, such as budgeting or purchasing. Nor would the course aim toward adding the weapon
of personal manipulation to the specialist's arsenal. Several
persons during the discussion lamented a tendency in some

circles to view administration as a narrow exercise in small group dynamics.

The consensus was that professionally-trained functional specialists would find real value in such a course. Noting that specialists who rise to administrative posts in government—particularly lawyers and controllers—are not infrequently damned by their associates, the panel expressed great sympathy for a broadly-oriented course as envisioned above.

Disagreement developed on some details. One participant was dogmatic in his opposition to proliferation of special courses in administration for particular clientele groups, e.g., hospital administration, engineering administration. Another participant was equally adamant that we are confronted with a practical, tactual situation, and that necessity requires giving the specialist the subject matter under a label calculated to appeal to his particular specialist interest. Question was raised as to whether teachers of administration have reached a point of acceptance where they have the prestige to offer material to specialist groups. There seems to be plenty of evidence that such acceptance is being achieved by teachers of administration, and that presently they are performing an important pump-priming role, which may later be followed up by specialist schools with their own courses in administration taught by members of their own faculties.

Representatives from the specialist fields, who participated in conference discussions, indicated that there was already a noticeable trend in the professional schools to include in the curriculum material on administration. This is particularly true of the public-service oriented professions, like social work and city planning. The doctoral thesis in social work not infrequently is concerned with a problem in administration. The program in city planning, though perhaps centered in a school of engineering or architecture, is likely to include a required course in municipal government and administration as offered by another department of the University. Recently the American Association of Land Grant Colleges and State Universities recommended that agricultural specialists be offered courses in public administration and human relations.

Public administration as a subject for study is less widely recognized in such professional schools as law and engineering, despite the fact that there is considerable mobility between private and public employment in these professions. In law schools there has been much talk but not much action. There is, of course, a great diversity among the schools, ranging all the way from Yale Law School's rich offerings by a unique faculty mixture of lawyers, social scientists, and researchers to schools with rigid, completely vocational curricula which permit no electives. Inter-disciplinary seminars in which public administration and specialist school teachers both participate may offer the most promising way of introducing administration.

The discussion was somewhat less specific and satisfactory when the matter of post-entry training was brought up. While university responsibilities at the pre-entry level are clear, there is no unanimity as to post-entry responsibilities. There was a feeling that here government departments must analyze their peculiar problems, accepting a major obligation to work them out internally, feeling free, of course, to call upon the universities for such assistance as they can properly give. In-service training, as contrasted with pre-entry training, is not what universities do best. Yet there have been some noteworthy successes in which university participation has played a prominent part. In Wisconsin there have been management seminars which have emphasized the mutual problems of high-level state administrators. In Pennsylvania, after initial skepticism had been overcome, a year's course in Pennsylvania state government for bureau chiefs and deputy secretaries was well received. The American Society for Public Administration under its expanded program has put on useful regional management institutes in which operating public administrators have exchanged experience while catching up on the latest ideas of the researchers and professions. The Rockefeller Public Service Awards have enabled high-level federal personnel to go to Harvard on a year's educational leave to receive broad-gauged training in administration. Scientists have been particular beneficiaries.

The tenor of discussion was perhaps more encouraging and optimistic than the paper on which it was based. The professional schools are definitely beginning to recognize the very real career opportunities offered by an expanding government. At the same time the need for broad orientation of professional school students in the role of government and administration is getting a sympathetic hearing. Teachers of administration may expect more and more calls from the professional schools for assistance. As this occurs, the give-and-take between the various faculties, and the mixing of students from various university units, will prove a fruitful experience for all concerned.

John W. Lederle

7

The Respective Roles of Higher Education and Governmental Employers in Preparing People for Professional Administrative Careers

THOMAS J. DAVY *
University of Pennsylvania

HENRY REINING, JR. *
University of Southern California

INTRODUCTION

As one reviews the discussions of the administrators' workshops and of this educators' conference, one is impressed by the quite general agreement on two points: (1) that "staffing democracy's top side" is a valid, indeed desirable, purpose of higher education; (2) that to realize this purpose higher education, public service organizations, and governmental employers must cooperate. It would be laboring the point unduly to offer further justification for assumptions so generally agreed to. To place these assumptions in proper perspective, it is well to note that they relate to all three of higher education's primary purposes: the intellectual self-development of the student, his voca-

* *Thomas J. Davy, Ph.D., is Educational and Research Associate, Fels Institute of Local and State Government, and Assistant Professor of Political Science, University of Pennsylvania; Henry Reining, Jr., Ph.D., is Professor of Public Administration and Dean of the School of Public Administration, University of Southern California.*

tional preparation, and the preparation of students generally for effective citizenship.

This conference has concentrated on one aspect of "staffing democracy's top side," the problems of providing the administrative leadership and competence needed by government. The "administrative top side" has been identified as those positions satisfying the criteria formulated by the administrators' workshops for distinguishing "administrative policy-making officers" from others in the public service. Such positions include both generalists (city managers, chiefs of administration, etc.) and line and staff specialists serving in higher administrative positions (heads of line departments, personnel directors, finance directors, etc.).

In several of the conference sessions it was pointed out that higher education also has an important responsibility for preparing administrative technicians, i.e., budget analysts, procedures analysts, personnel classifiers, etc. This responsibility appears to stem from a number of factors: (a) such positions, being relatively new in the public service, have captured the imagination of public administration teachers; (b) though such activities are vital to effective administration in a complex industrial society, training for them within the service has generally been inadequate; and (c) higher administrators often rise from this base.

It is interesting to speculate about the effect that the expected increase in college enrollments during the next decade may have upon the preparation of administrative technicians. If educational resources fail to keep pace with the growth in enrollments, public administration programs may have to establish priorities among their various emphases; they will most likely prefer the emphasis more closely related to their general educational purposes, the preparation of the administrative generalist. If this happens, then governmental employers will probably have to assume more responsibility than heretofore for training administrative technicians within the service, or for subsidizing colleges and universities to train them.

Another concept implied in these discussions which bears upon the question of respective roles is that of "total career development" as a point of view for analyzing the problems of qualifying people for public administration careers. The administrators especially emphasized that pre-service schooling could not fully qualify a person for the administrative policy-making levels—that much of the knowledge and most of the skills needed for higher administration require for their acquisition the maturity obtained through progressively responsible experience and additional training at each level of responsibility. This fact would suggest that those concerned with equipping people for leadership at the higher administrative levels in government should view the process as one extending from the start of career-oriented study to the completion of service; they should determine their most effective contributions to each stage of the process rather than limit themselves to any particular stage.

With these concepts, expressed or implied in previous discussion and apparently quite generally accepted, as the points of reference, the purpose of this discussion is to explore those aspects of administrative career development that may be of concern to both higher education and government, and in which some form of mutual relationship may be appropriate. Possibilities for cooperation are considered in pre-service education and training, in post-entry staff development, and in research. Because the location and organization of the public administration program in a school may have a bearing on the nature of the cooperation it can provide, this question is also considered.

It is to be noted that the terms "higher education" and "government" are abstractions; their use without qualification may be misleading. There is no general policy or philosophy of higher education, nor a general policy or philosophy common to all governmental employers. The policies of an educational institution are shaped by many factors: its traditions and those of its departments; the predilections of its faculties; its hierarchies of authority; its sources of support; and many others. The policies of a governmental jurisdiction or agency are influenced by a similar diversity of factors peculiar to it. All such factors have an important bearing upon policies regarding their respective roles in administrative career preparation and in other areas of cooperation.

This discussion analyzes the role of higher education in administrative career development from the point of view of the maximum contributions that can probably be made in terms of educational purposes and resources. In this sense, the paper presents an ideal or "model" of cooperation between education and government. It is hoped that such a model will be a useful guide to individual schools in selecting the most effective types of contributions they can make with resources undoubtedly more limited than those assumed in this discussion. A similar qualification applies to governmental employers.

COOPERATION IN PRE-SERVICE EDUCATION AND TRAINING FOR ADMINISTRATIVE CAREERS

There is need and opportunity for cooperation between educational institutions and governmental employers in the recruitment and selection of qualified young people for pre-service education and training, in the course program itself, and in internships.

Underlying the problem of recruiting and selecting able students is the more fundamental problem of creating favorable attitudes toward government among the public generally and among college students in particular. The battle for prestige in the public service has not yet been won. The study of attitudes toward public employment in the Detroit metropolitan area, conducted by the Detroit Area Study of the University of Michigan in 1954,[1] concluded "that since 1930 the prestige value of public employment has undergone a marked shift in the favorable direction." [2] However, this growth in prestige has occurred primarily among those on the lower levels of the social class structure. For this conference, the conclusion of the Detroit study on the relationship of prestige to educational level is especially significant:

. . . education is known to be associated with social class as well as income, and therefore it was to be expected that those with high education would hold more unfavorable attitudes than those with low education. Favorable attitudes were concentrated in those with lower education, but the link was not direct. Education up to the completion of high school presented a fairly uniform proportion of individuals favorable to public employment with the exception of those with less than six years of schooling. Strikingly enough, only for those individuals with some college or with completed college education did the reputation of government employment drop off sharply. These findings raise a strong presumption about the inability of higher education to foster a balanced evaluation of the prestige of government employment.[3]

Professor Philip E. Jacob's study of the influence of college teaching on the values of students also produced some disturbing conclusions. While noting that American students are "dutifully responsive towards government," Professor Jacob concluded:

[1] Morris Janowitz and Deil Wright, "The Prestige of Public Employment: 1929 and 1954," 16 *Public Administration Review* 15, Winter 1956.
[2] *Ibid.,* p. 21.
[3] *Ibid.,* p. 20.

"Except for the ritual of voting, they are content to abdicate the citizen's role in the political process and to leave to others the effective power of governmental decision. They are politically irresponsible, and often politically illiterate as well." [4]

The study found that the apathy of college students toward public affairs is "particularly pronounced in regard to local government and politics." [5]

Public attitudes of indifference and antagonism toward government, especially among the well-educated, are serious deterrents to effective recruitment for public service education. An all-out effort to change such attitudes is essential not only for improving the quality of public administration, but more importantly for strengthening democratic values. Both higher education and governmental employers can be effective in creating more favorable attitudes toward government among the public at large, present and prospective teachers, and college students. In the long run, the prestige of government will depend upon the extent to which it increases its competence, broadens its perspective, and refines its responsiveness. These are long-term objectives for all concerned with improvement of the public service. In the short run, colleges and universities, governmental employers, and others interested in these objectives should make a special effort to increase public knowledge and understanding of the nature and role of government at all levels. They should try to persuade people to take a more active interest in governmental affairs. An effort of this kind for college students appears especially necessary.

[4] Philip E. Jacob, *Changing Values in College*, New Haven, Conn.: Edward W. Hazen Foundation, 1956, p. 4.
[5] *Ibid.*, p. 27.

RECRUITMENT AND SELECTION OF STUDENTS

Both educators and employers can do more to bring to the attention of students career opportunities in the public service and both undergraduate and graduate programs of preparation for them. They can also explore the possibilities of making such opportunities and programs more attractive to the superior college students. A program for administration similar to that of the Citizenship Clearing House for encouraging student interest in politics would be desirable.

Discussions with representatives of many public administration programs throughout the country indicate that far too few young people of superior intellect and leadership potential are being attracted to such programs. An important reason for this condition is undoubtedly the keen competition for talented college youth among business, the professions, engineering, science, and other fields, and the excellent opportunities for advanced training offered in these fields. A study of the exact nature of such competition and the methods used in other fields to attract students is desirable. Such a study would indicate the steps that should be taken, in the form of scholarships, fellowships, and other assistance, to meet this competition.

There is little reason to expect that recruitment for public administration will improve without special effort and more resources. The national security controversy implies that a greater proportion of the country's educational resources will probably be allocated in the next few years to fields most directly related to the technological requirements of the defense program; recruitment of outstanding students for these fields will be even more aggressive than in the past. Certainly most political scientists would agree that competent administrative leadership at all levels of government is as important to the security and well-being of the country as any other consideration. Greater effort is needed to win the public generally, governmental leaders, and our superior young people to this point of view.

The apparent lack of general interest in public administration among college students may also stem partly from the fact that they may not be sufficiently aware of career opportunities in government and of the special educational programs available to prepare for them when choosing their majors or careers. Representatives of public administration programs, governmental employers, and staff members of public service organizations could by working with guidance counselors and their assistants in high schools, junior colleges, and colleges help to bring the pertinent facts about public service careers forcefully to the attention of young people at the time many of them are making vital decisions regarding their futures.

Career conferences provide excellent opportunity to bring career opportunities in public administration to the attention of students. Such conferences in many schools appear to concentrate on business, engineering, and science. Yet schools should feel obligated to acquaint their students with career opportunities in all major fields, including public service. The failure to cover government in career conferences may reflect the failure of government authorities and others concerned with public administration to show a sufficient interest in them. All government administrators should be willing to participate in such conferences; indeed, they should volunteer their services to colleges and universities in their areas. Public service organizations—ASPA, ICMA, APHA, APWA, and others—could effectively promote this idea. They could also prepare general materials on career opportunities in the public service and on related training programs for distribution to students, and background materials for those who take part in career counseling. It may be noted that the International

City Managers' Association has just published an excellent brochure on career opportunities in city management with these purposes in mind.[6]

In selecting students for undergraduate and graduate study in public administration, the schools are, of course, fully responsible. Since most schools recruit nation-wide, the use of the personal interview—perhaps the most effective basis for evaluating prospective candidates—is limited. Governmental employers and professional associations might provide a valuable service to colleges and universities in this regard. If the schools could call upon leading administrators in various parts of the country to interview applicants from their regions and to submit to the schools in which such applicants are interested comprehensive evaluations, such independent and competent judgments might be especially helpful in selecting students.[7]

CAMPUS INSTRUCTION

There are also important values to cooperation between colleges and universities and governmental employers in the public administration program itself. Campus instruction is obviously the responsibility of the school. Yet public administrators can contribute materially to the effectiveness of the course program. Many schools invite outstanding administrators and other governmental leaders to give

[6] The International City Managers' Association, *City Management—A Growing Profession*, Report of the Committee on Professional Training, 1957. An excellent pamphlet covering career opportunities in government, primarily in the national government and in New York State, is Jay B. Westcott, *Government Careers—Opportunities for College Graduates*, Syracuse University Press, 1957.

[7] This whole question of recruitment and selection for pre-service education and training is an extremely important one. It is unfortunate that more consideration could not be given to it in this conference. Those who participated in the planning of this conference hope that meetings like this can be held more frequently than in the past. Perhaps the problems of recruitment and selection of students could be the subject of the next conference. A broad and comprehensive analysis of the problems by representatives of pre-service programs, professional associations, and government is needed.

special lectures and to participate in seminars. If administrators are properly oriented to the purposes of a course or seminar and if the mental processes and assumptions underlying the administrative decisions and actions they describe are drawn out by discussion, they can contribute unique insights into the administrative process. The case method of presentation rather than the general lecture is probably the easiest and most effective form of class participation for most administrators.

In this connection, some comments with respect to the qualifications of the public administration faculty may be appropriate. Since public administration is an applied field and is considered an art from the point of view of performance, it can be argued that those who train students for the field should combine both "can do" as well as "can teach" qualifications. It is difficult to see how a teacher can communicate to his students the subtle intangibles that the workshops indicated were such essential elements of the administrator's art without having experienced them himself, either directly as an administrator, or vicariously through close association with higher administrative levels.

The case method, valuable though it is, is not a substitute for experiential deficiency. For the value of case analysis depends to a large extent upon the administrative insight of the person who interprets the case situation with and for the students. Insight of this kind comes primarily from direct observation and experience. Lack of administrative experience in the faculty is an additional reason for seeking the cooperation of higher-level administrators in the academic program.

Administrators can also help to strengthen the course program by arranging and conducting field trips and demonstrations for the students. An on-the-spot explanation and demonstration of a police communications system or mental health clinic may have more impact upon a student's appreciation and understanding than many hours of library study on such matters.

Another area of possible cooperation is student research. Research in problem areas of significance to principal administrative officers is probably the most valuable form of research for students from the point of view of their career objectives. If they can consult with such officers regarding their research problems and have access to data often available only in governmental agencies, the preparation of their term papers or theses should prove to be a more beneficial experience for them. Such studies can often be of real value also to administrators who cooperate in their preparation.

Governmental employers have a primary role in the planning and supervision of the internship, even when the internship is an integral part of the academic program. Since field experience is discussed in another paper in this conference, it will not be elaborated on here.

COOPERATION IN POST-ENTRY STAFF DEVELOPMENT

Further qualification of people for positions after they enter the public service is obviously the responsibility of governmental employers. Yet colleges and universities can make valuable contributions to more effective post-entry staff development. Just as educational institutions should seek and welcome assistance from governmental administrators in making pre-service education and training most effective, so government should request and receive assistance from higher education in making in-service education and training most effective. Pre-service and in-service education and training are but parts of a whole. The objective of improving continually the quality and competence of the public service, to which both government and higher education in a democracy should be dedicated, implies that close cooperation should be maintained between them in efforts to achieve that objective.

EXECUTIVE DEVELOPMENT

One type of post-entry program that appears to benefit from such cooperation is executive development. Carefully planned development programs for higher administrative positions would appear to be essential to an adequate career service. The qualifications of a principal administrative officer are his native abilities as they have been conditioned by his education and experience. The formation of such an officer is thus a process that continues throughout his professional life. If the quality of administrative leadership is to be improved, then attention must be given to each stage of this process. Appropriate experience and additional education and training for each stage of development—induction, supervision, middle management, top management—should be considered by the employer and cooperating school in devising development programs for the higher administrative levels. The plural "programs" is used because executive development is appropriate for both administrative generalists and program specialists who are potential candidates for the top-level positions. Such programs should, of course, be open to all employees with the necessary qualifications and potential, not merely to college graduates.

The induction stage of an executive development program is especially important. It has been suggested that in large jurisdictions and agencies this stage should probably extend over a three to five year period. Internships served by graduates of public administration programs and others would be part of this period. This stage should be characterized by the following elements: close direction of the inductee by the top administrative levels, so that early in his career he will develop a sensitivity to the administrative milieu of the higher levels; work assignments that would broaden his understanding of the particular function in which he is building his career and of related functions;

development of basic administrative skills; and advanced study and seminars.

At each stage of development following the induction period, those who prove capable should receive career guidance and counseling, progressively responsible and diversified experience, and graduated study, in addition to any on-the-job training that may be appropriate for the duties of their specific positions. Rotation in jobs, educational leaves, participation in the activities of pertinent professional organizations, and the understudying of outstanding administrators are but some of the arrangements that have proven effective in executive development.

There are many ways in which higher education can assist governmental employers in executive development. First would be to take the initiative in promoting among governmental employers generally the broad-gauged approach to a career service upon which such a program rests. As employers become interested in the idea, the college or university can advise them on appropriate programs and assist them in the research necessary for establishing them. The school could probably also assist in the selection and counseling of candidates, and could participate in conferences and seminars that may be parts of the programs. It might also be appropriate for the school to provide formal course work, full-time or part-time, for people in these programs. It might also be possible for a number of institutions in a region to join together in the establishment of an "administrative staff college" for executive development service to all governmental jurisdictions and agencies in the region.[8] Co-sponsorship of training courses and management institutes for principal administrators prepared by professional organizations could also be a service to employ-

[8] For a detailed discussion of the administrative staff college see Marshall E. Dimock, "The Administrative Staff College: Executive Development in Government and Industry," 50 *American Political Science Review* 166, March 1956.

ers in the region served by a school. The training courses of the International City Managers' Association and the week-long regional Management Institutes conducted by the American Society for Public Administration in cooperation with various universities throughout the country are examples of this type of executive development activity.

Education's possible contributions to executive development have been discussed at such length because this kind of assistance appears to be most closely related to the specific interests of schools with public administration programs and because the faculty would probably have special competence for it. However, there are, of course, types of careers in the public service other than administrative to which higher education can often make valuable contributions. It can provide basic technical courses for people selected for specific positions requiring limited educational background: criminology and related courses for police officers; social work theory and practice for welfare visitors and supervisors of various kinds; etc. It can also provide refresher and up-dating courses in both technical and administrative subjects. Several schools also offer in-service education courses in general governmental services and processes for governmental employees who have not had the advantages of higher education or who have not had such courses in specialized curricula. Most universities offer in evening classes post-entry opportunities of this kind through their extension divisions. In some schools, employees can earn certificates in public administration through such study.

STAFF ASSISTANCE TO EMPLOYERS IN IN-SERVICE TRAINING

An educational institution can often provide an especially valuable service to governmental employers in in-service training. By in-service training is meant programs and activities planned and conducted by the employer to help his employees improve the knowledge, skills, and attitudes needed for their specific duties and responsibilities. The public administration faculty, by virtue of its extensive knowledge of administrative theory and practice, governmental services, and instructional methods, may be especially qualified to assist employers to establish the training function in their jurisdictions.

It is questionable whether members of the faculty should themselves conduct in-service courses. Such courses in a well-rounded job-training program will be so diversified that the faculty could easily dissipate its resources if it assumed instructional responsibility for them. In addition, such courses usually involve detailed technical knowledge peculiar to the jurisdiction or agency which the faculty does not have, and which, from the point of view of its educational purposes, is not to its interest to master. The role of the school in in-service training should be to provide the employer with what may be termed the "training staff service." Employers, particularly in the smaller jurisdictions and agencies, cannot usually afford to employ training specialists and have to seek outside assistance for organizing the training function. In providing such assistance, the aim of the school should be to help the employer establish the training function, and to develop the staff service and instructional resources within the jurisdiction or agency, so that after a time its assistance will no longer be needed. As the employer's temporary training staff, the school could work with him in identifying his training needs and establishing priorities among them, planning training courses and activities to meet these needs in close cooperation with the responsible officers in the agency, developing instructional materials and aids, selecting and training the trainers, and in evaluating the effectiveness of such training. Since an educational institution can provide services of this type only to the extent of its resources, it must usually establish priorities for itself. First consideration should in most cases be given to improving the higher administrative levels.

Even if a school does not have the resources to engage in the several forms of assistance suggested above, there is one important contribution it can make to governmental employers in in-service training with relatively little investment of time and energy. The approach that the employer takes to in-service staff development determines the kind of a program that results. Governmental employers, especially when they have had little experience with training, tend to take a short-term approach; they generally seek specific courses to meet only their most urgent needs; they are happy if "packaged" programs are available that are taught by outsiders and that do not require very much of their time. When such programs are completed, many employers are inclined to feel that they have adequately discharged their responsibility for in-service staff development. It takes time and experience for the employer to realize that almost all employees, because of changes in laws and regulations, in the nature and scope of programs, and in technology, require frequent refresher training for their positions; that, therefore, training should be a continuing function in government, like budgeting, planning, and other staff services.

The ideal of an in-service training operation is a comprehensive training plan covering all classes and levels of positions in the jurisdiction. For each position such a plan would present in detail the orientation and indoctrination to be given new employees in that position, the job knowledge and skills required and the training to be provided for their acquisition, and the types of additional training and broadening experience to be offered outstanding incumbents of the position to qualify them for higher responsibilities. The plan would also delineate the responsibilities of the training unit and of administrators and supervisors in the training process. The executive development program would be an integral part of the plan. Like most ideals, this ideal can rarely be realized. Yet if the school that is advising employers on training keeps this kind of long-term objective in mind and promotes it as it can with employers, its efforts, however limited they may have to be, should in the long run produce sounder and more lasting results than would a short-term objective of merely helping employers to "put out their training fires."

These then are some of the kinds of contributions that colleges and universities can make to post-entry staff development. An important question remains, however. Who pays? Ideally, the governmental employer or employee, depending upon which benefits the most from such services should pay the full cost of them. Often, though, it may be necessary for the college or university to underwrite, if it can, at least part of the cost until employers recognize the values of such staff development activities. Various foundations have assisted schools for the initial stages of such services to governmental jurisdictions in their regions. But there is no question that at the earliest possible time the school should seek to place the full financial burden for such services upon the employer, since there is no justification for it to subsidize the training function after it is established any more than there is to subsidize budgeting, procedures analysis, planning, or any other staff function.

There are two other questions about costs of post-entry staff development, which, though the school has no authority with regard to them, may affect appreciably the effectiveness of its services: (1) should the agency or should the employee pay the costs of instruction and instructional materials for courses provided for employees by the school? (2) should training be conducted on "company time" or during the employees' leisure? Two criteria appear to gov-

ern policies on these questions: (1) the benefit of the training to the organization versus the degree of personal advantage to the employee; (2) the level of responsibility of
the employee. The first criterion implies that if training
contributes to the immediate production needs of the organization, then management should pay all the costs of
training; if it is for promotion, it is to the personal advantage of the employee and he should pay for it. The second
criterion suggests that training for lower level positions
should be given on paid time, for higher positions on the
employees' own time, and for middle positions half on company, half on employee time.

However, in interpreting these criteria, certain considerations are pertinent. Organized training for promotion
is as important to an agency as training for the immediate
job; therefore, management should pay for the promotional
training that it deems essential. Also, training is important
for all levels of administration, not merely the lowest levels. If administrators decide that training is necessary for
subordinates, whether they be street cleaners or department
heads, then the employer should probably pay the costs
thereof. Then too, when employees take courses related to
government and their jobs on their own time, they are contributing time and often money to the interests of their
employer, even though such training will undoubtedly
produce personal benefits for themselves. All training, if
it is planned and conducted properly, produces personal
benefits for the employee, whether they be in the form of
better morale resulting from increased competence for the
job or from wider opportunities for promotion. Therefore,
the criterion of personal benefit is a rather tenuous one,
and may sometimes be an unfair one. The primary criterion should be the degree to which training, either on-
the-job or outside, contributes to the competence and potential of the employee. For higher level positions this

criterion should be interpreted broadly. Leadership is as broad as its perspective.

With regard to training cost, it may be noted that a growing number of governmental jurisdictions are adopting tuition reimbursement plans. Upon successful completion of a work-related course, the jurisdiction or agency reimburses the employee for the tuition, and sometimes course materials, costs. No recent statistics concerning this practice are available. A considerable proportion of the public employees studying at the University of Southern California's Civic Center is being supported through tuition reimbursement plans of this kind.

COOPERATION IN RESEARCH

Research may seem tangential to a discussion of administrative career preparation, but since it is related to the level of knowledge in the field and to the qualifications of the faculty preparing students for administrative careers, it is appropriate to discuss it briefly in this paper. It is obvious that both the governmental employer and the educational institution have need for research in public administration: the former because the continuing changes in the character and scope of governmental functions are constantly creating new problems in administration; the latter because these changes in government must be examined and understood by scholars if instruction in public administration is to keep abreast of the times.

The possibilities for research in public administration cover a wide range. It is beyond the scope of this paper to consider the substantive nature of these possibilities.[9] However, it is useful for the purposes of this discussion to iden-

[9] For recent statements on the subject, see Frederick C. Mosher, "Research in Public Administration: Some Notes and Suggestions," 16 *Public Administration Review* 169, Summer 1956; and John C. Honey, "Research in Public Administration: A Further Note," 17 *Public Administration Review* 238, Autumn 1957.

tify the primary interests of employers and educators in public administration research. The employer's primary interest is operational; he seeks information that will help him solve his immediate administrative and technical problems. The educator's primary interest in research is intellectual; he seeks an ever-widening and more fundamental knowledge and understanding of government and administration, and whether or not such study contributes to the solution of operational problems is incidental.

These are, of course, extreme positions on the scale of research interest. If the employer is professionally motivated and has a sense of obligation toward increasing knowledge of public administration, then he will probably be more interested in general and fundamental research than an employer not so motivated. If an educational institution includes service to government as a major purpose, it can justify specifically operational research more easily than a school that emphasizes exclusively the purely educational purposes of higher learning. As a general rule, the research interest of governmental employers will tend to be operations-oriented and they will be willing to give greater cooperation and support to research that serves their operational needs; the research interest of educators will tend to be intellectual and operational research will be only a means of obtaining data and formulating hypotheses for more fundamental research.

Yet between the extremes of research on specific operational problems and fundamental research, there can be a broad area of mutual interest between governmental employers and educators that justifies close and continuing cooperation. Even at the extremes cooperation is desirable, since the distinction between operational and fundamental research is not as definite as might be implied by these observations, and since each is often necessary for the adequate realization of the other.

With these general observations in mind, the following propositions regarding the possible contributions of government and education to research in public administration are submitted.

1. A college or university should promote among the governmental employers in its region the importance of research and the need for cooperation. It should emphasize the fact that research is as important a staff function in government as personnel or budget. It should assist employers to establish sound research organization and procedures. Since many jurisdictions and agencies may be too small to support a well-rounded research staff, it can provide such encouragement and assistance to state leagues or public service associations if they do not already offer a research service for their members.

2. To the extent that a school considers service to its governmental community a major purpose and to the extent that specific operational research may serve fundamental research in the long run, it may provide research assistance on specific problems to individual jurisdictions and agencies. From the point of view of its primary interest in research and for economy of effort, however, the institution should probably try to concentrate on those governmental problems that are major in character and that are common to a number of jurisdictions or agencies. The full cost of operational research by higher education should probably be borne by the employers who benefit from it. However, if such research directly serves the educational interests of the school (for example, when it is in the form of students' theses or term papers), or the school's interests in basic research, then the school should be willing to share the cost of such research with employers.

3. A school can serve as a clearing house of information regarding research problems and efforts for governmental employers, civic and professional organizations, and other

interested agencies in its region. This type of service could contribute considerably to more efficient and valuable research in public administration.

4. A school or a group of schools working together, could stimulate and correlate the research efforts of a number of groups or organizations working on the same basic problems in a region. This could be an especially valuable service in a metropolitan area.

5. The unit of the college or university most concerned with research in public administration could well serve as a liaison between governmental employers and other departments of the school that can contribute to such research. Cultural anthropology, sociology, social psychology, economics, education, and other fields can often make valuable contributions in this regard. Coordinated research by different faculties offers a real challenge to higher education.

6. From the point of view of higher education's major purposes, it is probably a sound maxim that the major responsibility of a college or university in public administration research is fundamental research and that a school should feel obliged to rationalize its research efforts in terms of this responsibility.

INSTITUTIONAL RESPONSIBILITY FOR CONTRIBUTING TO BETTER PUBLIC SERVICE

If a college or university considers the improvement of government as one of the major responsibilities of higher education in a democracy, this responsibility applies to all departments of the institution, not merely to the unit directly concerned with public administration. There should be an institution-wide awareness of this purpose. Since administrative positions in government are filled both by people trained in general administration and by people trained in professional and technical specializations, the largest number by far in the latter category, all departments should be concerned with the problems of "staffing democracy's top side" and should be willing to contribute some of their resources to the solution of such problems. To achieve such a broad approach, boards of trustees, presidents, deans, department chairmen, indeed all members of the faculties, should have constructive attitudes toward public service and an interest in improving it. However, such attitudes and interest do not generate themselves. The unit whose principal focus is the public service must assume responsibility for "the fostering of a greater awareness among all constituent schools of the public aspects of their fields and of specific recruitment opportunities." [10]

There is no question that primary interest and responsibility should reside in social science departments. In this regard, the question of whether public administration should be a separate curriculum, either as a separately organized element in a general social science department or as an integral part of the political science curriculum, should be considered. The relationship of public administration to the social sciences, and especially to specializations in political science, has been, and in some institutions still is, a matter of controversy. The field has had a difficult time in many schools in achieving equal status with political science, international relations, and other related fields. Some schools have established separate schools or departments of public administration. Regardless of its organizational status, however, it must be emphasized that a broad social science approach to instruction and research in public administration is imperative. So is focus on management. As the discussions of this conference so manifestly indicate, we are not doing an adequate job

[10] John M. Gaus, in *The Public Service and University Education* (Joseph E. McLean, editor), Princeton Univ. Press, 1949, p. 198.

if we limit our preparation of students for the public service to staff and management techniques, or if only theory and no management is taught.

A cogent reason for establishing public administration separately from other disciplines, at least on the graduate level, is that programs of preparation for administrative careers in government should be professional in nature. There are many implications to the word "professional," discussion of which is beyond the scope of this paper. But one important implication is the types of activities appropriate for a professional school. Judging from the example of other professions, it would seem that teaching-research-service is the ideal combination of activities for a professional school. This trilogy appears to be the secret of the effectiveness of our great medical schools. Yet it appears difficult to achieve this combination of activities in an environment based primarily upon a liberal arts approach to education. Therefore, it may be advisable for a public administration program aspiring to professional status to seek a separate identity. It would seem desirable at least for members of the public administration faculty to have research and service responsibilities in addition to teaching responsibilities.

If a school decides to conduct organized research along the lines suggested in this paper, or to provide the types of services in post-entry staff development suggested, it should also consider the advisability of establishing a special unit—a civic center, or institute, or bureau of public administration—for such activities. Such research and service activities require a close and continuing relationship with governmental employers. They also require special competences and interests in the faculty. To establish a special unit of this kind would in some schools require an exception to extension division jurisdiction.

SUMMARY

The purpose of this discussion has been to survey the possible contributions that higher education and government can cooperatively make to more effective preparation for administrative careers. The problem of raising the prestige of public employment among the public generally and among college students in particular is basic to all considerations for improving the public service. Colleges and universities, governmental employers, and public service organizations should cooperate closely in striving to change public attitudes of indifference or antagonism toward government and to further public understanding of and interest in governmental affairs.

The pre-service stage of administrative career development is the responsibility of higher education. However, governmental employers can contribute substantially to this stage by helping to bring career opportunities in the public service and the need of special preparation for them to the attention of high school and college students, by assisting schools to evaluate prospective students for public administration programs, by participating when requested in the course program itself, and by sponsoring broad-gauged internships.

Although post-entry staff development is the responsibility of the governmental employer, there are many opportunities for higher education to contribute to this stage. Executive development is an especially promising opportunity. Basic technical courses, refresher and up-dating courses, and general courses in governmental services and processes for employees are a service that some schools provide to help employers in their regions broaden the perspective and improve the competence of their organizations. Staff assistance to employers in establishing the training function and in planning well-rounded job-training programs is another type of service that a public administration faculty can often provide.

As to possible cooperation between government and education in research, it is well to keep in mind that the primary interest of the employer is operational, whereas the primary interest of the educator is intellectual. These interests, though, bridge a broad area of opportunities for cooperation. Higher education can promote the importance of research to effective administration among governmental employers and assist them to establish sound research organization and procedures. It can also do research on major problems of common concern to a number of employers in its area of service. Serving as a clearing house and correlator of research pertaining to governmental administration for its region could be an especially valuable contribution by a college or university. However, it is advisable for a school to challenge itself from time to time regarding the extent to which its efforts are contributing to fundamental research in public administration.

Responsibility for improving the public service should be shared by all units of the educational institution. However, the public administration faculty must assume primary responsibility. There are cogent arguments for establishing public administration as a separate curriculum, and, on the graduate level, as a separate school or department. Regardless of its status, though, it is imperative that instruction and research in public administration manifest a broad social science approach as well as a management focus. To make the kinds of research and service contributions suggested in this discussion most effective, it may be advisable for a school to create a special unit for such activities.

The Respective Roles of Higher Education and Governmental Employers in Preparing People for Professional Administrative Careers
Panel Discussion

Chairman: JOHN D. MILLETT, President, Miami University

Panel: JOHN H. FERGUSON, Secretary of Administration and Budget Secretary, Commonwealth of Pennsylvania; Professor of Political Science, Pennsylvania State University

ELMER D. GRAPER, Emeritus Professor of Political Science, and former Director of the Institute of Local Government, University of Pittsburgh; Chairman of the Civil Service Commission of Pennsylvania

ROBERT J. M. MATTESON, Executive Director, American Society for Public Administration

HENRY REINING, JR., Professor of Public Administration and Dean, School of Public Administration, University of Southern California; President, American Society for Public Administration

At the outset I should like to express my personal appreciation for the excellent papers which have been prepared for this session of the conference, and for the conference as a whole. The material made available to all of us has been most helpful. At the same time, I should make it clear that any resemblance between my remarks and these papers, or for that matter between my remarks and the discussion we have just had, will be purely coincidental.

We are all agreed, I believe, that in the preparation of persons for careers in government service both universities and governmental employers have their part. These roles should be complementary rather than competing. There is too much for each to do without having any sense of rivalry or of duplication.

It is often said that the beginning of a science is classification. The essence of art is to put the bits and pieces back together again in a coherent and meaningful whole. This is the task we confront in arriving at some general understanding and prescription about the preparation of persons for careers in government service. There are certain distinctions which we should make. Yet we must also be able to bring the parts together in a flexible pattern of mutually supporting inter-relationship.

First of all, our attention here has been focused largely upon educational preparation, that is, upon the instruction or teaching of persons going into government service. The educational enterprise of our society, of course, extends beyond instruction as such. It also embraces research—the search for and acquisition of new knowledge—and service. The educational process depends upon familiarity with research methods and achievements. Furthermore, our system of education gives a good deal of emphasis to the practical utilization of knowledge, and here the element of educational service enters in. Insofar as our knowledge about public administration is concerned, the university must frequently depend upon the cooperation and good will of the governmental employer in advancing the frontiers of knowledge. In turn, the university has an obligation to assist in the application of knowledge to specific problems. Thus the university and the governmental employer are joined in the very basic features of the educational process.

Secondly, a good deal of attention has been given here to a distinction between education and training. Some of the papers have preferred to use the terms knowledge and skill. The words embody the same conceptions. It has been suggested that the task of education belongs to the university, the task of training to the governmental employer. Obviously, the suggestion here is that education is concerned with the broader aspects of knowledge, such as organizational theory, while training deals with the actual mechanics of operation in a particular job and agency. The distinction is undoubtedly useful as a frame of reference. As a distinction it has the fault of all such endeavor; it is not always easy to draw such differences in any fixed, uncompromising way.

The papers considered here have suggested another distinction, that between pre-entry and post-entry education. The former refers to undergraduate or graduate education programs which the person may undertake before his actual recruitment into the public service. The latter refers to educational activity which the person may undertake after he has begun his career in governmental service as a means for enhancing his own individual abilities and consequently for advancing his own career. I for one am not entirely satisfied with this distinction.

To be sure, government has some responsibility to encourage its servants to improve their knowledge and so prepare to take on greater duties. In this process government obtains the services of a person who has greater satisfaction with his career, and who can contribute more effectively to the mission of the enterprise. All of this is worth while. Yet I for one believe that much of this post-entry education can best be realized through our universities rather than through elaborate in-service educational facilities. In particular, where the education involves professional competencies which are in demand both within and without the realm of government service, then I believe much of the burden of post-entry education should be left to the initiative of the individual and the performance of the university. Yet even here there is a need for close cooperation and mutual assistance between the governmental employer and the university. The responsibility of the university is to give impetus to the educational process under whatever circumstances it may arise.

Certainly it is clear that university initiative in education for public service is called for. Some of our group here felt that this was impossible without some specially organized device, such as an Institute of Public Administration, which could cut across and bring together the several disciplines of the social sciences. There was some fear expressed that an Institute of Public Administration might in its separate status become too much involved in service and training and so neglect its educational task. There is danger that such an agency may actually become a part of management in the public service rather than an integral part of the university community. The answer, as that to so many problems, appears to be eternal vigilance.

It seems essential for government in turn to provide some focal point of leadership which will encourage cooperation with universities in their educational activities of benefit to the public service. Rather than wander about in a wilderness of bureaucratic activity, the university must have a central point of assistance if it is to work cooperatively with government. Here in Pennsylvania this focal point has been the governor's office itself. The long association of the present governor with this Institute led him to recognize the need for cooperative effort by government and universities in the areas of education and service. The Institute of Local Government at the University of Pittsburgh was formed through the initiative of local government officials themselves. They have continued in various ways to assist and support that undertaking.

Inevitably it must be asked: How shall the university's role in education for the public service be financed? Here again there is no ready-made, simple solution. There appears to be a growing tendency for government to help. This is good. Some here have stressed that the student should pay at least part of the bill. Such an arrangement would be consistent with the prevailing practice in higher education. Our universities need general support as well. Education for the public service is just one part of the whole endeavor by which our universities serve American society.

A corollary issue is that of time. Insofar as post-entry education is concerned, should this be obtained entirely outside the regular hours or periods of government service? The opinion has been frequently expressed here that a sharing of the time between the governmental employer and the individual is desirable.

The question of faculty has also occupied our attention. The work offered by the university in the field of public administration requires more than the traditional scholar-instructor type of person. The university needs individuals also of broad experience, of proven ability in oral and written communication, and of recognized capacity as consultants. The ideal type is seldom available. We can only hope to meet many of our needs through a number of different persons. We in the universities cannot afford to overlook the staffing assistance we can obtain on a part-time basis from within government itself.

Fortunately, it has not been within the province of our particular discussion to define a body of knowledge to be labelled "public administration." I am confident that had we been called upon to do so, we could have accomplished that task. As a political scientist I insist that there is both a general body of knowledge within the broad scope of the study of government properly identified as public administration, and also a specialized body of professional knowledge to be imparted to the prospective or active practitioner.

We who teach in the field of public administration can well afford to keep two broadly related but nonetheless separate goals in mind. One task of higher education is to provide all students with some comprehension of the broad segments of man's knowledge. For lack of a better identification we frequently refer to this objective as that of general education. I hold that the student in higher education has not had a proper exposure to the social sciences if he has not obtained some understanding of the status and majesty of the public service in modern society. I feel that those of us specially interested in public administration have been remiss in providing the materials for this part of a general education.

In the second place, we are concerned with professional education. This means instruction in the knowledge and technique of public administration for practical use. Here again we must recognize a dual task. In a narrow sense public administration embraces the technical performance of such work as that done by the organizational and procedural analyst, the budget examiner, the personnel officer, and related components of the managerial function in the public service. But this definition alone of our professional interest in public administration is too narrow.

We who specialize in public administration must communicate our knowledge and our enthusiasm to other professionally educated persons, especially those educated in medicine, law, engineering, public finance, science, forestry, and other fields. We may call this, if we please, education for general administration, but the importance of our responsibility in this phase of higher education for the public service is immense indeed.

Insofar as the prestige of governmental service is concerned, the battle is not yet won. Here we fight in a peculiar cultural context all our own. A basic concept of our society is that government assumes a limited role, performing only certain vital tasks. Much of our social energy still flows in non-governmental channels. It is not easy to present the challenges of governmental service in their true light and still not appear to be aggrandizing the role of government in our society. Here is a fundamental task for our universities.

Perhaps it is worth mentioning also that all of our concern with preparation for professional administrative careers in no ways presupposes a politically irresponsible bureaucracy. Rather, part of the job of education is to stress the political responsibility of the public servant. While our political system places the essential duties of administrative oversight upon the legislature, the executive, and the judiciary, the work of day-to-day supervision of the bureaucracy must necessarily fall upon the small group who make up the political leadership of our great departments and agencies. Our general educational efforts, the bureaucratic tradition, and our social customs must provide the necessary guide lines for political leadership within public administration. All of our professions, our great corporations, and other walks of life as well must come to recognize public service at the political level as vital to our free society. Community service enjoys prestige today; tomorrow it is not too much to hope that governmental service at the state and federal level in particular will achieve a similar recognition. Our university efforts at education in public administration will achieve their goal only if this additional condition of an intelligent, forward-looking political leadership is realized in the public service.

Our universities face one of their greatest opportunities and one of their heaviest responsibilities in preparing people for professional administrative careers. The job cannot be performed alone. It requires governmental collaboration as well. It requires support from many segments of society. From the combined endeavors of us all we may look forward to still further accomplishment in the professionalization and effective performance of our governmental bureaucracy.

John D. Millett

8

Higher Education and Training for Administrative Careers— Retrospect and Prospect

JOHN A. PERKINS *
University of Delaware

Most of the basic questions facing education for the public service have been discussed during the past two days. Yet, some of these questions are so vital to the well-being of education—indeed, to the very future of our society—that we are directed to devote our deliberations in this final session to "Higher Education and Training for Administrative Careers."

I propose to approach this topic in its broadest context. Higher education in any of its manifestations cannot be properly considered apart from the social climate. Conversely, education's responsibility is to help the social order overcome its shortcomings. In this reciprocity, education for public administration is no exception. In fact, the relationship between education and social progress is brought into sharpest focus when government and education for public administration are considered. Our discussion should proceed out of a realistic look at the past and the present. We must also set forth goals for the future that are illuminated by ideals. With this approach, a very respectable quantity of practical progress should evolve.

First of all, we must forthrightly face up to prevalent at-

* John A. Perkins, Ph.D., is President of the University of Delaware and Under Secretary of Health, Education and Welfare of the United States.

titudes and conditions affecting both the Government and higher education.

Ours is an era of bigness. We have a big country, a big population, big business, big labor, one world. To speak of "little" government, as some good people would, is a *non sequitur*. Abraham Lincoln understood that the size of government is an outgrowth of needs. He stated:

> "The legitimate object of government is to do for a community of people whatever they need to have done, but cannot so well do for themselves. . . ."

Today's government is a product of the needs of our civilization. That it is big reflects the complexity of our modern society and our leadership role in world affairs.

Economic, social, and political inevitabilities indicate that government, if it is to meet the needs of our time, will hardly play a shrinking role in our society. This fact affects the obligations of citizenship by a self-governing people and their educational programs as well.

In the fact of big government, a dilemma is posed. Can we fulfill the governmental needs of an increasingly complex society without sacrificing essential democratic freedoms? Not only do we fear loss of present freedom; we want *more* security and *more* freedom. There is apprehension lest expansion of government impair the individual's economic well-being and personal freedom—apprehension lest today's public servant becomes 1984's "Big Brother."

Government in the United States has of course expanded at all levels, especially in recent decades. Between 1902 and 1955, State and local expenditures expanded thirtyfold, while our gross national product expanded only twentyfold. Localities employ more than 5 million persons, 10 percent of the Nation's nonfarm workers. Similar statistics can be cited without end. However, they present only one side of the picture. Such figures can be countered by equally significant ones indicating the growing number and improving quality of services rendered—services producing a healthier, better educated, more economically secure society. Professor Sumner H. Slichter admonishes: "It is wrong to regard the government merely or even primarily as an expense. It is a service-rendering organization. Its services are badly needed and are worth many times their costs. . . . It is just as desirable to increase government outlays where increases will produce adequate additional services as it is to cut spending where cuts can be made without curtailing useful services." But, students of governmental administration need not engage in a battle of statistics.

Since the days of William McKinley, we have experienced two world wars, subsequent periods of economic boom and bust, international tension, and phenomenally swift scientific and industrial advancement, with accompanying population growth and shifts. The late Frederick Lewis Allen characterized the first 50 years of our century as the era of "The Big Change." Significantly, one of his early chapter headings reads "Government on the Sidelines," a later one is entitled "Reluctant World Power."

The American people have had to look increasingly to government. They have, however reluctantly, enlarged the functions and role of government at all levels.

In all this, the real issue is not so much the size and complexity of government, important as that is, but the responsible control of government by the whole people. In other words, has big democracy gone hand-in-hand with big government? A subsidiary question is, can big government be staffed to run in an efficient and responsible way? It is anticipatory to interject here that the first question relates to education of the whole citizenry. The second relates to the education of officeholders, be they political officials or civil servants.

Happily, this half-century has witnessed a tremendous expansion in suffrage, both in law and in practice. The voters are better informed and better educated.

INHERENT DANGERS OF COMPLEX GOVERNMENT

These developments are commendable. The inherent danger, however, is that the citizen's interest in government may become acute and active only when related directly to his self-interest; that he will be disinterested and fail to participate when the general well-being is at stake. Two quite different illustrations come to mind. A recent *New Yorker* cartoon depicts a considerably inebriated gentleman hammering on the bar for service and declaring to the disapproving bartender, "In a democracy the *customer* decides when he has had enough." In Edith Hamilton's new book, "The Echo of Greece," Isocrates laments that the Athenians of his day were thinking not of their *duties* as citizens but of their *rights*. They were looking to the state to guarantee not *freedom* as in the old days but *privilege*.

Another inherent danger is that as government grows bigger, whether at local, State, or Federal level, it will become tradition-bound. The *status quo* is defended out of a misconceived patriotism. Hence, there may be a failure to change our governments when there is need to do so. The requirements of responsibility and efficiency so well known to students of public administration may go unheeded. In other American enterprises it is acknowledged that greater efficiency is often associated with bigness. Cannot large-scale government operations also bring greater efficiency? They can and they have. The Bureau of Old-Age and Survivors Insurance in the Department of Health, Education, and Welfare illustrates what can be done. There the productivity per employee has increased 35 percent since 1950. Employees of the Bureau of Internal Revenue in 1953, in spite of increased salaries and other costs, were collecting $100 in taxes for every 49 cents of expenditure. In 1939, it cost $1.13 to collect the same revenue.

Responsible government, efficient administration—these are, essentially, a matter of qualified, competent, dedicated public officials supported by intelligent citizens. Present and future shortage of qualified personnel for business and industry, for teaching, and the other professions has been well-documented. Moreover, positive programs to alleviate these shortages have been initiated.

THE SHORTAGE OF QUALIFIED PERSONNEL

Yet, there has been little concern over the equally serious shortage of qualified personnel for government and its administration. Considering the essential role of government in our society, this failure to attract enough able people may prove fatal. Newcomers to the Federal Government inevitably are favorably impressed with the quality of administrative talent. To a great extent, these administrators are the youth of the depression grown to maturity and responsibility. Before long, many of them will be eligible for retirement. One hears it said, by those who know Washington well, that, at the present time and for some years past, sufficient numbers of men of similar quality and dedication have not been entering government service.

I shall let one of these highly respected professional public administrators speak for me: "In the last dozen years or so there has been nothing like the same number and talent recruited into government that there was in the thirties. Yet, the need for top flight people is great. Government needs administrators with special talent in analysis and synthesis, with the ability to tear problems apart and put them together again with good horse sense. Beware of the doctrinaire fellow. Public administration requires men who can knit together the contributions of the specialists, who can achieve coordination through reason instead of by means of the big stick. Such administrators must be socially and psychologically healthy. For those who are qualified government is an exceedingly exciting and challenging place to work."

PUBLIC ATTITUDES TOWARD GOVERNMENT

Given such an attractive job description, why is public service not overwhelmed with applicants? Political scientists have sought explanations. With respect to pay levels, recruitment and promotion practices, training, and employee motivation, government service, especially at the upper levels, runs a poor second to private pursuits. These facts are but a syndrome. The malady is public attitudes toward government. Except in times of crisis many people are indifferent to government. When they do take an interest, it is in a spirit of indignation; too often disloyalty, corruption, or inefficiency are assumed. The worst gets printed. Contrary evidence doesn't make news.

Such attitudes toward government make understandable the abuse of public servants. Alexander Hamilton was not the last official who could complain of "the malicious intrigues to stab me in the dark." The clubmen who cautioned Theodore Roosevelt that politics was the domain of saloonkeepers and horsecar conductors and was therefore to be shunned by gentlemen had only brought their epithets up to date.

Admittedly, it is dangerous to generalize about public attitudes. Actually, there has been noticeable increase in the prestige of public employment since Leonard White's pioneering study in 1929. For the population as a whole, private employment *per se* is no longer held in higher esteem. But the appeal of government service remains low among college graduates, the very group most essential to the complex tasks of big government.

A recent survey of college students reveals self-contented indifference to politics and self-centered conformity to the mores of our business society. Only 17 percent of the collegians thought that participation in community affairs would be one of the three activities from which they would derive most satisfaction. Only 3 percent gave useful citizenship top place in their plans for the future. The satisfactions of career, family, and leisure were overwhelming favorites.

The roots of such attitudes lie, of course, in our history. Our country was born in protest against overbearing monarchy. In exploiting the great promises of the industrial revolution in a land of economic virginity, opportunity did not welcome restrictions of any kind, especially from government. Then too, the "Shame of the Cities" a few decades ago tarred public employment as a disreputable means of livelihood, a misconception which has not been altogether dispelled. As a result, those most needed as participants in government service shun it. It is interesting to speculate, too, whether Americans, joiners by nature, have not so widely proliferated their loyalties among service clubs, social groups, humane causes, even institutions of learning, as to make it difficult for them to sense the primacy of loyalty to government.

We must also recognize several characteristics of our economic system at midcentury which add to the difficulty of recruitment for government service, particularly for policy level jobs. Taxes on individual income and inheritances probably give fewer people financial independence in the prime of life. Ever fewer people enjoy the freedom of self-employment. Instead, most work for large corporations. There the prize jobs with accompanying high income are to be achieved by career-long devotion. Job security and company-sponsored retirement plans also militate against sacrificing security to do public service.

To sum up, we have growing needs to be met by government. Yet, the process of government is unattractive owing to our attitudes, our history, and our economy.

THE COMMUNITY OF INTEREST BETWEEN THE CAMPUS AND THE CAPITOL

At bottom, the problem of staffing government depends upon changing public attitudes and individual sense of duty. Realizing this, we are suddenly and belatedly awakened to the community of interest between the campus and the capitol. Unfortunately, there has been all too much of a hiatus between government and politics and the colleges and universities. This is especially hard to explain. Our so-called liberal education professes classical orientation. But has it? Pericles, speaking for the Athenians, declared: "We do not allow absorption in our own affairs to interfere with participation in the city's. We regard the man who holds aloof from public affairs as useless. . . ." The avowed purpose of education in the schools of Athens was to prepare men for public service. No one could assert that American schools of higher learning have had as a first purpose inculcating a dutiful sense of public service. Are we to conclude that the history and the languages of the Romans and the Greeks are of greater pertinence to American higher education than what these ancient self-governing peoples thought and wrote about? What we teach as philosophy they practiced as politics. To them humanism was not simply language. It was the day-to-day wrestling with human affairs.

If undergraduate higher education is to be truly liberal, its core subject might well be the study of government in all its aspects and the related social sciences. The social sciences, properly organized and taught, should create an indigenous 20th century humanism of the true classical tradition. Personal participation in public affairs will then be the role of the educated man. Only if this emphasis is made in our colleges on social science and those social subjects evolve this new humanism, will self-government be properly safeguarded. Walter Lippmann rightly objects to the tacit assumption of present day higher education. It assumes that "while education can do something to enable the individual to make a success of his own career, the instinctive rightness and righteousness of the people can be relied upon for everything else." What a dangerous assumption for a self-governing people!

IMPORTANCE OF HIGHER EDUCATION AT THE UNDERGRADUATE LEVEL

In view of the danger, what ideally should happen within higher education for the benefit of all students and especially for those committed to careers in public service? In fact, training for public careers cannot be considered apart from undergraduate education. Insofar as education is instrumental in determining values, it happens in the undergraduate years. The values inculcated and the subject-matter interest generated among undergraduates also determine to a great extent who will go into what fields of graduate study and what types of employment.

If public administration is to recruit sufficient numbers of talented youth, it may be that undergraduate education needs a little reformation, particularly political science and other social sciences. Since World War II, the glamorous fields for students, faculty, and administration alike have been the physical sciences, pure and applied. Recognizing this and determined not to lose their place in the academic sun, the classical subjects—languages, history, philosophy, and literature—have played upon the conscience of higher education. They have staged a rear-guard action under the guise of general education.

Meanwhile, the social sciences lacking tradition and without glamour may have languished rather than flowered. Mind you, I am not adverse to the physical sciences or the most traditional liberal arts subjects. My concern is, first, that the subjects most capable of preparing modern citizens for the kind of life so much admired in the Ancients are not receiving due attention now. The entire citizenry needs the background the social sciences offer. In fact, political science and cognate subjects, properly organized and taught, constitute the true general education for the 20th century. If Plato, Isocrates, or Aristotle were teaching today, would their courses be in the departments of languages or literature? Neither history nor philosophy (as now taught) would be likely to attract them. Yet, the subjects to which these classical greats would naturally gravitate, the social sciences which should constitute the core of humanism in the world's greatest democracy, are far from dominant in undergraduate education.

Many undergraduates who go into professional fields other than public administration ultimately find employment in public service. But, given our present undergraduate curricula, they may have never been exposed to the rudiments of government and administration. Those undergraduates who never go into public service will, of course, be citizens. But without considerably more background in political and other social sciences than many of them now have, they will not provide the enlightened, high-minded base in the citizenry needed if professional public administrators are to function effectively.

Whose fault is it if faculty colleagues don't give the social sciences an appropriate place in the curriculum, if presidents and deans don't accommodate their budgetary needs, if the abler students choose other majors? In striving for objectivity and "scientific" respectability, social scientists have neglected even to propagandize their subject matter, not to mention admitting to its high social purpose. Perhaps the political science curriculum in general and courses in introductory public administration in particular are falling short of their opportunities—indeed, of their responsibilities. Might I mention, too, the wisdom of a new rapprochment between political science and public administration?

GRADUATE EDUCATION FOR PUBLIC ADMINISTRATION

It is with considerable temerity that I approach the meat of the matter: graduate programs in public administration. These programs have been somewhat on the periphery of my attention in recent years. My professional colleagues have given far more thought than I have to detailed curricular matters and their execution.

Nothing would please me more than to open my eyes, Rip Van Winkle-like, and find everything changed—for the better. However, it is my impression that, for the most part, the conceptions and conundrums remain much the same. Indeed, some of the impetus of a decade or two ago may have declined. A few new courses, or at least course titles, may have been added out of a desire to emphasize the complexities and sophistication of this field. We are all anxious to gain for it highest professional status. At the same time, some curricula in public administration are still an eclectic congeries of courses offered by the sundry departments and schools composing a major campus. Public administration programs are often a patchwork. Courses and the professors offering them often do not have as their major purpose education for public administration. The faculty in public administration *per se* is still a very small albeit devoted one. It is augmented by conscripts from other disciplines and from operating units in the more respectable and efficient local, public jurisdiction. That the Nation's capital is still without a full-time graduate school of public administration also indicates less than to-be-expected progress.

Whether the proper curriculum emphasis of professional students should be upon the fundamental and theoretical aspects of the subject or upon the intensely practical tool courses plagues public administration as it does training for other professions. To enrich their teaching, programs in public administration continue to affiliate themselves with the governments, mostly State and local. This has benefited faculty, students, and public officials. The National Government, which is our "teaching hospital" *par excellence,* is seldom utilized, to the detriment of both the profession and the Government.

Students in public administration are of two types and too few. There are those with determination, zeal, and capabilities who, somewhat mysteriously, in spite of more fellowships and better employment opportunities elsewhere, still want to be public servants. There are those who, incidentally to their main professional objectives, elect a few courses in public administration. They are aware that government is a major employer of those trained in such professions as forestry, welfare, health, and education. They wisely recognize the need to become somewhat acquainted with administrative theory and practice as related to government.

DOES PUBLIC ADMINISTRATION MEASURE UP TO THE NEEDS OF OUR TIME?

It is my impression that public administration has not measured up to the needs of our time. Yet, the fault primarily is that our time does not recognize its needs. You have already gathered that I admire the ancient Athenians. They did, however, make a fatal mistake which we should not repeat. Their Golden Age was the 5th century B.C. The great schools, the Academy, the Lyceum, and that of Isocrates, did not flourish until the 4th century. Athens became full of educational fervor, particularly with respect to education for public affairs, as if in answer to a broad realization of governmental failure. This unfortunate historical sequence constitutes a lesson for America. We must not let misunderstanding, inefficiency, and neglect of government so impair our national strength that we belatedly look to higher education simply for an autopsy of failure. We must bring public affairs and public administration to the forefront in our universities as a sort of preventive medicine in this period of early national maturity. While ideally we might wish someone else could take the lead, the responsibility is inescapably that of those who teach public administration.

How are we to find the great strength for the task before us? Alfred North Whitehead offers one suggestion. Teachers of public administration are in a happy position to follow it—". . . firsthand knowledge," Whitehead writes, "is the ultimate basis of intellectual life. To a large extent book learning conveys second-hand information, and as such can never rise to the importance of immediate practice. Our goal is to see the immediate events of our lives as instances of our general ideas. What the learned world tends to offer is one second-hand scrap of information illustrating ideas derived from another second-hand scrap of information. The second-handedness of the learned world is the secret of its mediocrity. It is tame because it has never been scared by facts."

TOWARD A SYNTHESIS OF RESEARCH, TEACHING, AND PRACTICE

For the large assignment facing them, teachers in public administration cannot be tame and they must have facts. In their intimate relationships with government, they are in a position, unique in academia, to relate themselves to the great problems of our day and their solution. Still more personal public service and governmental research is called for. Research is the elixir of professional leadership. As a nation we are devoting about 1¼ percent of our gross national product to research. Of this $5.4 billion, not more than 1 percent is for research in the social sciences; moreover, only a very small part of this $55 million goes for projects that will advance the art and science of government. Medicine offers a sharp contrast. It spends about $340 million annually on research, a 275-percent increase in the last decade.

The medical schools, too, have evolved an enviable synthesis of research, teaching, and practice. From the basic sciences and preclinical studies, new facts are discovered. They are carried into the clinics and related to human ills. Many cures are effected in practice owing to these facts. In the process, new problems are discovered by teaching clinicians and new theories are developed. These hypotheses are investigated in the laboratory, and the cycle repeats itself. Medical education has thus become highly respected for its enlarged contributions to mankind. There is a striking parallelism of opportunity and method between medicine and public administration.

Progress against disease requires clinical facilities in the greatest centers of population where medical problems exist in infinite variety. For the same reason, progress in public administration depends upon relating its teaching, research, and students clinically to the greatest center of government in the free world, our Nation's capital. There administration, its problems, and its facts will always abound. Second-handedness in studying them will never be adequate. What a wealth of as yet unrealized possibilities for education for public administration Washington, D. C., offers you and your universities. You need only relate yourselves in joint efforts with one another and existing institutions there. If public administration follows medicine's example, its esteem within higher education will approach that of medicine. But more important, public administration will make an equally enlarged contribution to society.

So much for facts. Now about being less tame. Within the graduate professional educational components of our great universities, public administration has been altogether too tame. The status of public administration on the campus is usually something less than a graduate professional school. It should be something more. Public administration must be brought from a kind of stepchild, Cinderella-before-the-ball circumstance to the ideal status of a queen among its presently dominating older sister schools of law, medicine and health, forestry, and social work. Here the analogy may break down. Even a fairy godfather or two like the late Mr. Samuel S. Fels will not in all likelihood be enough to work the needed transition. Obviously such magnificent financial help is needed. More important is the need for professional leaders of public administration with a large conception of their role and with the courage and ability to put carriage wheels under their ideas. The conception that must permeate the most conservative academic minds is that most education for most of the professions is not quite complete, owing to the great probability of graduates working either within big government or with big government, unless students have a few courses in public administration.

SUMMARY

By the way of summary—your subject-matter of public administration, considered ideally, should be in the heart center of undergraduate and graduate higher education.

In closing, conferences of this nature, and especially discussions like this one, take on the aspect of a whipping post. We tend to whip ourselves against the post of our ideal.

Self-flagellation is useful at times provided we do not succumb to the frustrations inherent in the process of comparing the actual and the ideal. To paraphrase Rheinhold Niebuhr, man must ever seek impossible victory and face inevitable defeat. Niebuhr has certainly not succumbed to his pessimism. Nor should we. Return to the campus and establish there what is practical of the ideal.

9

Partnership for a Better Public Service*

HONORABLE GEORGE M. LEADER
Governor of Pennsylvania

Thank you for the honor of this occasion. I thank you for myself and for the people of this great Commonwealth. It is as much a tribute to them as it is to me. For in a democracy, the State's Chief Executive embodies, during the period of his trust, the hopes and ideals of the people whom he serves.

This tribute to Chief Justice Jones and myself is a symbol of one of the great traditions of the University of Pennsylvania: the tradition of partnership between town and gown—the tradition of dedication to the proposition that one mission of a great university in a republic is to help government through education and service, to realize the highest purposes of democracy.

Not only in her men and women, but also in her schools and departments does Pennsylvania exemplify this great tradition.

The Wharton School, that for seventy-five years has been training men and women for leadership in both government and business; The Fels Institute of Local and State Government, whose many important contributions to better government I have come to value both as a student and more recently as Governor; Law, Medicine, Engineering, Education, and the other professional schools, whose significant research is helping us in meeting many of the great

* Commencement Address, University of Pennsylvania, February 8, 1957.

social needs of our times—these all manifest that tradition of mutual interest between the University and the government service.

This tradition has always been important. It is even more important today. The changing nature of our society and the challenges of world leadership are making new demands upon our partnership.

Our civilization is now facing, I believe, its crucial struggle. Will we, in Professor Toynbee's phrase, climb to a higher plateau? Or will we fall back into the abyss now occupied by all the civilizations that have preceded ours? Whether we in government and you in higher education adequately discharge our responsibilities in meeting this challenge may well determine the question. We must maintain and strengthen our partnership.

What is the challenge of our times? It is the ill-housed, the ill-clothed, the ill-fed—not only in this Country, but throughout the world. It is the sick and the lame and the halt. It is economic crises and their resulting poverty. It is political slavery. It is fear and distrust among peoples. It is war that will destroy civilization. Most important of all, it is the degradation of human life and the loss of human dignity that are the inevitable products of these conditions.

What is the challenge of our times? It is discovering the values and ideals common to all the peoples of the world upon which we can hope to build a just and lasting peace. It is finding the proper balance between liberty and authority. It is achieving security in a fear-ridden world while fulfilling our social and economic needs at the same time. It is inspiring politically enslaved people to seek liberty and helping them find the means to do so. It is overcoming the administrative difficulties stemming from the growing complexity of government.

What is the challenge of our times? It is developing the diverse professional, technical and administrative skills required for adequate and efficient government. It is making our public service even more sensitive and responsive to the needs and wishes of our citizens. It is achieving the vision needed to transcend the difficulties of the present, and to build, upon the values of the past, a new and better way of life, not only for ourselves but for all the peoples of the world. It is discovering and cultivating the superior intelligence, ability and leadership that government desperately needs.

In thinking about government, we tend, I believe, to overstress the responsibilities of the Federal Government. Its world-wide scope, the fact that its decisions are of common interest to the whole country, the impact of these decisions throughout the world and in our own lives—these characteristics of the Federal Government cause us to focus most of our attention on Washington.

There is a danger in this tendency. Ours is an integrated society. Our strength stems not from one segment of this society; it stems from all of our institutions, and all of our units of government. The smallest township shares in the responsibility for meeting the challenge of our times.

Traffic congestion, slums, juvenile delinquency, sanitary water supply, waste disposal, orderly land use development, integration in our schools, property assessment, care of the physically handicapped and mentally ill—these are only some of the matters for which local and state governments are primarily responsible. Our day-to-day decisions on such matters will, in their cumulative effect, have as much bearing on our success in the role of world leadership in the long run as will the size of our armed services or our policy in the Middle East.

Washington, then, should not be our only point of interest. Our borough and township offices, our city halls, our county courthouses and our state capitols should also claim our close attention.

Now the plain and distressing fact is that government—especially local and state government—is not attracting enough men and women with sufficient professional and administrative ability. Yet the highly complex services of these governments require superior ability.

My hardest job in Harrisburg has been—and still is—to find enough competent people for the key professional, technical and administrative positions. And this difficulty cannot be attributed solely to the undersirable aspects of employment in our State's service. Almost all municipal and state governments in the United States are having similar difficulty.

I do not intend by this point to discredit the thousands of able public servants who serve the people with competence and devotion. They work long hours and receive too little recognition. They are the first to admit that we need people even better qualified than themselves if we are to provide more adequate government services. For they are primarily the ones pressing me to find ways of attracting more capable people into government service.

Now if this were only a question of better recruitment methods, it would not be an appropriate subject for your attention on this occasion. The question is a much more basic one. It is a question of the attitudes of our colleges and universities toward governmental careers for their graduates. It is a question of the way in which our colleges and universities cultivate leadership potential for government service. It is a question of the way in which they equip all of their graduates for the obligations of citizenship. It is a question of the manner in which government employs college graduates and the opportunities it gives them to develop their abilities. Finally, and most important, it is a question of the attitudes of our citizens toward their public service.

If we are to improve government service—and we must do so—all of these questions must be considered.

Penn's tradition of partnership with government is the answer, I believe, to achieving the kind of public service we need. All of our colleges and universities must adopt improvement of government service as one of their principal missions. For the burden of developing the knowledges and skills and of educating the leadership that government needs will rest increasingly on them.

Yet, how many of our colleges and universities now accept this responsibility? How many of them have faculty members studying and teaching government full-time? How many of them encourage all students to take more than the first year introductory course in political science? How many of their students learn enough about local and state government to make the informed judgments on governmental issues that they as citizens in a republic must make? How many of our college graduates are schooled in that most precious talent of citizenship, responsible criticism? "Too few," is the answer on all counts, in my opinion.

It would be presumptuous indeed for an amateur like me to attempt a definition of the proper role of a university in its relationship to government. I shall not attempt to do so. However, some suggestions from my vantage point as Governor may be helpful to those in our colleges and universities who are responsible for defining this role.

Higher education's role in achieving an adequate public service has, I suggest, three elements: education, research, and service.

It is imperative, I think, that our institutions of learning raise their standards of higher education for government service.

It is significant that the Wharton School, through its Fels Institute of Local and State Government, is now making a comprehensive study of education and training for professional careers in government administration. This study will, I am sure, be a major contribution toward improving local and state government service.

Not only should our colleges and universities raise the standards of preparation for government service. They should also, I believe, lead the way in persuading political authorities to broaden the opportunities for educated people within the government service. Higher standards and broader opportunities for development necessarily go together.

I suggest that it is also vitally important that the professional schools—law, medicine, engineering, architecture, and the others—include intensive study of government in their curricula.

Many graduates of professional schools enter public service. Many more become leaders in their communities. I suggest that they should, during their college days, acquire knowledge of and sensitivity to the processes and broader problems of government.

The public health director is not only a doctor; he is also a government administrator. The highway executive is not only an engineer; he is also a government administrator. The welfare executive is not only a social worker; he is also a government administrator. The planning director is not only a designer; he is also a government administrator.

In passing may I say that we need more interest and activity in government by all our citizens. Our institutions of learning should encourage all students to become active in civic affairs; they should give their students the knowledge and understanding to do so.

All college graduates, in fact, should be better acquainted with government and the social needs with which it is concerned than most of them appear to be. They should know local and state government especially.

To the extent that you become actively interested in government after graduation, most of you will be involved in civic affairs of your communities and of your states. Public parks and playgrounds, health centers, land subdivision controls, zoning variances, slum clearance projects, radial highways, and similar quite mundane matters will be among your concerns. In college, therefore, all students ought to acquire some intimacy with the practical, everyday activities of government. These activities are government.

With regard to research, many of our colleges and universities are now devoting a considerable amount of time and energy to research for government. Most of this research, I believe, is technical and operational in nature—it is concerned with specific problems of immediate import.

There is need also, I suggest, for more basic, long-term research for government—the kind of pure research that in mathematics and physics has preceded the magnificent accomplishments of the physical sciences.

What, for example, is the probable future development of nuclear power and its use in the United States? How will this development affect the disposition and configuration of our cities? Our cities are now spending many millions of dollars on capital improvements. Yet nuclear power may develop at such a rate and in such a way that many of these improvements may become obsolete soon after the ink is dry on the contracts.

Or, we might ask, what is the relationship of population growth to industrial development, and what are the implications of this relationship to our policies of assistance to under-developed areas?

Perhaps research that I do not know about is already being done on these questions. But I feel certain there are many questions of a similar fundamental nature that are not now receiving conscious, systematic, long-term study. Industry, it may be noted, is allocating an increasing amount of its resources to basic research. Government has perhaps an even more vital need for such research.

It is unlikely that legislative bodies—their members must show results to get re-elected—will authorize funds for this type of research by government agencies. Nor can most of our civic agencies indulge in this kind of research. Their boards of trustees must also show relatively short-term accomplishments in order to attract members or subscribers.

We must look, therefore, to our colleges and universities for such research.

The third element of higher education's role in achieving more adequate government is, I suggest, direct service. To illustrate what I mean by direct service, I would cite the extraordinary cooperation and assistance that I have received from colleges and universities during the past two years.

Members of the faculties of these institutions served anonymously and without compensation as consultants to me and my department heads when we first took office. They surveyed all the major departments and agencies and recommended changes for improving their administration. Their invaluable assistance prevented much of the administrative chaos that usually accompanies a change in state administration. I believe that this type of assistance is unique in state government.

A member of your faculty organized and directed the efforts of these consultants. He has served as Chairman of my Advisory Committee on Administration. He is now principal consultant to the State Reorganization Commission and a member of the State Council of Education.

A member of your faculty was my first Secretary of Administration—in fact, the first Secretary of Administration in the history of Pennsylvania. Under his inspiration and guidance, we have reorganized many of our State agencies. We have also installed efficient accounting and budget systems, and have extended the merit principle to many key positions. Though he has now returned to his teaching duties, the Commonwealth continues to benefit from his wisdom and broad knowledge through his direction of the State Reorganization Commission.

May I take this opportunity, on behalf of the Commonwealth, to express publicly my deep appreciation to these men and their academic associates for the very significant contributions they are making to better government service, not only in this State, but throughout the Country. Their work is another example of Penn's tradition of partnership in government.

Though it is appropriate on this occasion to accord special recognition to Pennsylvania, we should at least note that other schools in the Commonwealth are also making important contributions to better government service. Faculty members from Pennsylvania State, Pittsburgh, Temple and several other institutions are providing, through research and direct service, vision and expert knowledge essential for solving our governmental problems.

It is unfortunate that because of the anti-intellectualism that prevails in some elements of our society, these contributions of higher education do not receive the full recognition they deserve.

To critics who try to condemn this developing partnership between higher education and government, by labeling it "egg-head" government, I say let's have more of it. For only by joining political responsibility with superior intellect and knowledge can we hope to raise our civilization to a higher plateau. In this partnership lies our hope of realizing democracy's adaptation of Plato's ideal—the philosopher-king.

I have been stressing to this point the role of higher education in equipping government to meet the challenge of our times. But both parties to a partnership share responsibility for the enterprise. Higher education cannot do the job alone. We in government must do some soul-searching of our own. We must reorient our attitudes toward the employment of college-trained people and the kinds of opportunities for career development that we afford them.

Our colleges and universities are, and should always remain, centers of basic research and higher thought. Their main task is intellectual and cultural development. Over-specialization in curricula tends to impede their performance of this primary task.

Yet colleges and universities must take some account of job-opportunities for their graduates. One assumption of governmental personnel policy has been that we should recruit for specific positions and promote through narrow functional hierarchies. This assumption tends to limit the opportunities we can offer to superior, broadly-educated young people for career development in the public service. It has also tended to force institutions of higher learning that educate men and women for government service to over-specialize their curricula. They have to specialize if their graduates are to have the specific knowledge and skills required to compete for the narrow job-openings available.

One reason for the respect that the British civil service has won throughout the world is that the government recruits for its administrative class broadly-educated people. For numerous reasons they appear to be willing to serve a relatively long apprenticeship on humble assignments. Thus, they obtain the specific knowledge and skills required for eventual broad responsibilities.

We are gradually modifying our policies on recruitment for the public service in this Country. Through general intelligence and aptitude examinations, through internship and administrative assistant programs, and through service-wide promotional ladders, we are broadening the opportunities for college-trained people. It is heartening to see that local governments, especially those with the manager form of government, are among the leaders in this movement.

Public personnel policy has also generally assumed that the employe when hired should be fully qualified for his position. This assumption may have been valid in Andrew Jackson's day. It is certainly not valid today for many positions.

Government must, through in-service training, supplement the general knowledge obtained in school with the specific knowledge and skill required in each job. Some of you may have noticed the news item some days ago about the member of the General Assembly who criticized us for instituting rather modest in-service training programs within our departments and agencies. This attitude is all too prevalent. Preparation for public service careers cannot stop at the moment your President hands you your degree. Education, both for life and for government service, is a continuing, lifelong process.

Let us in government, then, accept responsibility for direct participation in the educational process. Let us establish in-service training, internships, executive development programs, and other forms of staff development. Let us provide more and broader opportunities for career development. Let us demand less specific vocational and technical preparation from college graduates entering the public service. Let us adopt other incentives that will attract the superior college graduates.

With special reference to local and state government in Pennsylvania, let us extend the principle of selection and promotion according to merit to all professional, technical, and principal administrative policy-making positions below the level of political responsibility. Since October, we have through executive act extended civil service status to over 8,000 positions. Politics has had no part in this action. Probably the majority of the people who have thus acquired civil service status are Republicans. I hope that our Legislature will see fit to extend statutory coverage to these and other positions.

These then are the roles of higher education and of government in achieving more adequate public service. There is one more role to consider, the role of the citizen.

The price of liberty, we say, is eternal vigilance. The price of good government, I submit, is also eternal vigilance. If the citizens of a republic do not take an active interest in their government—if they do not demand honest, competent and responsible public service—then subversion and corruption can, and do, gain the upper hand.

Responsibility for meeting our challenge rests ultimately upon each citizen. If our citizens are apathetic or irresponsible, neither government nor higher education can fulfill their respective roles in providing the competence and leadership needed for our tasks.

A rather disturbing paradox exists in this Country. On the one hand, our citizens take pride in having what they consider the best government in the world. They vehemently defend it against external criticisms. On the other hand, many of them tend to be overly suspicious and indiscriminately critical of their public service. Many more of them are apathetic about governmental matters. In the age of Pericles, government was the chief concern of every Athenian citizen. Our public service appears generally to be held in low esteem by many of our citizens.

Yet in a democracy, each citizen is, in a sense, in the public service. If he does a poor job in discharging his obligations of citizenship, he gets poor government. The level of ethics, competence, and adequacy of government tends, I think, to reflect the expectations and the vigilance of our citizens.

You who have graduated here today are the citizens of today and tomorrow. Because of the special educational advantages you have enjoyed, we look to you for the leadership we need. Let me urge you then:

Keep yourselves informed about the activities and problems of your local, State, and Federal Governments. How would you decide the major issues of your times if you were in the positions of immediate responsibility? You are in the position of ultimate responsibility.

Participate actively in the governmental affairs of your communities.

Demand of your government responsiveness, honesty, competence, and efficiency. Support actively proposals for strengthening these essentials of good government.

Be fair and constructive in your criticism of government. Give proper credit to the vast number of dedicated public officials and employes who serve honestly, selflessly, and competently.

Finally, consider government service as you plan your professional careers. Many people find the excitement of partisan competition for elective office distasteful. We may note that half of those competing for elective office are destined to be disappointed. We should keep in mind, however, that for every elective office there are thousands of positions in the public service that are, or should be, completely nonpartisan in nature. Over 90 percent of government is nonpolitical service to the people. This service offers many opportunities for rewarding careers to college-trained people. These opportunities merit your attention.

In closing, I would ask you to think for a moment about the ultimate goals of our society. Peace—is that really the ultimate goal? Rome enjoyed a long period of relative peace. Yet during those years of peace, her civilization disintegrated.

Our ultimate goals are the great social, economic, political, and religious aspirations that rise from the deep wellsprings of our civilization. Peace is a necessary, but not a sufficient, condition for achieving these goals. We need also superior, trained intellects devoted to the public interest.

Government, our colleges and universities, all of our citizens—we must all work together toward the improvement of government service and the achievement of our ultimate goals.

PART II

The Position and Role of the
Administrative Policy-Making Officer

10

Introduction:
The Position and Role of the
Administrative Policy-Making Officers*

STEPHEN B. SWEENEY
University of Pennsylvania

There has been no systematic and extensive study of education for the public service since George Graham's work of twenty years ago. During the past few years, a number of political scientists have discussed informally the possibility of cooperating in a rather thorough re-consideration of the fundamental assumptions and elements of preparation public service careers. Experience to date should suggest guide-lines for the improvement of education and training efforts, both pre-service and in-service.

As a result of these discussions, cooperative arrangements were made with the American Society for Public Administration and the International City Managers' Association for intensive, year-long research culminating in a program of workshops and conferences on administrative career development.

* *Summary of remarks by Stephen B. Sweeney, Ph.D., Director, Fels Institute of Local and State Government, and Professor of Governmental Administration, University of Pennsylvania, at panel, "Education for Public Administration," American Society for Public Administration Annual Conference, Chicago, March 22, 1957. This statement was distributed in advance to all participants in the educator's conference.*

FRAMEWORK FOR EVALUATION

The purpose of this research program is to provide colleges and universities with a specific and comprehensive frame of reference for them to evaluate their pre-service programs. Furthermore, the research program should prove equally valuable to governmental employers in planning career development programs within the service. This effort represents a fresh approach to the problem, and the essential elements of it may be of special interest.

The basic assumption of this program is that education and training should be related directly to the requirements of the level of positions for which colleges and universities are preparing people. For the administratiive policy-making officer, what are the meaning, conditions, and obligations of leadership? What are his responsibilities? What are the activities involved and the problems encountered in discharging these responsibilities?

ADMINISTRATORS DEFINE ELEMENTS OF POSITIONS

A second assumption of the program is that the people best qualified to provide answers to these questions—in both present and future terms—are the people who have achieved success in administrative policy-making positions. This has been the purpose of the two workshops, the one in St. Louis in November composed primarily of leading city managers and the one in Chicago in March composed of an intermixture of state and local administrators, and of staff and line department heads.

A third assumption relates to the use by educators of the administrators' definition of the position. In devising programs to equip students with some of the basic knowledges and skills needed, the educators should analyze this definition carefully. This will be the purpose of the concluding portion of the joint program, the educators' conference.

Educators who are especially concerned with public administration training will consider desirable curricula patterns, effective course instruction methods, and types of field experiences. The respective roles of higher education and governmental employers in career preparation and development, and the problems of equipping the professionally trained functional specialist for general administrative responsibility will be considered as well.

A fourth assumption of the program should also be stressed. It has so far been agreed by all who have cooperated and participated thus far that education and training for administrative policy-making careers cannot be done by colleges and universities alone. In this work we should plan for total career development, which involves both pre-service and in-service preparation. Our workshops have made clear that many of the essential knowledges and skills require experience and maturity for their attainment; they cannot be obtained in pre-service programs.

CAREER DEVELOPMENT REQUIRES BOTH PRE-SERVICE AND IN-SERVICE PREPARATION

Therefore, career preparation and development demands a close and harmonious relationship between pre-service and in-service training. While pre-service programs should be strengthened, it is also important for government to strengthen its in-service career development programs. Since colleges and universities do have some concern with the job opportunities available to their graduates, it should be noted that if government fails to fulfill its responsibility for in-service training, then colleges and universities will be less able to provide the broad-gauged pre-service preparation that is in keeping with their role and traditions.

Sometimes there is a tendency to assume that the "job-analysis" approach to education and training will produce a narrowly vocational outlook. But the narrowness or

breadth of educational programs depends upon the narrowness or breadth of the concept of the positions for which
people are being trained. The workshops have delineated
a concept of the administrative policy-making officer that is
comparable to principal positions in other significant fields
of endeavor in our society.

The St. Louis and Chicago workshops included approximately fifty administrators and consumed approximately
twenty-five hours of intensive discussion. All of this was
based on many days of preparation and discussion by the
academic and service staffs of the Fels Institute.

In such a short presentation, it is not possible to sum-
marize adequately even the major elements of the position
and role of administrative policy-making officers as defined
by the administrator groups. But perhaps a few of the
points they developed will provide some useful ideas for
later discussion.

LEADERSHIP ROLE DISCUSSED IN CONTEXTS OF INTERNAL AND EXTERNAL RELATIONSHIPS

The leadership role was described as the ability to guide
and direct effectively the work of the unit or agency. The
subject of leadership was divided into two broad categories:
the leadership role in external affairs, that is, toward the
legislative body, clientele groups, and the general public;
and the leadership role in internal or institutional matters.

The group concluded that leadership should be thought
of in terms of the major responsibilities of the office, the
conditions of administration in democratic society, and the
obligations of professional status.

Some of the differences in emphases between the two
workshop groups are interesting. For example, the city
managers assumed that a generalized training for leadership could be provided. Line department heads believed
generally that leadership was inextricably related to func-

tional responsibilities. Ability for leadership had to be developed within each functional context: leadership in public works is enough different from leadership in public welfare that specialized training for each is necessary.

The contributions of practical administrators to an academic understanding of the scope and depth of administrative leadership cannot be over-emphasized. Although disagreement often took place among the participants, it clearly brought home the complex variables in leadership which should be vivid in the minds of educators assuming the responsibility of training for the public service.

ADMINISTRATORS IDENTIFIED FOUR MAJOR CATEGORIES OF RESPONSIBILITIES

In the second session of each workshop, the major responsibilities of administrative policy-making officers were identified. Responsibilities were defined as the classes of activities for which they may be held accountable. Accountability, the workshops agreed, implies susceptibility to appropriate action by superiors for both unsatisfactory and meritorious performance.

In all, sixteen major responsibilities were identified and grouped under four categories:

1. Responsiveness to superiors and clientele
2. Articulation of objectives and programs
3. Procurement, organization, and control of administrative resources
4. Direction and supervision.

Both workshop groups agreed that no priority could be established among these responsibilities. However, it is interesting to note that the city managers tended to center their discussion on the responsibilities involved in responsiveness to superiors and clientele and in direction and supervision. The more diversified Chicago group concentrated on the articulation of objectives and programs.

The discussion of this latter point was especially interesting. The group agreed that the administrator is responsible for formulating and recommending to his superiors policies and programs that are both professionally sound *and* politically acceptable—to the extent that he is able to anticipate political acceptability. In developing these recommendations, they said, the administrator's main task is to reconcile and articulate the recommendations of his subordinates, his own best professional judgment, and the value preferences of his superiors and clientele.

ADMINISTRATOR HAS RESPONSIBILITY TO WORK WITH AGENCIES AND GROUPS OUTSIDE OF HIS JURISDICTION

Another significant point in the discussion was that the administrator has an obligation to work with those agencies and groups outside of his own jurisdiction whose efforts might have an important bearing upon the accomplishment of his objectives and programs. Such outside agencies and groups may include other line departments, staff and management units, neighboring jurisdictions, other levels of government, and civic groups. If such external groups have vital roles in meeting the administrative and social needs with which he is concerned, then the administrator should be accountable for coordinating their efforts with his. The group identified the many types of difficulties that can be encountered in discharging this responsibility. Despite such difficulties—some of which he often cannot overcome—he should seek such coordination, they agreed.

To the educator the emphasis placed upon this point implies that programs of career preparation should stress, perhaps more than many do now, the attitudes and techniques of cooperating with groups in which the administrator has little or no authority. It would seem that for administrators in metropolitan areas, as one example, this point is especially significant.

KNOWLEDGE OF GOVERNMENTAL ENVIRONMENT ESPECIALLY STRESSED

The third session considered the basic knowledge needed by administrative policy makers. Here, we avoided prescriptions of specific college or university courses and stressed the areas of knowledge which were deemed most important.

Five categories of knowledge were suggested: knowledge about

1. The political, social and economic environment
2. The administrative process
3. Human relations
4. General technical services (Finance, governmental planning, research methodology, statistics, public relations, etc.)
5. Governmental services.

As was expected, considerable diversity of opinion was expressed. There was apparent agreement on the need for knowledge of the political, social, and economic background. Indeed, this was thought to be most important. Nevertheless, it was unanimously agreed that the other categories of knowledge were all important if the administrator was to be fully equipped to assume the responsibilities inherent in his position.

The final session of each workshop considered basic administrative skills. These were defined as "mental and physical processes essential to the discharge of responsibilities, habitual in performance, and developed through observation, practice and experience."

Skill must be distinguished from knowledge for purposes of education and training because the conditions and methods of achieving them differ. One is *educated* to knowledge; one is *trained* in skills. Skill is developed through step-by-step demonstration and guidance, practice, correction—until, at the acceptable level of competence, the process is performed without conscious thought of the process as such. Skill is obtained in an actual or stimulated work situation.

SIX CLASSES OF ESSENTIAL ADMINISTRATIVE SKILLS IDENTIFIED

The workshops identified six classes of essential administrative skills

First: *Problem identification and analysis,* or the processes of decision-making;

Second: *Situational analysis,* i.e., the skills involved in "sizing up" his administrative and political milieu, his organization, and his subordinates;

Third: *Operational analysis.* These are the skills needed for analyzing technical and substantive matters underlying planning, organization, direction, and control.

For example, the workshops agreed that the administrator should be skilled in the following processes: analyzing positions; interpreting financial documents and conditions; interpreting statistical compilations; reading, visualizing, and interpreting various forms of visual representation of spatial relationships, such as engineering and architectural plans and maps, work simplification charts, etc. He should be skilled also in scanning large masses of written materials and in distilling and categorizing the useful ideas and facts they contain. Finally, the administrator should be trained to recognize in his day-to-day decisions broader policies and objectives, as well as the more fundamental economic, social, and political problems of his community and society.

Fourth: *Audience-oriented interpretation and presentation.* Leadership, the workshops agreed, involved primarily the securing of favorable responses from people whose decisions and efforts affect the success of the administrative endeavor. The administrator must be skilled in analyzing his various audiences and in presenting, both orally and in writing, his ideas in such a way that they motivate the particular audiences with which he deals.

Fifth: *Delegation and review.* These are the skills involved in assigning authority, responsibility and work to subordinates and in reviewing their performance. These skills of delegation and review were the subject of considerable discussion by both workshop groups. The administrators felt that skills of delegation and review were perhaps the most important, and yet the least understood and perfected, of the various categories. Both groups took the time to spell out the steps they thought were essential for adequate delegation.

Sixth: *Negotiation and conference.* These skills were discussed in the contexts of interviewing and group conferences.

DIFFERENCES ACCORDING TO BASIC VARIABLES NOTED

In all of the workshop discussions the administrators identified differences in emphases among the elements of the top administrative level positions according to size of jurisdiction, staff or line character of the agency, types of political superiors, state or local government, and other significant variables.

These are only some of the highlights of the two workshops. They have provided the educators with a broad, comprehensive, specifically spelled-out definition of the position and role of administrators.

One of the most satisfying aspects of this program has been the remarkable teamwork among the administrators, the educators, and the professional associations. If we can maintain and develop further over the years this very constructive relationship, we can together improve not only education and training, but many other aspects of governmental administration in which we share common aspirations

I I

The Administrator's Leadership Role

FREDRICK T. BENT *

University of Pennsylvania

INTRODUCTION

Staff Presentation. In recent years, writers of texts in public administration have given recognition, long overdue, to the importance of administrative leadership in government. Prior to the beginning of the depression, primary emphasis was placed on administrative principles and techniques, formal organizational structure, and the legal framework within which administration operates. Discussion of administrative leadership was largely concerned with desirable personal characteristics. Partially as a result of important changes in the patterns of goverment caused by the depression and the second world war, and partially as a result of empirical studies of how administrative organizations actually do function, there has come an awareness of the singular significance of individuals who occupy positions of administrative responsibility. There is, then, need for intensive study of today's administrator at the state and local levels of government.

The leadership role of administrative policy making officers cannot be defined easily. In its broadest terms it is to guide and direct efficiently the work of the agency toward agreed upon objectives. Some writers stress the importance

* *Fredrick T. Bent, Ph.D., is Educational and Research Associate, Fels Institute of Local and State Government, and Assistant Professor of Political Science, University of Pennsylvania.*

245

of the administrator's function in setting new goals, others stress coordinative functions, and some decision-making. Regardless of the emphasis given, it is clear that administrative leadership in government has many facets.

Two basic assumptions underlie the thinking in this paper. The first is that administrators must lead in creative thought, initiate and motivate action, and express positive interest in the formulation of policy within the organization they direct. The second is that administrators are not neutral toward program objectives, are not isolated from the political milieu of their politically appointed or elected superiors, and are not totally disinterested in matters other than the routine day by day administrative problems of their agency.

The leadership role can be approached in two ways. The first would emphasize certain *personal* qualities or qualifications which adhere to the person and not to his title, position or salary. These, such as courage, initiative, sense of balance, integrity, and judgment, to mention only a few, have already been considered at length by many writers and will not be discussed here. Personal qualities can only be evaluated in terms of concrete action taken in a given administrative context.[1] Thus, leadership is situational; certain qualities appear to be demanded at one time and not at others. Leadership can also be thought of in *organizational* terms—the administrator's capacity to develop through his organization a concrete program of action which will be both imaginative and practical, and to carry out or implement the program efficiently and fairly. This paper will be primarily concerned with organizational leadership.

This does not imply that the leadership role of administrative policy-making officers is exercised exclusively in the

[1] Chester Barnard, *Organization and Management.* Cambridge: Harvard University Press, 1949, pp. 101-102.

particular organization they direct and that it ignores the equally important "outside" relations with other public agencies, clientele groups, or citizens. Thus, the leadership role of administrative officials can be said to be both external and internal.

External leadership refers to an administrator's responsibilities toward organizations and groups (such as legislatures, clientele groups, and the general public) which are physically outside the agency he directs. Although the ways in which these groups affect, and in turn are affected by, administrative action vary considerably, it is clear that the development and implementation of policies concern, in varying degrees of intensity, sizable portions of American society.

The exercise of *internal* leadership refers to the administrator's responsibilities within the agency he directs. Although by definition this is a more narrow area of activity, it makes up in depth and intensity what it may lack (particularly in small agencies) in breadth and dimension. Neither the external nor the internal aspects of leadership exercise are mutually exclusive since one clearly impinges upon the other. Administrative leadership in its fullest dimension demands both, and success or failure in one may qualify success or failure in the other.

Administrators' Discussions. The members of both workshops were unwilling to discard the importance of personal qualities which they felt were important for administrators to have. In addition to those suggested in the outline they proposed the need for intense interest and preoccupation with the job to be done, integrity, the ability to withstand the pressure of daily work, the ability to know when to compromise, sensitivity to community needs and wants, and the desire to advance.

The participants in one workshop were asked to address

themselves specifically to the question whether it was more important for administrators to possess certain tangible evidences of leadership or to possess substantive knowledge of a particular field of endeavor. There was general agreement here that, particularly in state and local government, substantive knowledge was fundamental and that leadership could only be exercised if it were directed to programs.

Although there was general approval for recruiting the broadly trained liberal arts college graduate into the public service, the administrators pointed out that despite their leadership potential the college graduates often presented problems to the administrator. These included their lack of intimate knowledge about the operational aspects of government work, their predilection to prefer staff to line agencies, and their restiveness under close supervision. The problem of keeping students in their proper channel without dulling their enthusiasm was also mentioned. However, it was pointed out that part of the difficulty brought about by recruiting college graduates was caused by a failure to determine in advance whether the particular job was repetitive or routine, or whether it would require imagination and leadership.

Several administrators also expressed the strong conviction that graduates from professional schools, such as medicine and engineering, were just as apt to possess leadership qualities as the liberal arts graduate and that, in addition, they possessed factual knowledge which was so urgently needed. Lines of promotion to top administrative positions, they insisted, should not be closed to the functionally-trained person.

GOAL-ORIENTED GUIDANCE AND DIRECTION

Staff Presentation. The leadership role of administrative policy-making officers can be studied under four broad headings:

1. Goal-oriented guidance and direction.
2. The democratic framework.
3. The human values.
4. Professional status

It is no longer seriously questioned that administrators play a positive role in the formulation as well as in the execution of policy. The International City Managers' Association in its recently-amended Code of Ethics now also recognizes the policy-making role of city managers and has taken a stand quite at variance with its position twenty-five years ago.[2] Contemporary writers of administration also place greater emphasis than their predecessors on the policy role of public administrators. The pertinent question is no longer whether or not this is an obligation of administrative leadership, but rather how and in what ways this responsibility can be met to give sensible and realistic guidance and direction to the legislature. At the very minimum it would include:

1. A sense of organizational relevance.
2. Public relations or a political sense.
3. Sensitivity to clientele responses and individual reactions.

Sense of organizational relevance or ability to conceptualize. One of the most compelling problems facing an administrator is to ensure that the specific objectives and programs of his agency are integrally related to the total services supplied by the government to meet community needs. The greater the diversity of administrative activities, the more difficult it becomes to fit in the organiza-

[2] In 1924, Section 5 of the Code of Ethics stated: "Loyalty to his employment recognizes that it is the council, the elected representative of the people, who primarily determine the municipal policies, and are entitled to the credit for their fulfillment." Quoted from VI *City Manager Magazine* October, 1924, p. 10. The 1952 Code reads: "The city manager as a community leader submits policy proposals to the council and provides the council with facts and advice on matters of policy to give the council a basis for making decisions on community goals."

tional objectives of his agency with those of other agencies which also provide community services. An awareness and an anticipation of the objectives and plans of other departments of government are essential. Knowledge of what other agencies are doing or hope to do and of how their plans supplement his own is necessary before the administrator can formulate policies intelligently for legislative consideration. This ability to conceptualize is thus not sporadic but continuous since community needs normally transcend the jurisdiction and competence of a single department. The ability to relate the objectives of one agency of government with the objectives of other agencies requires a depth of understanding about the total public policy which increases in importance despite improvements in administrative techniques.

Public relations or political sense. Government officials and government action must be exposed to the citizens. These officials must have an ability to anticipate and make allowance for probable public reaction, and must feel an obligation to sell the public on the need for having good administrative services rendered by the government.

It is unrealistic to assume that an administrator can intelligently advise the legislative body on policies without understanding currents of public opinion. If administrators are now expected to be participators in the formulation of policies, they can ill afford to assume that it is the sole responsibility of the legislature to anticipate likely community objections. "Administrative foresight must be as good as public hindsight."

Sensitivity to clientele responses. The increased responsibility of the administrator in the formulation of policy and the actual administration of those policies which have legislative approval brings to the foreground two related obligations. First, an administrator must acknowledge ultimate political executive or political legislative direction and control. Second, he is obliged to be aware of and concerned with the reactions of clientele groups and the general public. It would not be difficult to envisage a situation where administrative leadership was abdicated because of vacillation and hesitancy in the face of hostile public opinion. However, having avoided the one extreme of knuckling under to selfish pressures, the administrator must also avoid the other extreme of substituting his own value judgments for those of the public he serves.

Whether the value judgments of the administrator are right or wrong is immaterial at this point; but whether he is overstepping his position as a public servant is not. There must be an awareness of the need for the adjustment of value systems—those of the administrator and those of the public.

Administrators' Discussion. The administrators consistently stressed the fact that they did not work in a political vacuum and therefore emphasized the importance of knowing the community well enough to anticipate probable public reaction to projected policies. Although recognizing the value of informing the public on the need for proposed changes in plans and programs, they emphasized the practical limits to an administrator's public relations functions. Not only may some legislators look upon this as infringing upon their responsibilities, but in addition, there are times when it is of vital importance to move ahead even though public reaction is apt to be hostile. An unpopular stand will be immeasurably strengthened if it has support of council and recognized community leaders. Several of the workshop participants expressed the opinion that council may sometimes be less aware of community feelings than the city administrator. The importance of the timing of administrative decisions was also mentioned as crucial in securing public acceptance.

Despite the emphasis on the administrator's role in the formulation of policy, some explained that there are times when the administrator should caution against precipitous changes in policy. In these instances, administrative leadership may in fact mean the adoption of "delaying tactics" on policies which are believed to be unwise or needless.

LEADERSHIP ABILITIES

Staff Presentation. The role of the administrator in giving guidance and direction in *internal matters* has already received considerable attention from both writers and practitioners. However, the problem of determining how an administrative policy-making officer can fulfill this role is as yet unanswered. Listed below are five prerequisite abilities which are most often stressed in public administration literature. They indicate that supplying goal-oriented guidance and direction within the organization is as taxing as supplying them to external affairs. The five are: [3]

1. To see the enterprise as a whole.
2. To make decisions.
3. To plan ahead.
4. To delegate.
5. To secure loyalty.

To see the enterprise as a whole. This means that an administrator must thoroughly understand the agency's common purposes so that its programs will be geared to common, agreed upon objectives. However determined the effort, most administrators find it far from easy to visualize their departmental programs as a part of the governmental program. To do this, an administrator cannot be so immersed in the detailed operation of a single part of the total program that he fails to support and direct its other ac-

[3] These five categories and subsequent discussion in this section have been taken from chapters two and three of John Millett, *Management in the Public Service,* New York: McGraw-Hill, 1954.

tivities. To see the enterprise as a whole means that an administrator must operate at his "proper level" to use the expression of Paul Appleby.[4] The ability of the administrator to do this is of singular importance if the agency is to fulfill the expectations of the legislature and the public. The ability to make decisions, to plan ahead, and to delegate intelligently are all dependent upon seeing the enterprise as a whole.

To make decisions. In the literature of public administration, it is frequently stated that decision-making is the one distinguishing characteristic of the administrative leader. Certainly, indecision at the top soon drags down the entire organization, leading to confusion, inertia and low morale. In common with all human activities, decisions can never be based upon an analysis of "all" the facts necessary to justify them. This is especially true in public administration where decisions must be made rapidly and cannot await the accumulation of detailed data. Some facts will not emerge until after the decision is made, concrete action taken, and results observed.

Although decision-making exists at all levels of the hierarchy, the higher the echelon the less firm are the guide lines upon which a decision can be based. Here the personal judgment and values of the administrator (coupled with the advice of subordinates) and his comprehension of what the agency should and can do have repercussions throughout the organization. The establishment of priorities results in the allocation of material and personnel resources and these are seldom sufficient for the total purposes of the agency.

Despite the universality of decision-making, numerous factors limit its frequency, decisiveness, and scope. Personality differences between administrators are obviously a variable factor. Legal restraints on authority are a second.

[4] Paul Appleby, *Big Democracy*. New York: Alfred A. Knopf, 1945, p. 45.

Familiarity with the objectives of the agency and legislative confidence are other qualifying factors. Also the traditions or power structure of an agency may discourage vigorous decision-making at the top and protect decision-making prerogatives at lower levels. Finally, absence of a modicum of reliable facts, and hesitancy to move too quickly before opinion has "jelled" may influence an administrator to avoid taking a stand.

To plan ahead. The planning process involves two interrelated activities. The first is program planning in which the substantive objectives of administrative effort are determined; the second is administrative planning which is the devising of means to achieve them. By the ability to plan ahead, however, we are referring primarily to program planning. This is a highly varied activity, part of which is certainly budgeting, a form of monetary planning. But program planning may also be local, regional, or statewide in its scope encompassing such fields as economic development, conservation, water resources, highways and streets and many others.

Mary Parker Follett has stressed the importance to administrators of not merely "meeting the next situation" but rather of "making the next situation." [5] To do this requires not only imaginative anticipation of what future programs need to be planned, but also the allocation of time during the day for this activity. Unfortunately, the pressure of daily routine and deadlines often means that the future must take care of itself. Appleby's admonition to administrators to operate at their proper level places a high priority on program planning.

To delegate. The assertion that the administrator should freely delegate so that nothing is done at the top of an or-

[5] Henry C. Metcalf and L. Urwick (eds.), *Dynamic Administration, the Collected Papers of Mary Parker Follett.* London: Sir Isaac Pitman and Co., 1952, p. 263.

ganization which could not be done farther down the line is generally accepted as an important canon of administration. Frederick Lawton has written that "in order to keep his mind free for large matters and fresh enough to show an inventive turn in dealing with them, he should push down to lower levels responsibility for final action where in the nature of things such responsibility can best be assumed." [6] Yet the very practical reason why executives fail in this responsibility is infinitely more complex. It is in part governed by the ability of subordinates. Statutes and ordinances may limit the opportunity for delegation, and the nature of the problem may preclude handing it to subordinates. In addition, there are doubtless personal reasons which account for the failure to delegate. Significant among these could be the egoistic temperament of the administrator, the belief that delegation is inimical to leadership, and inability to trust anyone but himself, to mention only three.

Regardless of causes, the consequences are usually predictable. If an administrator feels that he must assume detailed operating responsibility for all aspects of an agency's total operations, not only will he not have time to plan ahead, but he may also fail to provide the type of guidance and direction which is so essential.

To secure loyalty. The ability to delegate and the ability to secure loyalty from subordinates are perhaps closely interrelated. One of the more important consequences of leadership occurs when subordinates are encouraged to accept functions delegated to them by the executive. "In effect," Millett has written, "leadership is dependence, dependence upon the faithful performance of one's associates and subordinates." [7] To the extent that subordinates are

[6] Frederick W. Lawton, "The Role of the Administrator in the Federal Government." 14 *Public Administration Review* (1954), p. 117.

[7] Millett, *op. cit.,* p. 45.

encouraged to accept this responsibility, will management and others be convinced of the importance of the work being done." [8] This means getting employees to understand the purposes and objectives of the organization and to appreciate how things get done and why. Therefore, loyalty should not be thought of in terms of personal obeisance to the administrator, but to the agency itself. Loyalty to the agency can best be secured if both workers and management feel that they play integral parts in the accomplishment of the goals of the organization.

Administrators' Discussion. Most of the discussion centered about the decision-making responsibilities of administrative officers. Some felt that experience in making decisions could be best acquired in line departments rather than in staff agencies, and consequently, that new employees should be assigned there. Others took vigorous exception to this, asserting that staff agencies provide as much experience in developing the ability to make decisions as do the operational units of government. All participants were in general agreement on the importance of decision-making as an indication of administrative leadership; disagreement occurred over where this ability can be best developed.

Nevertheless, a cautionary note was sounded by some over the emphasis on decision-making, by pointing out that not making a decision was oftentimes as important as making one. The timing of the decision on some occasions is crucial; sometimes the administrator should postpone taking a stand as long as possible. It was also pointed out that too much emphasis on decision-making may lead to an unwillingness to delegate responsibilities to subordinates.

The question was also raised whether the typical civil service regulations inhibit or encourage the making of decisions. Some of the participants felt that oftentimes civil

[8] *Ibid.,* p. 47.

service regulations tend to discourage initiative since a mistake may endanger tenure. It was suggested that there was a need for a rebel in most organizations—someone with drive, initiative, ideas, and a willingness to upset traditions. Too often, it was contended, civil service regulations placed a premium on security and complaisance.

This point of view was vigorously questioned by other administrators who maintained that this was an unfair evaluation of typical civil service systems, that if administrators are willing to delegate they are generally authorized to do so. The fault was thus a personal one and had nothing to do with personnel regulations. Employees' initiative cannot be developed unless they are given responsibility, but too often administrators want to make all the decisions themselves.

THE DEMOCRATIC FRAMEWORK

Staff Presentation. The democratic setting is so accepted that its importance is often overlooked or minimized. Yet this factor alone markedly distinguishes private from public administration. An administrator must be aware of the limitations on administrative action in a democracy. The obligations to the public, to the popularly elected legislature, and to the politically selected government or agency head may restrain or hamper executive initiative, discretion, and control. An administrator may at times doubt the vision or even the motives of his departmental superior; he may also chafe under legislative surveillance; and he may question whether or not the legislature accurately represents the needs or the aspirations of the public. However, unless the administrator is able to adjust to these political controls, he does not belong in government.

Legislative relations. Although the administrator has increasingly important responsibilities in the formulation and initiation of policies, nevertheless, it is still the primary job of the legislature to indicate the direction and establish the general standards for administrative action. The influence of the legislature over the administrator is a variable one. At times the city manager or the bureau chief may be given almost free rein in the development and implementation of policy, and at other times he may be tightly haltered. Irrespective of the remoteness or intimacy of legislative control, the administrator needs to recognize that the legislative branch is not an institution which exists primarily to impede or obstruct the exercise of administrative discretion, but rather that it acts as a complement and equal to the executive function in the finely developed checks and balances which are integral to the operation of state and most local government.

Relations with clientele groups. The democratic framework within which American public administration operates affects not only the relationship of the administrator to his political superiors and to the legislature, but also acts as a tempering factor in dealing with clientele groups. These groups are the ones whose interests are most strongly affected by the program of an agency; consequently they provide the principal source of political support and opposition. It is more than being "politic" to be aware of their interests. It is rather to ensure community acceptance of administrative programs.

Although the administrator cannot be held responsible to non-official agencies, he must be responsive to clientele groups so long as this does not jeopardize his obligations to the public as a whole. Obviously accommodating the demands of all special interests would be humanly impossible, even if desirable. Not only are their interests apt to be contradictory, but over-solicitous concern for their demands would lead to an abdication of the responsibility which the administrator has for the general community. Nevertheless, their view must be heard. Administrative devices to assure that citizens, individually or in groups, can have their day in court are imperative. The degree to which their demands can be accommodated without detracting from the public good will tax the ingenuity of the administrator and clearly emphasizes the delicacy of the art of administrative leadership within the democratic framework.

Concern for the general welfare. This is the overriding imperative of all public officials if democratic institutions are to be maintained. In theory, at least, the legislature should not need the assistance of anyone in "divining" the public good. Thus, one authority has written that should concessions have to be made in public policy in order to secure acceptance, they should be made by the political rather than the administrative organs of government.[9] On the other hand, other writers have stressed the responsibility of the administrator in determining the public good by injecting his own considerations of the public interest ". . . in the face of a natural inclination of spokesmen for private interests to see those interests as the undiluted public interest." [10]

Although there is an admitted danger of the administrator's substituting his own value judgments for those of the legislative branch, this is less apt to be serious in this country where democratic values prevail than in those countries that have had little experience with democratic institutions. Thus, most administrators feel that their decisions ought to be responsive to democratic values. However, the practical problem is to determine what the general welfare really is. For the principal administrative officer Schubert's interpretation of Avery Leiserson's observation is perhaps the most practical. "An administrator best serves the public

[9] Quoted in Glendon A. Schubert, " 'The Public Interest' in Administrative Decision-Making," LI *American Political Science Review* (1957), p. 352.
[10] *Ibid.*, p. 353.

interest when his action creates or restores an equilibrium among all the affected group interests, or if this is not possible, when the disequilibrium following his act is minimized." [11] Admittedly, this "equilibrium" definition evades any a priori judgment in advance of what the general interest is. Nevertheless, it does provide an operational frame of reference which is probably superior to the admonition that administrators "must acknowledge a general obligation to direct their actions toward promoting the healthy growth of a free society dedicated to the common good." [12]

Administrators' Discussion. Neither of the two workshop sessions discussed extensively the points suggested by the outline on the democratic framework. In most instances, their remarks were directed toward a further clarification of what had been written, or a reiteration with minor modifications of remarks which had been made earlier. Three of their observations are pertinent, however, at this point.

The administrators strongly re-affirmed the necessity for administrative officials to be loyal to their superiors—whether a city council or a politically-appointed executive or department head. Without this, their usefulness as advisors and counselors is virtually nullified. Should a policy be decided upon which the administrator in all due conscience cannot accept, his only alternative is to resign. "The ethics of the profession," to quote one participant, "leaves him with no other course of action."

The assumption sometimes made that the politicians are best qualified to know what the community wants was questioned by some of the discussants. Particularly the city manager, in his numerous contacts with citizen groups, may have a clearer understanding of what the community

[11] *Ibid.,* p. 362.
[12] Fritz Morstein Marx, "Administrative Ethics and the Rule of Law," XLIII *American Political Science Review* (1949), p. 1128.

is willing to accept than have members of council. However, the success with which the administrator's suggestions will be accepted by council is in large measure determined by the confidence which it has in him.

Several of the participants were concerned with the attitudes of young men just entering the municipal or state service toward their administrative and political superiors. It was felt that not infrequently the new employees do not consider themselves responsible to anyone other than themselves and that they tend to look upon the legislative branch with contempt.

HUMAN VALUES

Staff Presentation. Respect for human values within the organization is basic in much the same way as is respect for democratic institutions and processes mentioned above since both affect the ways in which administrative leadership can be exercised. Democratic government means democracy in administration as well as in legislation. However, the concept, human values, is exceedingly nebulous and is as difficult to define as the specific meaning of public interest. The admonition that the administrators should treat individuals as ends in themselves and not as means to something else provides little clarification.

Research which has been carried on by social scientists has forced administrators to give at least some recognition to the importance of group incentives, group dynamics, and individual fulfillment. Although, with few exceptions these insights into human motivation have yet to be accorded a firm place in the theory of administration, there is ground for optimism that some administrators are coming to realize that the most significant part of an organization is the people in it—how they work together, how they are led, and how they lead.[13]

[13] Luther Gulick, "Next Steps in Public Administration," XV *Public Administration Review* (1955), p. 75.

This places a new dimension on administrative leadership. Management's task is now viewed as being infinitely more important than the simple giving of orders. There needs to be an awareness on the part of the administrative officer that leadership involves reciprocal and inter-personal relationships with the other members of the staff and that his success as an administrator is dependent upon his ability to motivate them. Since leadership cannot be imposed upon the group, the administrator must exhibit those particular attitudes which the group already regards as essential.

What are these group values to which employees attach importance and which are essential to democratic leadership? One set is clustered around the satisfaction of certain basic emotional needs. These include a need for employees to have a sense of security, a sense of achievement and recognition, and a sense of belongingness. Although it is doubtful whether conditions of employment can ever be devised where these can be fully met to everyone's satisfaction, there is substantial proof that where recognition of these individual values has been secured (albeit to a limited extent) there has been a resultant improvement in morale and production.

The term "democratic management" has often been viewed with skepticism by "practical administrators." However, in recent years it has been accommodated to a limited extent with the more traditional theories of administrative leadership. It can be said that democracy is at work in management if these three conditions exist: first, if subordinates are convinced that the objectives of the agency are desirable; secondly, if there is an appreciation that these goals can be best accomplished through cooperation between labor and management; and thirdly, if the employees are consulted on the choice of methods taken to reach these goals.[14] Administrative devices designed to implement these suggestions are highly varied, but they could include regular and periodic staff discussions, labor-management committees similar to those encouraged by the War Production Board in the second world war, orientation programs for new employees, and in-service training.

Research in the importance of the informal social group in the formulation of individual attitudes has been carried on almost continuously since the Hawthorne Studies of Elton Mayo, which showed that increased work production was less dependent upon an opportunity for increased wages and improved working conditions, than it was upon congenially organized and congenially supervised work teams. Research by other industrial management experts has also shown how the work group can be crucial either in restricting group output or in achieving management-defined goals.[15] The administrative leader needs to recognize that the origin and strength of human motivation lies more in immediate and social values, and less in economic and individual appeals. It also should be observed that the administrative problems confronting an executive will be all the more difficult to solve if the goals of the group with which the individual identifies himself are antagonistic to the goals of the agency.[16]

Administrators' Discussion. The subject of how to create an atmosphere within the government office which is conducive to "good" human relations was not extensively discussed by the workshop participants. It was pointed out that few administrators have the time to think specifically about pro-

[14] O. Glenn Stahl, *Public Personnel Administration.* New York: Harper and Brothers, 1956, Ch. 11.

[15] Morton Grodzins, "Public Administration and the Science of Human Relations," 11 *Public Administration Review* (1951).

[16] Pfiffner and Presthus, *Public Administration.* New York: The Ronald Press Co., 1953, Chapters 9 and 10.

viding an atmosphere conducive to high morale since their immediate administrative problems are more pressing and demanding. Nevertheless, if administrators are willing to delegate functions to subordinates, if they call periodic staff conferences, and if they take time out to consult with their assistants on their work, office morale is likely to be satisfactory.

It was emphasized that in large organizations communication with all members of the staff is virtually impossible; it is impractical to try to talk with all members of the staff, and it is doubtful whether all people will understand what the administrator is trying to accomplish except in very general terms.

The responsibility of the administrator for the efficiency of his own organization may force him, at times, to dismiss those who are either inefficient or non-productive. If one employee is dismissed, it generally leads to a certain amount of insecurity on the part of the other employees who feel that the axe may fall next on them. This feeling can be moderated to some extent if the administrator has acquired a reputation for fairness and honesty. However, a newly-appointed administrator does not have this advantage. Few of his new employees know whether he is harsh or lenient, reserved or friendly. Consequently they are naturally "on edge" and will remain so until they become more acquainted with him. Since first impressions are often the ones held most tenaciously, the administrator should make a concerted effort to get to know his staff and what they are doing as quickly as possible even though this may delay "taking charge."

PROFESSIONAL STATUS

Staff Presentation. The implications of belonging to a profession have been the subject of considerable debate in the decade since the end of the second world war. This is evidenced by periodical discussions on the professionalization of the city manager in the ICMA annual meetings, the concern with ethics for the public service by Senator Paul Douglas and others, codification of ethics by a growing number of agencies and jurisdictions, and the growth in size of professional associations of public administrators. It is interesting to note that as late as 1947 in an article on professional associations, no mention was made of public officials, although the medical profession, engineers, economists, physical scientists, lawyers, and educators were specifically mentioned.[17]

Why is it that the public official has only lately been concerned with the professionalization of his employment? Several reasons can be suggested. First, and perhaps most important, has been the low prestige of government employment, and in too many instances, the low calibre of the public officials themselves. Assertion of the professionalization of public employment would not only have been out of keeping with the prevailing sentiment of many politically-sponsored public officials, but would have been received incredulously by the general public. A second reason that professionalization has been slow to take hold is the fact that the public service consists not only of heterogeneously-trained groups of men and women, but also an infinite variety of occupations. Under these circumstances it becomes difficult to set down rules of conduct or moral postulates concerning professionalization which will command widespread acceptance. A third factor stems from the absence of a career concept similar to that which is traditionally ascribed to the British civil service. Finally, there are the practical difficulties of observing and then enforcing

[17] Morris L. Cooke, "Professional Ethics and Social Change," 11 *Advanced Management* (1947).

what is generally thought to be the characteristics of a public service profession.[18]

The late Wallace Donham (speaking specifically of business administration) has written that to be called a profession there must be:

1. "The recognition of an intellectual unity based on intensive knowledge of a relevant body of experience, fact, and theory;
2. "The acceptance of responsibility by each member of the group to the group as a whole which transcends responsibility for mere money making and which may subordinate the individual's profits, or success in the usual sense of the word;
3. "The development of special standards and concepts of proper conduct growing out of the relation of the whole group to society of which it is a part." [19]

Although Donham was speaking of professionalization in business, as evidenced by his inclusion of "profits" in #2 above, it is highly doubtful whether, even with this word excluded, public administration fully meets either his first or second criterion. It is with the third that some progress has been made in the public service and it is here that the professional status obligations of the public administrator are relatively concrete.

The obligation for continued study. If administrators are expected and required to play a more positive and creative role in the initiation of policies for the legislature, it necessarily follows that they have the obligation of continued study and education. This does not mean study and education in the narrow sense of preoccupation with a particular concern of the organization he heads, but rather a more

[18] York Willbern, "Professionalization in the Public Service: Too Little or Too Much?" XIV *Public Administration Review* 13 (1954).

[19] Wallace Donham, *Administration and Blind Spots.* Cambridge: Harvard University Press, 1952, p. 11.

liberal orientation which will enable him to understand better the entire program of the agency as well as to have a more accurate comprehension of the agency's role with the total services provided by the government. There is always the danger that any agency head will be tempted to view its mandate in the narrow perspective of its immediate tasks. If this happens, the public official may become progressively absorbed in his own work and may find it increasingly difficult to be aware of the broader goals of public effort. In part, his grasp of the broad implications and responsibilities of his unique position can be strengthened through participation in seminars sponsored by ASPA and other professional associations, and in part through directed self-study in those areas which are of immediate concern to his agency.

Ethical considerations. Robert Walker has written that "The problem of balancing ethical standards against survival is one of the great unsolved questions of public administration." [20] This topic includes much of what has been said above and need not be repeated. It involves an administrator's responsibilities to the legislature, clientele groups, the general public, and individual citizen. It also includes what is commonly incorporated in codes of ethics. In this country, the most widely known code for public officials is that adopted by the ICMA. It is clear from this as well as from the others scattered throughout the country that enforcement provisions are lacking. This means that observance is largely a personal responsibility. Responsibility to the group as a whole about which Donham has written has only a shadowy existence and is virtually unrecognized for the entire public service. Observance of codes of ethics is, therefore, the individual (rather than the group) obligation of each administrator. Nevertheless, the

[20] Robert Walker, "The Universities and the Public Service," 39 *American Political Science Review* (1945), p. 930.

acceptance of group responsibility for the actions of its members as an ethical ideal is important irrespective of how far short administrators may fall of this goal. It is clear that it can be effectuated only after the development of a professional career philosophy in public administration.

Self-evaluation. The danger that the administrator, without community pressure, will do just enough to get by is a human failure which is not confined to the public service. Since the public is often totally unaware of what can be done, it is the obligation of the administrator continually to lift the sights not only of the legislature but of the community as well on the necessity for having good administrative services rendered by the government. This means that the administrator voluntarily places upon himself the obligation to be better than the minimum required by the legislature or by the public. As Marx has so well stated: [21] "Infinitely more important than compelling administrative officials to live up to minutely-defined requirements of control is their acceptance of an ethical obligation to account to themselves and to the public for the public character of their actions." [22]

[21] Marx, *op. cit.,* pp. 1134-1135.
[22] Due to time limitations there was no discussion of this section.

12

The Administrator's Responsibilities

THOMAS J. DAVY *
University of Pennsylvania

MEANING AND SCOPE OF RESPONSIBILITY

Staff Presentation. Positions at higher administrative levels are best described in terms of their responsibilities. By knowing the major responsibilities of a position, one can more easily determine the personal qualifications and the knowledge and skills needed for the position. The identification of these elements is facilitated if each responsibility is differentiated according to the types of activities involved and problems encountered in its discharge. Some of the personal qualifications appropriate for an administrative policy-making position are considered in the discussion of the administrator's leadership role. Knowledge and skills are also subjects of separate discussions. The purpose of this discussion is to discover the principal responsibilities of administrative policy-making positions and their corresponding types of activities and problems.

Responsibilities are those classes of activities for which administrative policy-making officers may be held accountable by superiors. Accountability implies liability to disciplinary sanction for unsatisfactory performance. In other words, the administrator's superiors evaluate his performance in terms of his responsibilities and, according to their

* Thomas J. Davy, Ph.D., is Educational and Research Associate, Fels Institute of Local and State Government, and Assistant Professor of Political Science, University of Pennsylvania.

standards, take whatever action they deem appropriate within their authority.

The fundamental responsibilities of all governmental administrators are the same. They are (1) to see that the laws governing their jurisdictions or agencies are faithfully enforced, (2) to use the resources available to them most efficiently for achieving the goals sought by their superiors, and (3) to make known to their superiors changes in goals, laws, and resources that in their judgment may appear necessary or desirable. The specific responsibilities of an administrator are established by laws, regulations, and delegations from superiors. They differ from jurisdiction to jurisdiction, and from position to position. They may change as problems and programs change.

Obviously the fundamental responsibilities are too general and the specific responsibilities of particular positions too varied for adequate guidance in educating and training people for administrative policy-making positions. The problem is to identify responsibilities applicable to *most* administrative policy-making positions. They should be defined in detail sufficient to provide an adequate basis for constructing general programs of education and training for such positions.

Analysis of the recent literature in public administration and of the other sources consulted for this discussion suggests that for the higher administrative positions there are four categories of responsibilities:

1. Responsiveness to superiors and clientele;
2. Articulation of objectives and programs;
3. Procurement, organization, and control of resources;
4. Direction and supervision.

Administrators' Discussion. The city managers' group in St. Louis and the mixed group of administrators in Chicago agreed substantially in their reactions to this part of the discussion. They questioned the limitation of the concept of accountability to "liability to disciplinary sanction for unsatisfactory performance"; they also found it difficult to agree on the nature of the superior to whom the administrator may be accountable.

The administrators felt generally that the term "disciplinary sanction" in the definition of administrative accountability was too strong or severe; it implied too drastic a form of action for all the varying degrees of liability implicit in administrative accountability. They also felt that from the point of view of the superior, accountability will often involve positive action, in the form of approbation or commendation of some kind, for meritorious performance. They therefore suggested that the definition of accountability be changed to read: "Accountability implies susceptibility to appropriate action for unsatisfactory and meritorious performance."

Opinions about the administrator's "superiors" to whom he might be accountable were quite diverse. Some discussants would include not only the appointing authority, but also the bureaucracy, the legislative body, the public, and perhaps others. However, the position was strongly maintained that probably most administrative policy-making officers are subject to an employer-employee relationship; it would be inadvisable and undesirable for them to assume that they are accountable to anyone other than the authority who appoints them. In the case of the city manager, for example, his recourse if he disagrees with the policies established by council is not to appeal over council's head to the people, but either to submit to council or to resign. This does not mean that the manager should not take his judgment of the public interest into account in formulating proposals for council; it means merely that he is accountable only to council for his actions. Both these points of view were extensively discussed in both workshops. The consensus appeared to be that the phrase "by superiors" should be deleted from the definition of responsibilities, and it should read: "Responsibilities are the classes of activities for which administrative policy-making officers may be held accountable."

Some workshop participants questioned whether the administrator should be responsible for enforcing all the laws governing its jurisdiction. Since legislative bodies rarely repeal outmoded laws, it was felt that this statement was too sweeping. In the managers' workshop the following alternative wording was proposed, to which most of the managers seemed to agree: "The fundamental responsibility of all administrators is to achieve the results desired by, and attain the goals set by, the person or persons to whom they are accountable. (This includes, as well, responsibility for developing facts and recommendations for changing goals and results desired)."

RESPONSIVENESS TO SUPERIORS AND CLIENTELE

Staff Presentation.

Responsibilities

1. To assist and service superiors in discharging their responsibilities efficiently and effectively.
2. To maximize clientele understanding of, compliance with, and support for the policies and programs under his supervision.

Examples of Activities That May Be Involved in Discharging These Responsibilities

—prepares and presents written and oral reports on special problems, on progress and results of policies and programs, and on emerging needs and alternative programs for meeting them.

—analyzes proposed policies and programs in terms of their potential difficulties for the superior, and deter-

mines the form and timing of presentation to minimize these difficulties.

—with reference to legislative superiors, prepares agenda
for and participates, as requested, in meetings.

—organizes and participates in public hearings.

—prepares and reviews reports and educational materials to be distributed to clientele.

—confers with and speaks before clientele groups.

—establishes and generally supervises a system for handling and analyzing complaints.

—makes employees aware of the opportunities for constructive public relations in their day-to-day contacts
with clientele.

—checks the appearance and convenience of facilities
and equipment observed or used by clientele.

—confers with newspaper reporters and representatives
of other mass communication media.

Examples of Problems That May Be Encountered

—determining the matters and situations, beyond those
legally specified, for which consideration and action
by superiors are necessary or desirable.

—judging the appropriate level on which superiors
should consider matters to be brought to their attention, and presenting the matter in a form that
facilitates this level of consideration.

—establishing a policy on presentations by subordinates
to the legislative body and its committees.

—handling requests from individual legislators that may
conflict with established policy.

—judging the kind and extent of knowledge, understanding, and interest of clientiele with respect to
matters to be presented for their consideration, and
adapting the language and form of presentation to
these factors.

—making oneself personally available to clientele with-

out impeding the expeditious discharge of other responsibilities.

—obtaining fair and accurate press coverage.

—establishing policies regarding employee membership
and participation in clientele groups, especially those
that seek to influence decisions made by the administrative officer and his subordinates.

—reacting to irrational or political attack.

Administrators' Discussion. The workshop participants
agreed generally with the statement of responsibilities and
with the examples of activities and problems as typical of
those involved in discharging the responsibilities. Exception
was taken to the point that the administrator's responsibility
for maximizing clientele understanding, compliance, and
support was limited to the policies and programs "under
his supervision." It was generally felt that his responsibility
was much broader than this—that though his immediate
responsibility was certainly to his own program, he, and
every other member of top management in the jurisdiction,
had an obligation to seek greater cooperation of the general
public and of special groups in carrying out all of the major
policies and programs of the whole enterprise. Limiting
this responsibility to the administrator's immediate concerns might tend to foster rather than discourage administrative parochialism.

There was some discussion also of the meaning of "clientele." It was agreed that all administrators should consider
the public represented by the governmental jurisdiction as
their clientele. Every administrator should seek the understanding and support of the entire community. He should
also feel obligated to serve "the public interest" in the
programs he directs. It was also noted, however, that almost all governmental functions serve or regulate specific
classes or groups of people, and that the administrator must

make a special effort to further the understanding, compliance, and support of those who are his "special clientele."

Staff Presentation.

Responsibilities

1. To formulate and present to his superiors policy and program proposals that are professionally sound and politically acceptable. A correlative responsibility is to reconcile and articulate the recommendations of subordinates, his own best professional judgment, and the value preferences of superiors and clientele.
2. To seek and to facilitate correlation of those activities of agencies and groups outside of his jurisdiction that have a significant bearing upon the accomplishment of his objectives and programs.

Examples of Activities

—formulates long-term capital improvement, financial, and work programs, or assists central staff agencies in this work.

—prepares instructions and procedures for the preparation and submission of budget estimates by subordinates.

—confers with subordinates regarding proposed work programs and budget requests, and reviews and correlates such matters for submission to superiors.

—consults with superiors and participates in hearings on plans and budgets.

—secures and utilizes the services of special consultants.

—interprets plans and budgets to clientele.

—cooperates with other departments, with neighboring jurisdictions, and with civic and special interest groups in achieving coordinated action on problems of common concern.

—works with jurisdictions and agencies of county, state, or federal levels for coordinated action on problems of common concern.

—confers with those staff and managerial units that may not be under his jurisdiction (planning, personnel, finance, purchasing, etc.) on those aspects of his operations in which they have agency responsibility.

Examples of Problems That May Be Encountered

—inducing subordinates to look upon budget preparation as a major opportunity for intensively re-appraising objectives and programs and for planning administrative improvements.

—inducing superiors to evaluate planning and budget proposals in terms of goals, programs, and standards of service.

—anticipating political reactions to proposals.

—minimizing the time-lag between emergence of needs and their recognition by superiors and clientele.

—developing quantity and quality standards on which to base budget proposals.

—clarifying the respective authority and responsibilities of overhead and line agencies in planning and budgeting, and building harmonious working relationships.

—helping technical subordinates to understand and appreciate the significance of the value judgments of superiors and clientele in deciding upon priorities of planning and budget proposals.

—inducing and assisting subordinates to base proposed plans and budgets on sound research.

—discovering common bases for communicating with other departments or neighboring jurisdictions.

—obtaining sympathetic treatment from higher levels of government.

—working with independent boards and commissions.

Administrators' Discussion. Both workshop groups discussed the term "articulation" at some length. Articulation was defined as the process of forming or fitting diverse elements into a systematically interrelated whole. The discussants were concerned that the concept might be interpreted to mean that the administrator was merely a "go-between" reconciling staff proposals and citizen acceptance. He is much more than this. He is the primary creative element in the process of formulating policy and program proposals. This creative element is the essence of community or agency leadership. In formulating a proposal for the consideration of his superiors, the administrator carefully considers the needs of his community or agency, the advice of his staff, the possible opposition and support from his superiors and from the community, and the advice and preferences of others who may be concerned with or affected by the proposal. To the greatest extent possible, he tries to reconcile and harmonize these considerations. But the proposal as presented to his superiors represents his own best professional judgment, which may at times be unpopular with his staff, superiors, and clientele. The workshops felt that as long as this creative element was recognized as an essential element of policy-formulation, the term "articulation" was adequate.

The extent to which the administrator can and should consider "political acceptability" in proposing policies and programs also was discussed. Accurate judgment regarding acceptability is sometimes very difficult; it was felt that the administrator might tend to underestimate public reaction on important and controversial questions. There is also the danger that he might overemphasize political feasibility and thereby allow his proposals to be dominated by considerations of expediency rather than soundness. At times he must aggressively promote unpopular programs because they are so desperately needed, even when it is apparent that they have no chance of being accepted. Thus if the municipal administrator knows that the water system will shortly become inadequate, his professional obligation is to propose an increase in taxes or borrowing for the needed improvement even though there is strong political opposition to such an increase in the community. Sometimes, it was suggested, vigorous advocacy of unpopular programs is the most effective means of educating the community to its needs. Such courage, it was felt, is an essential element of the administrator's leadership role. It was also pointed out that "timing" or "pacing" of proposals, which usually reflects political considerations, is an important aspect of the administrator's art.

The workshop groups discussed and elaborated upon the administrator's responsibility "to seek and to facilitate correlation of those activities of agencies and groups outside of his jurisdiction that have a significant bearing upon the accomplishment of his objectives and programs." Outside interests might include other departments, staff and management units, neighboring jurisdictions, and other levels of government. It was noted that an increasing number of the major problems of government require the close cooperation of many uncoordinated agencies for their solution. Thus the solution of the transportation problem in a metropolitan area requires effective cooperation among many departments of the central city, the local governments in the region, the state and federal governments, and often many citizen groups. Common action is desirable for such problems, yet usually there is no one authority that can effectively coordinate the programs and activities of these diverse interests. Recognition of their common concerns by such interests and willingness to cooperate are essential if regional needs of this kind are to be met.

Even in less complicated functions, it was noted, the administrator rarely if ever has complete authority over all of the elements involved in the solution of the problems for which he is responsible. The department head, for example, shares control of his budget with the finance department, control of his personnel with the personnel department, and control of many other aspects of his operation with other agencies. Then too, it was noted, problems which originate as the primary concern of one agency often become a major concern of other agencies within the jurisdiction. Thus in some large cities, prevention and control of juvenile delinquency start as a rather modest program of the police department; as the dimensions of the problem became apparent, it is realized that many other agencies have to participate in the program if it is to be effectiive. Until an organizational readjustment can be effected in such a situation, coordination by one authority is usually difficult; common action is achieved primarily through cooperation.

For these reasons, it was agreed that the administrator's responsibility to correlate his efforts with those of others concerned with his problem was an extremely important one. Not only should he be willing to cooperate with others, but he should also encourage such cooperation when appropriate. Aspects of an administrative situation that would make the discharge of this responsibility more or less difficult were brought out. If related agencies are independent, or under the leadership of the political opposition, or if—as in many state governments—the administration is "balkanized," or if administrators are by nature and inclination "empire-builders," or if the administrator is too parochial in his thinking about his operation, then correlation becomes very difficult. Nevertheless, it was agreed, the administrative policy-making officer should feel obligated to promote correlation or related efforts to the extent that he can.

While the workshop groups agreed that the administrator should relate his specific activities to those of the whole enterprise, it was suggested that he can become too selfless; an over-abundance of cooperative spirit may at times prove detrimental to his operation. The keen competition for scarce resources may require the administrator to be somewhat unreasonable and selfish. Otherwise, he may not obtain essential resources for his programs and poor morale may result if subordinates feel that he has let them down by not fighting aggressively for his programs. In most organizations, the administrator must indeed fight for his programs and staff. But in doing so, he should be governed by a sense of organizational relevance and by ethical principle. He should not act on the principle that his objective justifies any means. He should try to recognize the relationship of the total resources available to the jurisdiction or agency to the relative importance of the competing needs among which these resources must be allocated.

In other words, the workshop groups implied, the administrator had to maintain a nice balance between his responsibility to promote aggressively what he considered essential to his programs and his responsibility for relating his operation and needs to the whole enterprise. There was some discussion of whether there were any methods by which appreciation and understanding of the subtleties of these responsibilities could be developed in prospective administrators. The case method and the internship were cited as especially valuable opportunities in this regard.

After additional discussion, the workshop groups concluded that the administrator's responsibility for correlating his activities with other levels of government and with staff and managerial units is so important that it should be separately identified. His responsibility for forecasting long-term needs and planning for them should also be listed separately.

PROCUREMENT, ORGANIZATION, AND CONTROL OF RESOURCES

Staff Presentation.

Responsibilities

1. To organize and control his resources for optimum efficiency and responsiveness to the public interest.
2. To recruit and place the most competent people available and to promote people according to merit and potential.
3. To procure, distribute, utilize, and maintain physical resources economically, expeditiously, and with the maximum degree of organizational harmony.

Examples of Activities

—establishes, maintains, and adjusts the basic plan of organization for his jurisdiction or unit, and assists his subordinates in devising and adjusting the organization plans of their units.

—establishes policies regarding review and clearance procedures.

—specifies, within his authority, the policies and standards governing primary delegations of responsibility and authority, including the respective authority and responsibilities of overhead and line units in matters that may engender conflict between them.

—establishes or recommends policies, standards, and procedures governing the classification of positions under his supervision; suggests modifications in classifications as changes in the nature of positions require.

—establishes or recommends policies, standards, and procedures for the recruitment, examination, induction and appointment of personnel under his supervision.

—participates personally in the recruitment, examination and selection of his key subordinates.

—recommends policies pertaining to pay, holidays,

leaves and vacations, retirement, and other aspects of compensation that affect his ability to attract the personnel he needs.

—observes the adequacy of employee working conditions and makes or recommends improvements.

—establishes or recommends financial, personnel, and production control systems for his organization, and reviews systematically control reports.

—establishes or recommends policies and procedures governing the procurement, disposition, inspection and maintenance of facilities, equipment, and supplies for his organization.

—reviews and approves personally all major contracts and plans thereunder pertaining to his organization; establishes procedures for inspection of contract work.

—settles conflicts between using agencies and procurement and maintenance agencies.

Examples of Problems That May Be Encountered

—overcoming the relative rigidities of organization and classification plans in terms of the variable abilities and interests of employees, and of constantly changing needs and conditions.

—qualifying subordinates to accept delegations of responsibility and authority; determining the appropriate conditions of and controls over such delegations.

—solving the dilemma of recruiting for specific positions and building a career-service.

—developing competitive incentives to employment in the face of limited revenue possibilities.

—maintaining uniform and equitable pay policies in view of unequal bargaining positions among employee groups.

—discovering the most effective recruitment methods in the face of usually inadequate recruitment resources.

—getting competent people in the face of residence requirements, veterans' preference, patronage pressures, or similar difficulties.

—persuading subordinates to appreciate the importance of the probationary period.

—controlling without impeding.

—determining the benefits of overhead agencies in relation to their cost.

—devising budget and work control reports that are complete enough, yet simple to prepare and interpret.

—assuring that facilities and equipment are properly inspected and maintained.

—getting purchasing agents and operating personnel to work together harmoniously.

Administrators' Discussion. Both workshop groups accepted the statement of responsibilities without modification. It was noted that the criteria of efficiency and responsiveness had to be defined at least partly in terms of the operating conditions prevailing in the jurisdiction. Though these are general criteria by which the administrator evaluates his operation, he is sometimes required by his superiors or by the situation to carry out his responsibilities in a way that makes the optimum realization of these criteria difficult. Poor working conditions over which the administrator has little control may also interfere with the attainment of professional standards of efficiency. Such difficulties do not, of course, excuse the administrator from striving to make his operations ever more efficient and responsive.

There was also some discussion of the meaning of "public interest." Though this is an elusive concept and its expression may be the responsibility of the legislative body and political executive primarily, the participants thought that every administrator had to infuse a "sense of the public interest" into his operations. In this regard, it was agreed that requirements of due process of law should be strictly observed in all regulatory activities. Administrative due process, it was suggested, involves more than adherence to judicial prescriptions; for the administrator, it is a matter of philosophy, organization, and procedure.

It was mentioned several times during this session that though ultimate accountability for the activities listed under each class of responsibilities may reside in the principal administrator, actual "working responsibility" was usually assigned to specific units of the organization. It was also noted that in many jurisdictions some of the responsibilities listed were assigned by law to independent units or units over which the principal administrator has only partial authority, such as an autonomous civil service commission or a planning board. In such cases, the administrator cannot be held responsible for their performance.

DIRECTION AND SUPERVISION

Staff Presentation.
Responsibilities
1. To establish and maintain effective systems of communication for his organization.
2. To maximize his employees' acceptance of and enthusiasm for the policies, programs, and procedures with which they are concerned.
3. To help his employees improve their qualifications for present and potential responsibilities.
4. To assume direct leadership and supervision, when necessary, in major emergencies and in administrative situations of special political sensitivity.
5. To stimulate technician-administrators under his direction to improve continually the administrative and technical standards of their respective operations.
6. To evaluate systematically the adequacy and efficiency of the services under his direction.

Examples of Activities

—consults with subordinates, both individually and in groups, in arriving at decisions that affect them.

—reconciles conflicts among subordinates.

—establishes or recommends policies and procedures for accurately evaluating employee performance.

—analyzes the motivations and reactions of subordinates and adapts his approach in working with each to achieve maximum constructive response.

—establishes or recommends policies and procedures for the equitable application of the rewards and sanctions available to his organization.

—investigates charges against subordinates.

—makes major disciplinary decisions in situations not covered by general policies.

—reviews and authenticates communications to be distributed generally within his organization.

—confers with representatives of employee groups and unions.

—establishes or recommends policies regarding staff development within his organization; participates personally in planning, organizing, and conducting training programs for his immediate subordinates.

—organizes and conducts staff conferences.

—consults with subordinates on technical as well as administrative matters.

—takes direct action in emergencies (e.g., major disasters, riots, etc.), politically sensitive situations (e.g., location of incinerators, public attacks on subordinates, etc.), and "administrative vacuums" within the organization (e.g., incompetent key subordinates, breakdown in communication, etc.), until arrangements can be made for handling such problems through regular administrative channels and procedures.

—establishes standards and procedures for evaluating his services; visits and inspects operations periodically.

Examples of Problems That May Be Encountered

—leading subordinates to develop an attitude of "creative conflict" in matters of common interest, especially in staff meetings—building a "team" approach.

—deciding when and for what matters staff meetings are appropriate, and organizing and conducting them for maximum effectiveness.

—judging the nature and degree of confidence to place in subordinates.

—gaining the respect and loyalty of uniformed services.

—helping key subordinates who have risen through technical hierarchies to develop "governmental perspective" and general administrative competence.

—phrasing general communications so that the meaning intended is the meaning understood.

—devising an adequate performance rating system and gaining acceptance of it by the organization.

—getting administrators and supervisors at each level to recognize that it is their responsibility to see that their subordinates have the knowledge, skills and attitudes needed for their work.

—establishing a policy regarding attendance at technical and professional meetings by subordinates.

—protecting oneself from unnecessary involvement in detail when conferring on technical matters with subordinates.

—observing and protecting the channels of communication.

—defining adequacy and devising methods for evaluating it.

—defining efficiency and devising methods for evaluating it.

Administrators' Discussion. The workshop groups devoted most of their attention in this part of the discussion to administrative communication. The consensus appeared to be that developing and maintaining effective communication in his organization was certainly one of the most important and perhaps the most difficult of the administrator's responsibilities. Though it was agreed that communication is a general concept applying to all aspects of administration, some participants felt that it was so important that it should be identified as a separate category of responsibility. The title of this category might at least be amended to read "Direction, Communication, and Supervision."

Several of the participants believed that too many college graduates, including graduates of public administration programs, were poorly prepared in the skills of oral and written exposition. Since much of the administrator's time and energy is consumed in such activity, the participants suggested that the colleges and universities should devote more attention to this problem. The participants also felt that public administration programs should give their students a more sophisticated understanding and appreciation of the concepts and problems of administrative communication. Communication, both organizational and personal, is perhaps the most important element of effective organization and leadership.

The workshop groups also discussed the nature of the administrator's direct leadership and supervision in major emergencies and in situations of special political sensitivity. Obviously in a major disaster involving a significant portion of the jurisdiction and in situations threatening the life of the organization, he must take a direct hand. But even in such events, it was felt, he should exercise direct leadership and supervision cautiously. He must be careful not to undermine the authority and responsibility of his subordinates. The entire organization should be so geared that it can handle occurrences of this kind with a minimum of disruption. It is the chief administrator's responsibility to see that his organization is adequately prepared for emergencies and that it functions as an organization in such situations. It is perhaps even more important in emergencies, it was felt, that the chief administrator maintain his position as a generalist. The criteria by which the administrator can recognize occasions calling for his immediate supervision, it was implied, were the danger of breakdown in a vital function and threat to the existence of the enterprise.

GENERAL DISCUSSION AND SUMMARY

Both workshop groups were asked whether they thought that the responsibilities they had discussed could be ranked in any order of importance. The consensus was that such a ranking was neither possible nor desirable. Though we must differentiate administrative responsibility for systematic analysis and for the formulation of more effective programs of education and training for administrators, it is an "integrated totality" in practice. It was noted that though the responsibilities as stated placed heavy emphasis upon "the internal aspects of administration," it was generally the "external aspects" of his responsibility that posed the most difficult problems. But, it was added, this observation does not mean that therefore the external aspects of responsibility are the most important.

The workshop participants agreed that the responsibilities discussed applied generally to all administrative policy-making positions. Prospective administrators should be prepared through course study and field experience for all of these responsibilities to the extent that public administration programs can so prepare them.

Though these responsibilities will generally apply to most administrative policy-making positions, it was noted, the manner in which they are discharged will vary according to differences from one jurisdiction to another in such factors as size, type of political superior, administrative level, philosophy of the administrator, etc. In smaller local governments and at intermediate levels in large organizations, the administrator will perform or supervise directly more operational activities than an administrator in a larger jurisdiction and at the top level. Thus the city manager of a small community not only bears the responsibilities himself, but may also personally perform many of the activities involved in their discharge; in the large city, the manager is more of a staff advisor to his department heads. As long as the position meets most of the criteria accepted for identifying administrative policy-making positions, it is such a position whether it be in a town of only 5,000 people or in the largest state or Federal agency.

In summary, the following revised statement of responsibilities includes the modifications suggested by the consensus of both workshop groups.

Responsiveness to Superiors and Clientele

1. To assist and service superiors so that they can discharge their responsibilities efficiently and effectively.

2. To seek maximum understanding of, compliance with, and support for the policies and programs of the agency on the part of the general public and people especially served or regulated by the agency.

Articulation of Objectives and Programs

3. To formulate and present to his superiors policy and program proposals that are professionally sound and that are likely to be accepted politically, unless the proposal relates to a vital need that must be acted upon despite potential opposition.

4. In formulating policies and programs, to reconcile

and articulate when feasible the recommendations of subordinates, the values and preferences of superiors and clientele, and his own best professional judgment.

5. To anticipate community or agency trends and needs
through appropriate plans and programs.

6. To seek the cooperation of and work closely with
other departments and agencies, both line and staff, and with
private groups whose activities bear significantly upon the
accomplishment of his agency's objectives and programs.

7. To seek the cooperation of and work closely with
other governmental levels and jurisdictions whose activities bear significantly upon the accomplishments of his
agency's objectives and programs.

Procurement, Organization, and Control of Resources

8. To organize and control his resources for optimum
efficiency and responsiveness to the public interest.

9. To recruit and place the most competent people
available and to promote people according to merit and
potential.

10. To procure, distribute, utilize, and maintain the
physical resources of the agency economically, expeditiously, and with the maximum degree of organizational
harmony.

Direction, Communication, and Supervision

11. To establish and maintain effective communication
in his organization.

12. To seek maximum employee acceptance of and enthusiasm for the policies, programs, and procedures with
which they are concerned.

13. To help his employees improve their qualifications
for present and potential responsibilities.

14. To assume direct leadership and supervision in

major emergencies and politically sensitive situations which may threaten the breakdown of a vital function or the stability of the enterprise.

15. To stimulate subordinates to improve the technical and administrative standards of their operations.

16. To evaluate systematically the adequacy and efficiency of the services under his direction.

13
Knowledge Needed by the Administrator

FREDRICK T. BENT *
University of Pennsylvania

INTRODUCTION

Staff Presentation. As applied to administration, let us say that knowledge consists of those facts, theories, concepts, or techniques acquired through experience or study which enable the administrator to carry out the broad responsibilities of his office. Practitioners would be the first to assert that an administrator needs to know more than the processes and techniques of administration, important as they are. He must, in addition, be able to apply many disciplines in solving public problems for which he is held responsible.

In general, writers on administration say that an enlightened, imaginative public service needs the services of people who have had the benefit of a broad, liberal education. They are less precise in defining what they mean by "broad" or "liberal." Nevertheless, they imply that the ideal public servant should have a background in the liberal arts or in the social sciences rather than in a more rigorously restricted area of study such as statistiics or accounting, or in highly technical fields such as engineering or architecture. One author has written that the need for generalists and for broad training is a means of answering "The universal demand for synthesizing ability that is des-

* *Fredrick T. Bent, Ph.D., is Education and Research Associate, Fels Institute of Local and State Government, and Assistant Professor of Political Science, University of Pennsylvania.*

perately needed if man, his world, and his civilization is to survive." [1]

What areas of knowledge should an administrator master to meet his daily administrative problems and to give him perspective on the broad social ramifications of his office? To state that an administrator must have a judicious combination of both specialized and general knowledge does not advance us very far since the recipe does not say how much of either is needed. This vagueness is probably necessary, however, since knowledge ideally suited for one position might be comparatively irrelevant for another. A smoothly administered, well-established agency may desperately need an administrator with ideas, imagination, and impatience. Whereas another may be in greater need of the steadying hand of a person able to devise administrative procedures to translate into positive programs the flurry of ideas and plans generated by his predecessor.

The five areas of knowledge briefly described below are not listed in order of importance, nor do we say that knowledge in all areas is essential for administrative policy-making officers. It also should be kept in mind that these are areas of knowledge rather than specific courses which may be offered by colleges and universities. Although a strong case can be built for the ultimate usefulness and desirability of all the topics listed in the following pages, it is recognized that no one person could be expected to be conversant with all of them. Good administrators do not have the time to be walking enclyclopedias even if they had the inclination.

THE ECONOMIC, SOCIAL, AND POLITICAL ENVIRONMENT

Staff Presentation. The economic, social, and political environment is clearly the most comprehensive and extensive

---

[1] Joseph E. McLean (Ed.), *The Public Service and University Education.* Princeton University Press, 1949, p. 63.

area of knowledge. George Graham, in commenting on the need for knowledge here, wrote that the administrator ". . . is mastering a field of experience that will illuminate the problems confronting him in the future. He is preparing to understand the functional problems of administration." [2] Although administrators cannot be expected to be professional economists, sociologists, or political scientists, an awareness of the contributions of these subjects to administrative policy-making has high priority.

The economic environment. Three general areas of economics appear to be pertinent to administrators: economic principles and theory, economic institutions and processes, and business-government relationships. Subject matter contained in economic theory comes as close as any to a specific academic course. The necessity for some knowledge in this field is generally acknowledged as necessary if fiscal policies and programs are to be soundly based. Some knowledge of economic history and institutions both here and abroad is perhaps less immediately relevant, yet may provide perspective which otherwise would not be forthcoming if one's experience is confined to the immediate and the local. The impact of commerce and industry on governmental policies and programs and the consequences of government regulation of business or business activities through zoning, land use regulations, or taxation, are generally conceded. So too is interdependence of fiscal management and economics in such practical matters as tax schedules, planning programs, budgeting, and capital improvements. Intergovernmental fiscal relations affect so many substantive programs that familiarity with economics is of fundamental importance to administrators at all levels of government.

The social environment. Social problems, although most dramatically revealed in urban situations, concern all ad-

[2] George A. Graham, *Education for Public Administration.* Chicago: Public Administration Clearing House, 1941, p. 51.

ministrators and are not confined to those public officials employed in metropolitan areas. The existence of a more rigid social stratification, dislocation of neighborhood groups, increased juvenile delinquency, greater leisure, and many other phenomena are no longer isolated or purely local, but are variables which condition and influence governmental policy at all levels and in all sizes of jurisdiction.

An awareness of the social environment vastly enlarges the complexity of an administrator's job. He finds that the observations and conclusions of the social worker, the policeman, and the judge must be synthesized and translated into governmental action. The complexity of the social environment will certainly increase as will the need for specialists. The planners and zoners, police psychologists, criminologists, transportation experts and endless numbers of scientists and technicians become integral members of the administrator's entourage. Although he cannot be expected to master the technicalities or intricacies of these newly-developed disciplines—this would not be his role— yet he cannot be a dilettante.

While not being expected to hold their own with experts, administrators should be able nevertheless to utilize the skills and capacities of these people. Louis Brownlow has said that administrators must possess a "catholic curiosity" and, he continued, "he ought to know enough about everything to know where to go to get men who do know a great deal about particular subjects. . . ." [3] However, perhaps it should be added that not only should administrators appreciate the importance of these experts, but they must also be able to relate expert advice to the development and formulation of administrative policy.

The political environment. This is least foreign to the average administrator's previous education and present ex-

[3] Quoted in Felix A. Nigro (ed.), *Public Administration Readings and Documents.* New York: Rinehart and Co., 1951, p. 51.

perience, particularly since more and more administrators have a background which includes courses in government. Nevertheless, there is always the potential danger that administrators, preoccupied with administrative techniques and procedures, may minimize or disregard the political environment which permeates administrative decision making.

The areas of knowledge which could be included under the political environment are numerous and are often incorporated in courses found in the standard political science curriculum. Familiarity with the details is relatively unimportant: they assume importance only if they give an administrator an understanding of the ends of political action, the nature of political institutions, and of the interrelationships which condition the making of public policy. As Robert Walker has written: "The importance of this familiarity with the workings of government in our own and earlier times, and of being conversant with currents of political thought, emerges in the ability of the individual to relate everyday problems, policy proposals, and political issues to the evolutionary chain of events and thought out of which they arise." [4]

Administrators' Discussion. Several criticisms were directed to this section of the outline on the economic, social, and political environment. In the first place, it was felt the outline did not adequately recognize that, however important, the amount of knowledge needed by the administrator of the economic, social, and political environment varied widely depending upon the size of the jurisdiction, the level of responsibility, and the type of agency the administrator directed. Secondly, some of the administrators believed more emphasis should be placed on the economic rather

[4] Robert Walker, "The Universities and the Public Service," 39 *American Political Science Review* (1945), p. 933.

than on the social and political aspects, since, in the short run, economic considerations had the greatest effect on administrative policies and programs. Thirdly, it was suggested that a more appropriate heading would have been "governmental environment" rather than political environment.

The importance of knowledge in this area was not questioned. It was pointed out that it was particularly necessary for administrators who were functional specialists and who had not had the benefit of a liberal education. On the other hand, there was general agreement that even the liberal arts curriculum could not be expected to provide the type of education in the social sciences which would be most useful to the administrator. Consequently, if he is to provide the necessary perspective for community leadership he must be expected to continue his own education in this area.[5]

THE ADMINISTRATION PROCESS

Staff Presentation. Relevance of knowledge about the administrative process is seldom questioned by administrators. It is more difficult to get agreement on what this term means, what it includes, and how or whether the administrative process can be taught. For our purposes, the administrative process can be analysed into a sequence of

[5] The following comment written by Wallace Donham is pertinent here. In discussing the importance of having administrators act on the basis of the knowledge which they have acquired in a university education he writes: "This failure [to act] is not because what they have learned is useless. It is because the universities have not faced the problems that come up at the point where men must act; they have not shown the graduates of our colleges how they can translate theory into effective action while they are living their lives. Now in too many cases, when they try to act with reference to their social science training, they cannot do so. The abstractions they studied were made for other purposes and on other facts that have often changed with time. They must act with reference to all the present facts. The partial facts considered while they were in college may well have ceased to be sound for the determination of policies demanding action." Donham, *Administration and Blind Spots,* Harvard Univ. Press, 1952, p. 21.

steps whereby legislative enactments or administrative decisions are translated into policy or administrative action; in other words, a process which moves from the general to the specific.

In contrast to the other areas of knowledge which are included in this section, the subject of the administrative process seems to be least susceptible to definition. This is true not only because knowledge about it must be related to what is being administered, but also because one cannot separate knowledge needed for the administrative process from the other areas of knowledge which are listed in this section. Nevertheless, writers on this subject generally include the following five steps in the administrative process. These are: planning, organizing, assembling resources, directing, and controlling.

It would be redundant to define each of these. Nevertheless, it is clear that they broadly outline the position and role of administrative policy-making officers. Consequently, one can say that the administrative process is the underlying theme of the entire paper. Planning has already been mentioned as one of the leadership abilities needed by administrators. The assembling of resources, directing, and controlling were included in the preceding section on "responsibilities," and they also involve basic skills which are mentioned in the succeeding section. All three can also be included in this section on "knowledge" in that directing involves human relations and personal techniques, assembling of resources and controlling encompasses budgeting and finance, and so forth.

Much has been written about the specific techniques of organization and management which are integral parts of the administrative process. If we accept Dwight Waldo's dichotomy that organization is structure or anatomy and that management is physiology or functioning, a distinction may be made in the knowledge needed by the administrators.[6] Under organization would be included knowledge about departmental organization, service divisions, the role of staff and auxiliary units, the use of committees, over-all organizational structure, and the organization of top management functions. Under management techniques, knowledge needed might include administrative procedure and production analyses, office layout, measurement of governmental services, methods of program evaluation, methods of inspection, and many others.

None of these needs elaboration. Suffice it to say that knowledge about the techniques of management is most often acquired on the job where they can be related to the program objectives of the department. Since policy to be implemented often determines the procedure to be followed, the administrative process cannot be disassociated from the ends or objectives of administrative action.

Administrators' Discussion. Neither workshop discussed the knowledge needed about the administrative process. The opinion was expressed that the administrative process (for the administrator at least) should be thought of in terms of leadership abilities. These, as listed in the section on Leadership, included the ability to see the enterprise as a whole, to make decisions, to plan, to delegate, and to secure loyalty. It was thought that these abilities more adequately described the administrator's role in the administrative process than did planning, organizing, assembling resources, directing, and controlling.

HUMAN RELATIONS

Staff Presentation. The concept of human relations is subject to differing interpretations and emphases. It has been defined as that ". . . consideration of the face to face inter-

[6] Dwight Waldo, *The Study of Public Administration.* Garden City: Doubleday and Co., 1955, p. 6.

actions which occur between individual men and women in their immediate social environment." [7] Four fairly distinct approaches to human relations can be identified. Some writers equate human relations with internal communications in which communications become an analytical framework for the study of industrial relations. Others think of human relations as a problem in the study of social systems in organization. There are some who equate human relations with the problems of group performance and motivation, and a few who approach it from the point of view of reconciling democratic ideals with industrial organization.

Taken individually, each point of reference has its own limitations. Taken in toto, they strongly refute the notion that a native intuition will suffice to meet the requirements of sound human relations. The contributions of psychology, sociology, social psychology, anthropology, political science, economics, and philosophy can all be brought to bear upon the subject of human relations. Psychologists, for example, have pointed out the complex of emotional needs which must be satisfied in a well-balanced individual, and the inadequacy of organizational theory which stresses the position and ignores the individual. The need for worker self-expression has been shown to be as important in mass clerical operations as it is in an industrial environment. Social psychologists have analyzed the effect of group values on restriction of output, growth of status systems, standards of work, and many others. Other social scientists have been particularly concerned with the mores and attitudes of informal groups and have observed that informal group solidarity may prevent management from exacting full loyalty to the goals of management.

An administrator in dealing with his staff is concerned about human relations for three reasons. The first reason

[7] Cabot and Kahl, *Human Relations.* Vol. I, Cambridge: Harvard University Press, 1953, p. vii.

has been succinctly stated by Paul Appleby when he warns that only those organizations which appreciate the dignity of the individual worker can adopt a similar attitude to the public it serves.[8] The second reason is that the employer wants to secure maximum employee contributions toward the objectives of the agency, and this can better be guaranteed if employees gain a maximum amount of satisfaction from their work. Third, good human relations will minimize the disharmony which may exist between the objectives of the agency and the objectives of the informal group. To the extent that the interests of the informal group are coincident with those of the agency will the administrator's task be made less burdensome.

Knowledge about human relations demands more than a vague acceptance of the concepts of democratic management. Being a good fellow or having good intentions are hardly adequate in today's governmental organizations. The individual and social problems attendant in government are too vital to depend upon instinct. Although few psychologists or sociologists would assert that their investigations have isolated the specific and fundamental motivations of individuals or groups in all working situations, their research has clearly demonstrated that these factors cannot be treated as irrelevant or of marginal importance in administrative management.

Administrators' Discussion. The discussion on this topic was closely tied in with what had been said earlier about the leadership obligation of the administrator to secure the loyalty of his subordinates. The need for "good" human relations went unquestioned; how it can be achieved was left unanswered. Some of the administrators felt that, however important, few knew precisely what it meant. Considerable discussion took place over the question whether

[8] Paul Appleby, *Big Democracy.* New York: Alfred Knopf, 1945, p. 127.

human relations could be taught in the classroom. Some asserted that if it can be learned, it can be taught, citing the growing body of knowledge in the fields of psychology and sociology and motivational research. Others expressed the opinion that human relations can only be learned on the job and that in the last analysis the key to good human relations is found in the personality of the administrator and his fairness toward subordinates, rather than in formal schooling in the subject.

MANAGEMENT SERVICES

Staff Presentation. This rather vaguely phrased area of knowledge refers to the managerial as opposed to the substantive areas of knowledge which need to be understood by administrators.[9] The following areas of study appear to be applicable:

1. Principles and methods of public finance.
2. Theory and technical concepts of governmental planning.
3. Characteristics and major concepts of personnel administration.
4. Statistics.
5. Administrative law.
6. Research methodology and techniques.
7. Reporting and public relations.

It is clear that there is a close relationship between the knowledge needed in management services and the general knowledge about the economic, social and political environment which was described earlier in this section. The former is in large part derived from the broader, less differentiated subjects which were mentioned above. For example, public finance is derived from economics, administrative law from constitutional law, reporting and public relations from English composition, and research method-

[9] Although for finance directors, planners, personnel officers, and others, these are obviously "substantive areas of knowledge."

ology and technique from term reports and masters' theses. The major difference is in college ". . . the student is preparing himself for the institutional problems of administration" rather than providing himself with the background for the future problems which he may face.[10]

Fortunately, there is a vast amount of material available to the administrator on management services, The Management Manuals published by the International City Managers Association would be particularly useful as would publications by the American Municipal Association, American Society of Planning Officials, Federation of Tax Administrators, and others, many of which are associated with the 1313 group in Chicago. The practical question is not so much what should be known but rather how much of each. Here no general rules appear to be applicable.[11] Not only is there an apparent difference in the responsibilities of an administrative policy-making officer at the local and at the state level, but in addition, the unique circumstances of each agency may demand greater familiarity with finance, let us say, than with public relations, and it would be needlessly wasteful of time and facilities to attempt to prepare future administrators for all possible contingencies.[12]

The problem would be simplified if one could assume that city managers would always remain in cities of approximately the same size or that there would be little mobility between the state and local levels of government. Since neither of these assumptions can be made (particularly the first) the best advice would seem to be to get as broad a

[10] Graham, *op. cit.*, p. 51.

[11] However, Chester Barnard has written: "Usually leaders, even though not extraordinarily expert, appear to have an understanding of the technological or technical work which they guide, particularly in its relation to the activities and situations with which they deal. In fact, we usually assume that a leader will have considerable knowledge and experience in the specifically technical aspects of the work he directs. *Organization and Management.* Cambridge: Harvard University Press, 1949, p. 87.

[12] Walker, *op. cit.*, p. 926.

background as possible in these subjects at the university level and then utilize fully the publications and facilities of the various professional associations in governmental administration.

Administrators' Discussion. The participants in the workshops agreed on the importance of these subjects, although considerable emphasis was placed on the usefulness of reporting and public relations and less on administrative law. Some administrators raised doubt about the value of statistics. Throughout the discussion, continuing concern was expressed for fear that knowledge in these subjects (ordinarily obtained in the universities) will be unduly subordinated to the general cultural orientation of most universities. In particular, the city managers were worried about the under-emphasis given to the subjects included under Management Services. They probably would have concurred in this statement written by George Graham.

> . . . but in general they [municipalities] demand highly technical competence and finished training from the University man. Many local governments suffer from lack of specialists who can answer their technical problems. . . . The demand in local governments tends to be for a university man whose training is finished in the sense that it is comprehensive and balanced. He must be able to work with some independence without asking too much assistance, and he must begin to produce quickly.[13]

GOVERNMENTAL SERVICES

Staff Presentation. These services refer to the specific functions which government provides for its citizens. These may range from higher education to sewage disposal. Although it is true that a municipality or a state does more than merely provide "services," nevertheless, since administrators

[13] Graham, *op. cit.,* p. 18.

are held accountable by taxpayers and the legislature for their adequacy, administrators need to have reliable information and informed opinions about the functions provided by government.[14]

Although schools of higher education as well as prominent administrators continue to stress the importance of broadly educated public servants, this does not fully satisfy the needs of the public service. The type of knowledge described in the section on the economic, social and political environment is useful to all persons whether they become educators, businessmen or farmers. In addition there is the need for knowledge about the functions which government provides for its citizens. Lewis Merriam's criticism of "posdcorb" that one has "to plan something . . . organize something . . . direct something" summarizes this need.[15]

As a bare minimum, the administrator should be familiar with the terminology and the basic concepts underlying government services since he must judge the competence of his assistants in these fields and be able to appreciate their technical problems. Thus he should be familiar with the general problems associated with public health, education, recreation, public works, law enforcement, transportation, and many others. Knowledge of this nature is particularly important to city managers or those who have responsibilities which transcend more than one operating department.

The extent and depth of basic knowledge here would not meet the requirements of those who are expert in these functional fields. Thus, what a health officer would consider to be the irreducible minimum basic knowledge about public health would be doubtless far beyond what could be expected of an administrator who is equally involved in

[14] Lawrence J. R. Herson, "The Lost World of Municipal Government," LI *American Political Science Review* (1957), p. 335.

[15] Lewis Merriam, *Public Service and Special Training.* Chicago: University of Chicago Press, 1936, p. 2.

a myriad of other activities which the city or state carries on. To be more specific, an administrator needs to be familiar with the objectives and standards advocated by the various professional groups such as the National Recreational Association, the National Educational Association, and the National Association of Housing and Redevelopment Officials, for example. He needs also to know the extent to which these standards are met or cannot be met and why. On an earlier page Louis Brownlow was quoted as saying that an administrator ought to know enough about a subject to know where to get informed advice. This may not be enough, particularly if the administrator is to give the guidance and direction which his position demands. The administrator will always need expert staff advice, but such assistance can be utilized to greater advantage if the administrator has informed opinions of his own.[16]

[16] Due to time limitations, there was no discussion on this section.

14

The Administrator's Basic Skills

THOMAS J. DAVY *

University of Pennsylvania

DISTINCTIONS BETWEEN KNOWLEDGE AND SKILL

Staff Presentation. Administrative skills are the mental and physical processes essential to the proper discharge of responsibilities; their performance is habitual; they are developed through observation, practice, and experience to a professionally acceptable level of competence.

The distinctions between knowledge and skill will help to clarify the discussion that follows. Knowledge would appear to be essential to skill. Skills are applied in a substantive setting, and knowledge of the facts and theories pertinent to the problem or situation would seem to be required for effective application of a skill. Thus to analyze financial statements and reports meaningfully, one should understand the concepts and theories on which such documents are based. The typist becomes proficient not only by developing manual dexterity, but also by learning through instruction and observation the characteristics of her machine, the principles of layout, the peculiarities of the materials she is assigned to reproduce, and other information needed for her craft. Since skill is a matter of habit, we may tend to lose sight of the knowledge which underlies its application; the whole process of relating knowledge and skill becomes "second nature."

* *Thomas J. Davy, Ph.D., is Educational and Research Associate, Fels Institute of Local and State Government, and Assistant Professor of Political Science, University of Pennsylvania.*

However, one can have knowledge without possessing concomitant skills. One can know the theory of music, for example, and not be able to perform on a musical instrument. Or one can know theory of social psychology and not be skilled in group leadership. The essence of knowledge is reasoning and understanding; the essence of skill is performance and habit. Knowledge is obtained through observation, reading, lecture, discussion, analysis, synthesis. It is acquired in an atmosphere of study, intellectual curiosity, experiment, contemplation. Skill is developed through step-by-step demonstration and guidance, practice, correction—until, at the acceptable level of competence, the process is performed without conscious thought of the process as such. Skill is obtained in an actual or simulated work situation. In summary, one is educated to knowledge; one is trained in skills.

In terms of this concept of skill, there appears to be relatively little research in the field of public administration. "Administrative skill," "human relations skill," "leadership skill," "organizational skill," are terms commonly found in the literature. But these terms characterize complexes of skills. They provide only general guidance for devising pre-service and in-service education and training programs.

A skill has been defined as a mental or physical process. "Process denotes a progressive action, or a series of acts or steps, especially in the regular course of performing, producing, or making something." (Webster) For educational and training purposes, the "processes," or skills, we seek to discover should be discernible step-by-step actions to be taken by administrative policy-making officers for achieving desired ends. For the development of these skills, we may then be able to devise structured training experiences.

It is apparent that people develop high degrees of competence in skills essential to their work without conscious realization of the processes as such. Such skills are obtained through trial-and-error experience. They are often explained as "intuition," "pit-of-the-stomach feel," etc. Such explanations suggest that the best way for the prospective administrator to acquire skills may be by experience in an administrative environment conducive to their attainment. This may be the case. Yet in order to refine and make more efficient our educational and training efforts, it would seem worthwhile to try to identify the elements and processes encompassed by the term "administrative intuition" and to devise methods by which students can attain systematically the skills implied.

The purpose of this paper was to suggest a classification of basic administrative skills and to identify the principal elements of each class. Our present knowledge about administrative skills precludes precise delineation of the specific processes and steps in their performance. It was hoped that the administrators' discussions during the workshops and further research might enable us to define administrative skills more exactly. The classes of administrative skills suggested were problem identification and analysis, situational analysis, operational analysis, audience-oriented interpretation and presentation, delegation and review, and negotiation and conference.

Administrators' Discussion. Both workshops agreed with the definition of administrative skill. They also subscribed to the proposition that to achieve more effective education and training for administrative policy-making officers, it is highly desirable to classify and differentiate administrative skills and to devise structured training experiences for their attainment. Some participants in both workshops doubted the feasibility of structured training experience, but all agreed that it was worthwhile to try to do so.

After considerable discussion in both groups and some alternative proposals, there was substantial agreement that the six suggested categories of skills covered the requirements of the administrative policy-making officer. Both groups considered the relative importance of the six classes of skills, but no agreement was reached. Based upon the amount of time devoted to the discussion of each category and the intensity of discussion, the greatest interest was manifested in problem identification and analysis, delegation and review, situational analysis, and communication, in about that order. Both groups seemed to think that the skills of delegation and review were perhaps the least understood and the most difficult to practice.

While it was agreed that one can have knowledge without correlative skill, the idea that knowledge is essential to skill was challenged. Several examples were cited of people who had developed competence in various skills without schooling in related concepts and theories. After further discussion, the consensus seemed to be that skill does involve the application of knowledge, but that this knowledge is often absorbed on the job without conscious realization of its acquisition.

PROBLEM IDENTIFICATION AND ANALYSIS

Staff Presentation. Problem analysis is a primary skill for the administrative policy-making officer. It is the process used in decision-making, and thus is basic to all administrative situations. This skill is usually discussed in terms of five principal steps:

1. Obtaining agreement of those concerned on a specific definition of the problem to be solved;
2. Assembling the facts pertinent to the analysis of the problem;
3. Analyzing these facts and identifying the possible alternative solutions;

4. Evaluating each alternative in terms of its possible effects and results;
5. Selecting the most appropriate alternative as the solution.

These steps constitute a process of thought and action that is essential for the adequate discharge of administrative responsibilities, and that should be applied automatically by an administrator when confronted with difficulties. The steps, however, are probably more logical than accurate. For instance, we sometimes cannot define the problem specifically until we assemble and analyze some of the facts; the facts often force us to a re-definition of the problem. Then, too, we sometimes cannot know what facts are pertinent until we have formulated some of the alternative solutions. In actual practice, therefore, these steps tend to merge into one another. However, it would seem desirable for the prospective administrator to learn problem-analysis as a logical sequence, and then through experience to adapt this sequence where necessary for more effective decision-making. Structured training experiences, both in school and in-service, can be provided for the development of this skill. The case method in its various forms is especially effective for training in problem analysis.

Administrators' Discussion. Both workshop groups agreed that problem analysis was probably the primary skill of administration; no administrator can be successful without competence in this skill. With considerable elaboration and several illustrations, the participants agreed to the five steps of problem analysis suggested above. Many thought that the first two steps—definition of the problem and assembling of the pertinent facts—were the most important, and perhaps the most neglected, steps in the process. In this regard, it was noted that it is often impossible for an administrator to obtain all the facts he should know for a completely rational choice of alternatives. His major problems are usually too complex and involve too many intangibles for the kind of precise analysis implied in the steps as listed.

Recognizing this fact, however, the administrator should nevertheless train himself to follow the suggested pattern of analysis in arriving at his decisions. In doing so, he should beware of over-simplifying his problems; he should, the workshop groups suggested, realize that many of the problems on which he is called upon to make decisions involve conflicts of values which can be resolved only through political process rather than by logic. He should also recognize that his knowledge of personality and group-relations factors—important facts in almost every administrative problem—can rarely, if ever, be completely accurate. No matter how well-trained he is, the administrator's "hunch" will play an important part in his decisions.

The opinion was almost unanimous that every prospective administrator would benefit from a course in logic. Most of the participants also felt that the student would obtain valuable training in problem analysis in any course based upon analytical technique: courses in mathematics, the physical sciences, or engineering. However, some participants thought that such courses might tend to condition a person to expect a degree of precision in solving problems that is generally unattainable in public affairs. It was agreed that the case method was most effective for training students in problem-analysis within the public administration program itself. The participants suggested that the case description should be detailed enough to indicate at least some of the personality and other human factors involved in the case situation. The student should be led to recognize the types of assumptions he may have to make when he must make a decision without all the facts.

Ultimately, the workshop groups agreed, the best training in problem-analysis can be acquired in the field, provided there is proper supervision and guidance of the student. The participants suggested that an administrator who accepts responsibility for interns should help them formulate specific plans or schedules of career development. For training in problem analysis, he should lead his interns from easy to difficult problems over a period of several years. He should challenge them to analyze each assigned problem according to the five steps of the problem-solving process. The administrator should make it a point to discuss with his interns the problems he assigns them.

SITUATIONAL ANALYSIS

Staff Presentation. Most of the administrator's time is devoted to "sizing up" situations and people. The process or processes for this type of analysis are those most often characterized as "intuitive." Not much research has been done on the specific nature of situational analysis skills.

There seem to be three principal aspects of any administrative situation that are of most interest to the administrator.

First, the administrator relates his problems and decisions to his administrative and political milieu. He should consider the points of sensitivity and response of his superiors, whether they be administrative or political. He should analyze his community, especially its structure and processes of communication and decision-making. He should understand the nature of political conflict in the community and its relationship to his activities and programs. Many similar economic, social, and political characteristics of the environment must be analyzed by the administrator to discharge his responsibilities effectively.

Second, the administrator relates his ideas and actions to his organization. He, more than anyone else, should maintain the "sense of organizational relevance." He should interpret continually policies, programs, and results in terms of organizational structure, communication, clearance, relationships among subordinates, procedures, etc. The fact that the administrator analyzes not only the technical aspects of ideas and programs but also their potential impact and effect on the environment and the organization is one of his distinguishing characteristics. This process of thought presents him with some of his most difficult administrative problems.

Third, the administrator analyzes his staff. He should recognize their behavioral patterns, their motivations and effective incentives, their attitudes toward their responsibilities and other associates, the types of responses they make to direction and supervision, their capabilities, and many other considerations like these that are so essential to effective leadership.

More knowledge of the forms and processes of thought appropriate for analysis of this kind is needed. Greater collaboration between academicians and administrators in research on such matters is highly desirable. Such research should help considerably to improve both pre-service and in-service programs of education and training for administrative careers.

Administrators' Discussion. Both workshop groups agreed generally upon the nature and importance of situational analysis skills. They were asked to identify the specific processes the administrator uses in analyzing his milieu, his organization, and his staff. The participants were willing to pursue this line of discussion only to a limited extent and did not produce any specific suggestions. The discussion implied that the processes of a situational analysis probably differ according to the philosophy and approach of the individual administrator. It might be misleading, the groups thought, to define "a process of analysis." However, they did agree that research on this matter might produce valuable insights for improving the ability of schools and employers to train prospective administrators in situational analysis skills.

Some of the participants, in fact, seriously questioned the assumption that a person could be systematically trained in such skills. They believed that competence in these skills was primarily a matter of native ability and intuition derived from experience. However, others pointed out that some schools through skillful use of the case method have been quite successful in at least orienting their public administration students to the importance of situational analysis and in having them analyze the environmental, organizational, and behavioral factors of the case as part of the process of assembling the pertinent facts for effective decision-making. It was also noted that the internship is an excellent opportunity to develop the attitudes and habits of thought appropriate for situational analysis.

Some participants also suggested that inter-disciplinary research involving public administration, psychology, anthropology, and other social science fields might lead to a better understanding of the processes of situational analysis.

OPERATIONAL ANALYSIS

Staff Presentation. This category includes the skills needed by the administrator for analyzing the technical and substantive matters with which he deals in planning, organization, direction, and control. For purposes of discussion, five types of processes are suggested for this category.

1. Position analysis. Every administrator should be able to distinguish and define the responsibilities, duties, and tasks of a position, the knowledge, skills, and attitudes required for it, and the qualifications to be sought and developed in the incumbent. He should analyze the positions under his immediate direction in these terms. This

skill is basic to organization, supervision, recruitment, promotion, classification, and training. Though position analysis is often treated as a special tool of the personnel technician, it is in fact a primary skill for all administrators and supervisors.

2. Financial analysis. One of the criteria for identifying administrative policy-making position adopted by the workshops is that the incumbent "has an effective voice in the development of the budget of his agency or jurisdiction." This criterion implies that the administrator should be competent in reading and interpreting financial statements and reports, estimating revenues and expenditures, analyzing costs, and in other types of financial analysis.

3. Statistical analysis. Much of the information about his organization and its programs comes to the administrator in the form of tables, graphs, charts, and other forms of data compilation. It is his responsibility to interpret the significant aspects of such statistical presentations. Often too the administrator must decide on the types of numerical data and the form of their presentation required for the solution of various kinds of problems. Though for most situations, the administrator does not need a high degree of proficiency in the mathematics of statistics, it may be desirable for every administrator to have some knowledge of the elementary mathematics of statistics and skill in the preparation of statistical presentations. However, it may be noted that mathematical statistics provides excellent training in the kind of rigorous thinking that the workshop groups thought especially important in their discussions of problem analysis. In the workshop discussions of problem analysis and situational analysis, it was also emphasized that the administrator must often base his decisions on assumptions of probability rather than on exact information and well-defined cause-effect relationships; training in statistics would seem to provide special benefits in this regard.

4. Plan analysis. The administrative officer is often called upon in the course of his work to read and interpret engineering plans and maps, architectural plans, various types of work simplification charts, and other forms of visual representation of spatial relationships. Some special training in skills of this kind would appear desirable.

5. Rapid-reading. Most administrative policy-making officers have a great volume and diversity of materials cross their desks. They must keep in touch with the professional and technical journals in their areas of responsibility. They rarely, if ever, have the time to read and study such materials with the care they would like to. They should be skilled in "sizing up" masses of written materials, in capturing important concepts and significant points by rapid perusal, in placing these ideas and facts in the appropriate intellectual category for possible future use. "Rapid-reading" research indicates that this is a discernible mental process that can become habitual through practice.

Administrators' Discussion. The operational analysis skills as listed above were all considered extremely important by both workshop groups. Several participants thought that personal inspection of operations by the administrator was so important that it should be listed separately as an operational skill, even though its importance was implied in the discussion of other skills.

There was a difference of opinion in both workshop groups concerning the value of statistics to the administrator. Some of the participants thought that public administration programs tended to over-emphasize statistics; understanding of statistical concepts, they said, rather than technical competence in statistical analysis was the administrator's principal need. However, other participants, especially among the mixed group of administrators at the

Chicago workshop, thought that more time should be devoted to statistics in public administration programs. The participants thought that the pre-service education program could provide the prospective administrator with specific training in the skills of position analysis, financial analysis, statistical analysis, plan analysis, and rapid-reading.

DELEGATION AND REVIEW

Staff Presentation. This category covers the skills of assigning authority, responsibility, and work to subordinates, and of reviewing their performance. The processes of delegation and review include the following:

1. Establishing and maintaining personal priorities. The administrator must continually judge the relative importance of matters coming to his attention. In terms of the demands upon his time, he has to appraise the limits of personal time and energy he has available for these demands. This type of analysis will indicate to him those matters that should or must be delegated to subordinates.

2. Appraising and qualifying subordinates. Before assigning responsibilities to subordinates, the administrator must evaluate their competence for such responsibilities. He considers their competence, motivation, and reliability with respect to the matters to be delegated. If they are deficient in these elements, the administrator tries to help them prepare themselves for the additional responsibilities. Additional education and training, understudying, progressively responsible assignments under his direct supervision, and similar arrangements are used for this purpose.

3. Specifying the conditions and standards to be observed in performing the delegated function.

4. Reviewing, inspecting, and evaluating this performance in terms of the conditions and standards specified.

Administrators' Discussion. Both workshop groups discussed extensively the importance and difficulties of delegation and review. The consensus appeared to be that most administrators, though they give lip-service to delegation, do not in practice delegate sufficiently. Possible reasons for this fact were considered.

It is often difficult, the participants noted, for the administrator to specify accurately and precisely the conditions and standards of a delegation. In assigning projects to subordinates, he sometimes has only a general sense, or "hunch," about the assignment; he finds it difficult to articulate the purpose he has in mind, and he may have only an indistinct idea at best of the work that may be required to complete the project. In such cases, he can provide his subordinate only with general and indefinite guidance on appropriate conditions and standards. In such circumstances, the participants agreed, the administrator should review frequently the work on such projects as it progresses, and should make it a point to discuss the project with the subordinate at each of its major stages.

The importance of review and evaluation was stressed. Unless delegations are reviewed, there is danger either that the work will not be done or will be done improperly to the eventual embarrassment of the administrator; there is also danger that by failing to review delegations he may be abdicating his responsibility. Overwhelmed as he often is with the many work pressures on him, it was noted, the administrator may tend to neglect this very important step of the delegation process.

Some of the participants observed that the conditions under which the principal administrator operates may tend to inhibit his willingness to delegate. At the higher policy levels, it is sometimes impossible for the administrator "to be sure of himself." He can rarely be certain of the reactions of his superiors to the policies and activities of his agency; he tends to believe that he is better able to anticipate these reactions than anyone else in the organization. He also realizes that a mistake by a subordinate will sometimes cause public criticism far out of proportion to the significance of the mistake. The administrator is as much motivated by a sense of personal security a re his subordinates, and is perhaps more concerned wit organizational security than anyone else in the agency. It was also suggested that civil service regulations and independent channels of communication from the bureaucracy to the top policy levels may also present difficulties to delegation. For these and other reasons, the administrator's conscientiousness may prove to be an impediment to delegation.

Despite these difficulties, however, both for his own well-being and for the effectiveness of his organization, the administrator must make a conscious effort to delegate functions to the greatest extent possible. The more he concerns himself with details, it was stated, the less able is he to perform at the high administrative policy level required for the proper discharge of his responsibilities. Establishing personal priorities is the first, and perhaps most difficult, step for him. In this regard, the participants suggested that many administrators tend to under-estimate the capacities of their subordinates. Several examples were cited of subordinates who had met the challenge of new responsibilities in an excellent manner, though their superiors had at first had serious misgivings concerning their ability to meet the challenge.

In conclusion, the participants noted that delegation tends to "tone up" the organization. When subordinates realize that superiors have confidence in them, they tend to develop more constructive attitudes toward the organization and their work. The workshop groups suggested that more research effort be devoted to the nature and problems of the delegation process.

AUDIENCE-ORIENTED INTERPRETATION AND PRESENTATION

Staff Presentation. Leadership may be viewed as a process of securing favorable responses from people whose decisions and activities influence the success of the endeavor. Such people include superiors, the public generally, clientele groups, and the bureaucracy itself. The administrator, in one sense, is a "middleman" between the specialists whom he directs and the generalists to whom he reports. He interprets the specialized activities under his purview to the generalist and the layman; he interprets general policies and relatively abstract principles to his specialists. The forms of presentation are, of course, writing and speaking. His written and oral presentation should be adapted to his particular audience.

The process for this kind of communication includes the following steps:

1. Identifying the audience—its level of understanding and interest, its probable points of favorable response or opposition, etc.;
2. Interpreting the matter to be presented in terms of such factors—selecting the language, style, and format most likely to create a favorable response from the audience;
3. Presenting the matter orally or in writing;
4. Evaluating the effectiveness of the presentation.

It may be noted that audience-oriented communication is not usually a "natural" process for most people. People tend to express their ideas as they come to mind without realizing the relationship between language and form of presentation and audience understanding and response. Special training in this skill is generally required.

Administrators' Discussion. The summaries of the preceding sessions of the workshops indicate that communication was an important emphasis throughout all of the meetings.

Much of the discussion in this particular session reiterated points previously noted: effective communication as an essential aspect of leadership; communication as a major responsibility of the administrative policy-making officer; the importance of training in the techniques of communication; the relationship of communication to practically all of the administrators' activities; the generally unsatisfactory academic preparation in communication that many college graduates manifest in the field. Exception was again taken to the concept of the administrator as a "middleman" or channel of communication rather than as an initiator of ideas and programs.

Several other ideas were also discussed in this session. Both workshop groups emphasized the importance of effective public speaking to the administrator. The participants noted, however, that this skill was used in a variety of settings—council meetings, staff meetings, committee meetings of various kinds, in addition to public assemblages. The administrator deals most often with relatively small groups. Therefore, training in this skill should be related to the kinds of situations in which the administrator most often uses it. Role-playing in typical situations was cited as perhaps the most effective form of training for this skill.

Principal administrators are being called upon increasingly to perform over radio and television, the participants noted. Therefore, they should become familiar with the skills of presentation through these media during their period of academic preparation. Some of the participants also suggested that analysis of his "audience"—superiors, public, subordinates—and anticipation of their probable responses is a continuing process for the administrator, rather than merely one step he observes on occasions when he communicates with them. This kind of analysis, it was suggested, is perhaps the principal mental process of the administrative policy-making officer. However, it was noted, audience-analysis is not a "natural" process and prospective administrators should be consciously trained in this skill.

NEGOTIATION AND CONFERENCE

Staff Presentation. Negotiation and conference may be other names for the skills already discussed under previous categories. But since every administrative policy-making officer spends a great deal of his time in such activities, it was decided that the workshop groups should be asked whether there are skills peculiar to negotiation and conference that have not been covered thus far.

The administrator exercises the skills of negotiation and conference primarily in two types of situations, interviews and group discussions of various kinds. He should therefore be trained in the techniques of interviewing in relation to the major purposes of administrative interviews (eliciting information, disciplining, evaluating activities and people, etc.) and to the types of people he will most frequently interview (superiors, subordinates, citizens, press, etc.). Similarly he should be trained in the techniques of group discussion in terms of the major purposes of such discussion in administration (public hearings, staff conferences, training conferences, etc.), and in the various roles that the administrator may assume in such discussions (conference leader, resource person, working participant).

Administrators' Discussion. The workshop groups thought that negotiation and conference were such important activities of the administrator that they should be listed as a separate category of administrative skills, even though there was probably some overlapping of skills previously discussed. Rather than being separate skills, the participants thought, negotiation and conference referred to specific and very important administrative settings in which practically all of the skills previously discussed would be exercised.

Role-playing was mentioned again as an effective method of training in the skills of negotiation and conference. Such role-playing should be under the guidance of a person who has proven his ability in such activities. The concept of the administrator's role in various kinds of interviews and group meetings was discussed at some length. The importance of the administrator's consciously identifying his role in various kinds of meetings and with the various kinds of groups with whom he meets was stressed. The importance of planning for meetings in terms of both agenda and strategy was mentioned.

CONCLUSION

This session on administrative skills was the final session of both workshops, and time was allocated for some general discussion. It was emphasized in these general discussions, as it had been many times throughout all the sessions of both workshops, that education and training for administrative policy-making careers is a matter of total career development. Many elements of the administrator's position and role analyzed during the workshops required broad administrative experience and maturity; training for them will have to be deferred until such experience and maturity are obtained.

Therefore, career development must be a joint responsibility of colleges and universities and of governmental employers. Higher education can provide only some of the basic knowledge and skills in pre-service educational programs. In-service training, guided career experience, executive development programs—all primarily responsibilities of governmental employers—are necessary if a student is to become the kind of administrative policy-making officer that the workshops delineated.

Finally, it was noted that fundamental to administrative effectiveness is a well-rounded philosophy of government. As one of the city managers expressed it: "One of the essentials is a basic philosophy of government. I have heard councilmen say that they are not concerned so much with the detailed management ability of a manager—they take that for granted. They say they are concerned with the manager's general philosophy of government. They want to know what his attitudes will be toward various general public questions. These attitudes certainly have a profound effect on the direction of the administrative unit."

15

Administrative Leadership in Local and State Government: Its Meaning and Educational Implications

STEPHEN K. BAILEY *
Princeton University

(An address at the annual dinner for in-service students and award of certificates and plaques, Fels Institute of Local and State Government, University of Pennsylvania, September 13, 1956)

In order to be gracious on this important occasion, my first words must necessarily be ones of congratulations.

My first thoughts, however, are ones of uncharitable envy. I am one of those unfortunate human beings who served as a local official without so much as having read a book on local government or administration—let alone having taken systematic courses of the kind that so many of you have recently completed here at Fels Center.

Actually, as a former elected official, I am sorely tempted to picket this place! There is nothing that gives an elected official more of an inferiority complex than to be deferred to by people who know more about anything and everything than he does. There is always a slightly supercilious edge, for example, on the voice of the budget director who

* Stephen K. Bailey, Ph.D., is Professor of Public Affairs, Princeton University.

asks a Governor whether the six new trucks should go on the "capital account." The budget director knows that the Governor doesn't know a capital account from a parking meter. It is only the sophisticated Governor who can look the budget director straight in the eye and say with an imperturbable expression, "I tend to agree with you." This irrelevant reply gets the budget director off the hot seat, and pleases the Governor who figures that the budget director knows more about what should go on a "capital account" than anyone of the opposition legislators—who probably won't raise the issue anyway.

Some day one of you will write a notable treatise on "The Care and Feeding of Elected Officials" in which you will discuss frankly and openly the various ploys and techniques used by career administrators to convince elected officials that it is really *they*—not you—who make policy and run the world.

One of my favorite ploys is the one in which the career administrator goes ahead on his own with some major policy decision—like tearing down the east wall of the city hall. A brick falls on someone's head and the Mayor hears about it. He calls the careerist in and the conversation goes something like this:

The Mayor says, "John, I wish you had coordinated with me before you proceeded to implement your plans." (Note the Mayor's mastery of the careerist's native tongue.)

The careerist replies with a perfectly straight and innocent face—as the east wall crashes to the earth: "Gee, Mayor, I'm sorry. I didn't know you wanted to be bothered with administrative details."

Or the more complicated gambit, when the Police Chief wants three new cruisers. The conversation goes likes this:

The Chief says, "Mayor, don't you think that the Board of Estimates would appreciate it if we got rid of those five old Harley Davidsons which we haven't used since Truman came to town in 1948?"

The Mayor says, "Chief, you're inspired. Economy and efficiency are what we're after."

The Chief replies, "Mayor, economy and efficiency are the words. As a matter of fact, Mayor, I've decided because of the financial situation in this election year that I'm not going to ask for all of the ten additional cruisers we need. We may have to tighten our belts a bit, Mayor; but I figure this way: if I don't ask for seven of those ten additional cruisers, and if I get a good turn-in on the five old motorcycles, we'll save the city $15,000—and that's worth doing, Mayor."

Of course, by the time the Mayor has this one figured out, the Chief has his three new cruisers.

There's quite a science in all this, and I only wish that I'd had a chance to study a few of these basic principles of administration before I was mouse-trapped by them.

However, that is by the by. I am an egghead once again, and so can speak expertly, irresponsibly, and vaguely on almost anything, including tonight's topic: "Administrative Leadership in Local and State Government: Its Meaning and Educational Implications."

Let me start by roaming a bit in the forest of definition. What is a leader? More specifically what is an administrative leader?

Webster's is of only limited help here. Among the dictionary definitions of the word "leader" are the following:

a. a horse placed in advance of others;
b. a pipe for conducting fluid;
c. a net for leading fish into a pound;
d. a short line of transparent fiber used to attach the end of a fish line to the lure;
e. a block of hardwood pierced with suitable holes; and
f. a row of dots or hyphens used to lead the eye across space.

Webster's *is* helpful, however, in defining the verb "to lead." The dictionary uses such equivalent phrases as, "To precede and direct in movement," "To draw or direct by influence," "To induce," "To tend or reach in a certain direction."

In this definitional context, any official in local and State government who can do these things is an administrative leader. An administrative leader may not have the formal power or legal responsibility of a political leader; a low— or middle—level administrator may not have the scope of discretion or of delegated authority of his division or bureau chief; but I am contending here that leadership has nothing to do with formal status of rank, grade, or pay. Administrative leadership in our kind of society is made up of a series of qualities and qualifications which adhere to the person not to his title, position, or salary. Leadership, in short, is not where you are, but what you do with where you are.

In these terms, administrative leadership becomes a series of attitudes and skills which can be exercised by anyone with the capacity and the training.

The question before us, I suppose, is what are some of these attitudes and skills at the local and state level, and to what extent are such attitudes and skills trainable.

I think the first part of this question is easier to answer than the last part.

From direct observation I think I can identify at least four major attitudes or skills which most administrative leaders in my experience have had:

The first is what I should call a sense of organizational relevance. There are some administrators who never get the feel of their precise role in the common purpose of a large and variegated enterprise; but an administrative leader always does. When a lifeguard for the State Park Department saves a kid's life, the true administrative leader sees in his mind's eye not one, but a dozen heroes: the lifeguard himself; the girl in the personnel office who processed the lifeguard's initial papers; the secretary to the head of the Park Department who typed out the lifeguard's assignment; the messenger boy who delivered it; the purchasing agent who made out the "specs" for the pulmotor used by the lifeguard; the truck driver who delivered the pulmotor to the shed near the swimming pool; the clerk in the Treasurer's office who made out the checks for the pulmotor and for the salaries of all those mentioned so far; the tax collector who collected the funds part of which were used to make the payments possible;—and I could go on and on.

The successful administrative leader, like the successful pilot, is the one who always takes account of what's above him, what's below him, and what's on both sides of him, in relation to what is in front of him.

The administrative leader, putting this same point another way, has a sense of community—a sense of common purpose—a sense that it is only in relationship to those above, below, and on both sides that the problems ahead can really be solved.

The most effective coordination of policy is not the result of mechanical instruments of coordination operating at the level of the Mayor, Manager, or Governor. It is the result of the quiet leadership of men down the line who have a sense of organizational relevance.

You and I can think of scores of examples: the school superintendent who cooperates with the Park Department in the joint use of recreation facilities for young people; the Welfare director who tries to work with the police, the courts, and with private agencies in handling more intelligently the complex problems of alcoholism; the highway department clerk who has a new idea for a safety sticker on number plates and sells the idea to a clerk in the motor vehicle department during the coffee break.

But this sense of organizational relevance is of no importance whatsoever unless it is coupled with human warmth and understanding. I once knew a director of health who had a fine sense of organizational relevance but who pursued his objectives with such self-righteous vigor that he raised the ire of every other department head in sight. What, if approached in the right spirit could have been cooperation and coordination, turned into nothing but a series of jurisdictional squabbles. Skill in human relations—the capacity to induce rather than order consent—is a necessary quality in the administrative leader at all levels. This is drummed into our heads so often that it has become a banality. The trouble is we accept the proposition and then do little about it. It is always the other fellow who needs to change his ways. I think it is Gordon Gray, in the Department of Defense, who has in his office a little sign reading, "If I could only kick the fellow who is responsible for nine-tenths of my troubles, I wouldn't be able to sit down for a month."

The third requisite of an administrative leader is enthusiasm coupled with courage. I suppose in any large organization it is possible to find a variety of administrative types. There are some administrators who spend their working days plotting how to avoid work. There are others who are not particularly lazy, but who roll with punches thrown by others. They do the job assigned faithfully, never stick their necks out, and drone their life away. There are still others who go along with suggestions for change, but do so reluctantly—hedging bets between the old and the new.

The administrative leader is none of these. He is the man who exudes contagious excitement about his work. He is the man who is never entirely satisfied with the way things are going and has the courage to say so. He is the man who is concerned with procedure not as an end in itself, but as a means of achieving certain values in his organization and in society generally. As I have said in a related context, "Leadership is not just the anticipation of tomorrow; it is the creation of tomorrow." Leadership is dreaming dreams and making those dreams come true.

The man who has lost enthusiasm, who has lost vision and drive and the courage of his convictions, has no right to hang out his slate as an administrative leader.

Finally, the administrative leader at most levels of local and state government must be technically proficient in the procedural as well as the substantive aspects of his job. The stuff of modern government is complex. One definition of a "do-gooder" is a man who feels strongly but doesn't know how. Just as there is a danger in having personnel or budget officers who believe that organizational symmetry and strict conformity to the rule book are the goals of all administration, so there is a danger in having in our local and state governments administrative officials who are well-intentioned but unskilled and careless of channels.

To paraphrase Dwight L. Moody, "Government is too important to be left to duffers."

If what I have said so far makes any sense: that administrative leadership involves (1) a sense of organizational relevance; (2) a capacity for human warmth and understanding; (3) a spirit of enthusiasm and courage; and (4) technical proficiency—the tough assignment remains of relating these qualities and skills to our present and prospective educational purposes and endeavors.

I am frank to admit that I do not know whether human warmth and understanding and qualities like enthusiasm and courage are trainable in any formal sense. As one who heads a Graduate Program designed to train "leaders," I can only admit rather shamefacedly that I hedge my bets on this one by trying to make sure that those I admit to the School have some of these desirable qualities to begin with. Perhaps the first educational implication of my four-fold definition of administrative leadership is that we had better spend at least as much time in discovering and recruiting leaders as in training them.

But this leads into an even more distressing admission. As far as I know, no one yet has invented a Geiger counter to identify potential leaders. If there were some way of trotting through Wanamaker's or the Upper Darby High School on a busy day with a little electronic device that would shout "Eureka" every time we passed a potential leader, you and I could be in business. As a matter of fact, business could be in business. Industrial firms are presently spending hundreds of thousands of dollars every year in an attempt to discover through various tests and experiments the elusive qualities which make for "executive leadership." Maybe they are further ahead than I think. I am dubious that we are on the verge of turning human selection into a science.

But I am not totally convinced that education is irrelevant to the formulation of attitudes and sympathies. If I were so convinced, I'm not sure I'd stick with my present profession. The question is, however, have most educational institutions taken seriously this responsibility of motivating students, and cultivating their attitudes and sympathies? Actually, if there is one thunderbolt I should like to hurl generally at educators and practitioners in the field of local and state government over the past 50 years it is that all too often they have succeeded in transforming some of the most exciting enterprises in the world into dull problems in bookkeeping. Unless this process is reversed, local and state governments will fall increasingly into the hands of men and women equipped with photostatic lenses

instead of eyes and Friedens instead of hearts. I have a suspicion that the reason why we are pushing to analyse the
meaning and dimensions of leadership at the local and state
level is because we are frightened by the homogenized grey
fog which seems to have settled over so much of our state
and local government—turning everything into a kind of
emotionless limbo.

The blame for this limbo is not easily placed. But some
blame, at least, must fall upon the educational institutions
which have established curricula in government and administration seemingly devoid of any purpose but that of
choking life and enthusiasm in a quagmire of figures,
charts, procedural routines, and forms.

Why is it that so many able students can get excited
about saving the Belgian Congo; but so few can get excited about saving Newark? It is in part because no one
traipses around to the various schools and colleges trying
to make Newark exciting. But even if someone succeeded
in making Newark exciting, the young student enthusiast
would then ask, "How can I best train for a career in
Newark?" Like as not, the answer would come, "Take a
course in administration or budgeting or personnel some-
where." If nothing else does, this anwer, for many students,
will kill the will-to-go-on deader than a mackerel.

Too often we forget that local and state governments
have jobs for architects and engineers, educators and scientists, lawyers and social workers, doctors and economists,
law enforcement officers and psychiatrists—in fact, for almost every kind of technically-qualified man or woman in
our society. The State of New York lists 2700 different
kinds of jobs in state employment. Many of these jobs involve satisfactions unmatched in private enterprise or in
the federal service. The rewards are often intangible, but
they are nonetheless real: educating the young; protecting

the community against diseases; caring for and curing the sick and the mentally ill and handicapped; protecting the citizenry against fraud and greed and violence; abating nuisances; abolishing slums; building schools and playgrounds; promoting safety; planning highways; attracting new commerce and industry; reforming penal codes and practices; rehabilitating alcoholics; changing the lives of potential delinquents; healing the wounds of social, racial, and religious intolerance; creating parks; conserving and identifying sources of potable water; in short sustaining and creating the conditions of a decent future for ourselves and our posterity.

If we are to capture the imagination of potential administrative leaders we must do so in large measure by getting them to sense the enormous excitement of the various enterprises of government. And specialists in public administration must proselytize in—and insinuate themselves into—those educational institutions where motivation is already high, but not particularly directed towards local or state government: schools of architecture, education, medicine, law, physical education, theology, business, engineering, foresty, and social work. Furthermore, the frontiers of knowledge in these professional schools must somehow be communicated to our schools of public administration and public affairs. As this new knowledge becomes available, new kinds of budgetary questions will almost certainly be framed in our state and local governments. For example, if we raise the recreation, housing, welfare, and psychiatric budgets by 50% for the next ten years, by what percentage should we be able by the end of that time to cut our budgets for police, prisons, and mental institutions? Surely this is not an impossible kind of question. The answer may be inexact; but if we took this kind of question seriously, it would knock the stuffing out of the whole custodial concept which has kept us from improving our penal and other institutional practices in line with the dictates of humaneness and common sense.

We desperately need men of compassion and knowledge from other professional schools and university departments loaned to our schools and institutes of public administration to keep before our students' eyes the human goals of our local and state governments, and the new skills and knowledge available for reaching these goals.

Among other things, this may mean that we must rely more heavily than in the past upon apprenticeship-on-the-job for the mastery of some of the technical details of administration. I suppose this is heresy; but in a college senior about to enter public service, at the local or state level, I should be willing any day in the week to sacrifice a sophisticated knowledge of "personnel classification systems since 1883" for a good healthy understanding of the medical, psychiatric, and sociological problems of alcoholism or old age. I'd sacrifice a knowledge of six different ways of preparing a performance budget for even a partial comprehension of the relationship of economics to aesthetics in city planning. This does not mean that the housekeeping details of government are unimportant; it only means that a girl does not have to be a cooking expert before her wedding day in order to be a good wife and mother later on. There are some things she will learn on the job because she has to. We can't learn everything in school.

This, of course, is not an either-or proposition. What I have been trying to suggest is that if we wish to turn to our educational institutions to supply motivations, attitudes and sympathies for the public servant, we must not permit them to make the mistake that so many of our teachers colleges have made—of placing almost total emphasis upon techniques at the sacrifice of substance. Excitement and courage come from a belief in some value—some goal; not simply in the knowledge of administrative process.

Once the enthusiasm is aroused or identified, however, our institutes and schools of administration and government can contribute mightily in giving the actual or potential administrator a greater sense of organizational relevance and a greater sophistication in human relations and administrative techniques. The administrative leader is always faced with the twin problems of managing old programs and building consent for new ones. Our educational institutions and our in-service training programs must supply him with the tools and organizational concepts for accomplishing the ends he seeks.

What I said facetiously at the beginning of this paper I now return to in conclusion with dead seriousness. Elected officials come and go. This is as it should be in a representative democracy. But the Jacksonian myth that anyone can run the business of government has never been true. Today such a myth is preposterous. Policy leadership at the state and local level must increasingly come from career administrative officials who see the needs and who knock on the doors of their elected superiors until the latter assume public responsibility for action. This function of policy initiation must be exercised with discretion, with attention to channels, and with ultimate deference to the priorities set by elected officials. But it must be exercised nonetheless. The idea that career administrators have no responsibility except to carry out someone else's wishes is a tragically negative concept; and has limited the attractiveness of important positions at the local and state level. You people are in the most important enterprise on earth. Don't sell it short by waiting around for orders to come from above. The orders you want won't come unless you help make them come.

Let me say one final word: I am sure that some of you,

like some of my present and former students, have had
moments of thinking that careers in local and state governments are very low-voltage affairs; that all of the important
and exciting things really happen at the national or international levels of government. As one who has worked in
the local, state, and national arenas of government I can
only say that my experience has led me to realize that the
satisfactions and deferences attendant upon identification
with big-name organizations—public and private—exact
their own cost: in the very frustrations of size; in limitations upon individuality; in the coldness and loneliness of
power. The philosopher William James, who had known
unusual fame and prestige, wrote towards the end of his
life the following relevant words:

> I am done with great things and big things, great institu-
> tions and big success, and I am for those tiny, invisible,
> molecular moral forces that work from individual to indi-
> vidual, creeping through the crannies of the world like so
> many soft rootlets, or like the capillary oozing of water, yet
> which, if you will give them time, will rend the hardest
> monuments of men's pride.

This many of you know and understand. The recreation
director in Podunk, the state commissioner of education,
the county welfare worker—none of these may sign the
treaty of peace which will end all war. But theirs will be
the final glory; for it will be they, and others like them—
like you—who will help make possible the eventual victory
of man over himself—to which any meaningful treaty of
peace will be but a ceremonial flourish.

Appendix I.
Survey of Graduate Education Programs in Public Administration*

INTRODUCTION

This is a report on the results of a limited survey of graduate education programs in public administration. The study was limited to programs of a general character—excluding professional education, such as law, engineering, social work, or public health. The survey techniques were limited to a questionnaire sent to some 132 educational institutions designed to elicit fundamental program data—such as degree title, degree requirements, course requirements, thesis requirements, internship requirements, and institutional organization arrangements —and a review and analysis of the catalogs and program announcements which were readily available. The study was not designed to provide definitive answers to specific questions but rather to provide background data for this conference on training.

OVER-ALL QUESTIONNAIRE RESULTS

The questionnaires were sent to 132 educational institutions in the United States, Hawaii and Puerto Rico. The list of schools was primarily compiled from the 105 schools listed in the 1952 Public Administration Service report titled, "Educational Preparation for Public Administration." In addition, 27 other schools were included in an attempt to broaden the survey base.

Replies were received from 86 schools or approximately 65 percent of the survey base. An initial classification was made as follows:

* This survey was made and report prepared by Stanley Guild under the supervision of George S. Blair, Fels Institute of Local and State Government, University of Pennsylvania.

Group I. 45 schools which offer a Master's degree in Public Administration.

Group II. 30 schools which offer a Master's degree with some courses in Public Administration.

Group III. 11 schools which do not offer graduate study.

All of the schools in Group I indicated that preparation of graduates for the public service was a recognized objective, while three schools in each of the other two groups indicated that this training is not a recognized objective. Therefore, a second classification was made which eliminated all of Group III and the three schools in Group II which indicated that training for the public service was not an objective. The remainder of this report will be confined to 72 schools, 45 in Group I and 27 in Group II.

DETAILED QUESTIONNAIRE RESULTS

GROUP I—SCHOOLS OFFERING A MASTER'S DEGREE IN PUBLIC ADMINISTRATION

A. *Title of the degree*

The traditional title "Master of Arts" was the most common being used at 17 institutions or 38 percent of the schools while the "Master of Public Administration" is granted at 13 schools or 30 percent. For the remaining 15 schools, a wide range of degree titles is evident with only one common trend being apparent—the use of the traditional "Master of Arts" title and the addition of the words "in Public Administration," or "in Government." The following is a summary of the titles used:

Title	No. of Schools Using
Master of Arts	17
Master of Public Administration	13
Master of Arts in Public Administration	5
Master of Arts in Government	3
Master of Science in Public Administration	2

Master of Governmental Administration 1
Master of Arts in Public Management 1
Master of Public Affairs 1
Master of Political Science 1
Master of Science 1

B. *Semester hours required for degree*

The number of semester hours required for the degree ranged from a high of 62 hours to a low of 24. The normal requirement of 30 hours of graduate study was by far the most prevalent, being required at 23 schools or slightly over 50 percent. Cornell University, one of the schools requiring 62 semester hours, indicated this to be a minimum requirement which is "apt to run up to 70 hours over a two-year period." Several of the schools which require 24 hours for the degree indicated this to be a minimum that did not include credits for a required thesis. The University of Connecticut indicated a 24-hour requirement without a thesis or "15 hours with thesis, which is unusual." The following is a summary of the requirements:

Semester Hours	*No. of Schools Requiring*
62*	2
42	1
32	1
38	2
36	5
35	1
34	1
32	3
30	23
29	1
28	1
24	5

* For the University of Pennsylvania this includes: 30 academic hours, 16 field work credits and 16 prerequisite credits.

C. *Level of government*

In response to this question 17 schools or 38 percent indicated that their programs were designed to prepare students for all levels. Typical statements were: "All, and about equal," "no differentiation," and "program not focused in this way." In addition, three schools indicated at least partial emphasis on international. The one school which indicated state emphasis only was Puerto Rico. The following is a summary of the responses to this question:

Level	No. of Schools	Percent
All levels	17	38
State-local	9	20
Federal	7	15
Local	5	11
Federal-state	3	
State	1	
No answer	2	

D. *Course of study*

Thirty-three schools or 68 percent of the total indicated prescribed core subjects, plus some electives, while 9 schools or 20 percent indicated a prescribed curriculum and 6 schools or 12 percent do not have specific course requirements. It is interesting to note that of the 9 schools which have a prescribed curriculum, 5 indicate that they emphasize state and local government, 2 local government and 2 all levels. Of the 6 schools indicating "all electives," 2 prepare students for all levels, 2 for federal service and 2 for state and local government. Of the 33 schools which have prescribed "core subjects, plus electives," 17 schools or slightly over 50 percent prepare students for all levels of government, while the remaining 16 schools in this category are about evenly divided between preparation for federal, state and local and local government. A summary of the responses to this question follows:

Course of Study	No. of Schools
All electives	6
Prescribed curriculum	9
Core subjects, plus electives	33

E. *Number of semester hours of core subjects*

Of the 29 * schools which indicated a prescribed curriculum of "core subjects, plus electives," 17 schools or 58 percent prescribed 50 percent or more of the required hours in core subjects. A summary follows:

Approx. Percent Core Hours of Total Hours Required	No. of Schools
25 or less	5
33	6
50 or more	17

A tabulation of the number of core-subject hours and the number of schools reporting is as follows:

No. of Core Hours	No. of Schools
30	2
27	2
24	1
20	2
18	4
15	7
12	5
10	1
9	1
8	1
6	4
No answer	3

F. *Analysis of catalog and program materials of 16 schools reporting "core subjects, plus electives" or prescribed curriculum or both*

* *Four questionnaires could not be considered on this question because of inadequate answers.*

An analysis of catalog materials of 16 schools indicated that three courses, Organization and Management, Public Personnel and Public Finance, are required in 12 schools or 75 percent of the base group. A course in law, either constitutional or administrative, was found to be required in 10 schools. In addition, a seminar in public administration, which may be titled as "Theory and Practice of Public Administration," "Administrative Policy," "Problems in Public Administration," or "Principles of Public Administration" is a required course at 10 schools.. A tabulation of the frequency of like or similar course titles follows:

Course Title	No. of Schools Requiring
Organization and Management	12
Public Personnel	12
Public Finance	12
Law—Administrative, Constitutional, etc.	10
Seminar in Public Administration	10
Research and Writing	6
State and Local Administrative Problems	6
Public Budgeting	5
Accounting	5
Planning	5
Purchasing	3
Line Functions	3
Statistics	2

G. *Internship requirements*

Regarding an internship or field-work requirement, the schools are divided almost equally with 23 requiring either an internship or governmental experience and 22 schools not having any requirements. One school in the latter group, Illinois, indicated that an internship program is being planned. A tabulation of internship requirements follows:

No. of Schools

22	Do not require
18	Do require
2	Recommend, and in practice becomes mandatory
2	Require if student does not have government experience
1	Requires governmental experience prior to entry

H. *Time of internship*

A tabulation of the answers to this question follows:

No. of Schools	*Time*	*Length*
6	After completion of residence	(1½-12 mos.—aver. 6 mos.)
3	Prior to residence	(3 and 6 mos.)
2	During residence	(2 and 18 mos.)
4	During and after residence	(Part-time employment and after res. 3, 6 and 12 month internships)
2	Summer between years	(3 mos.)
1	Optional	(6 mos. during res. and 6 mos. after res.)

I. *Academic credit for internship*

Of the 18 schools which specifically require an internship, 6 give academic credit for this work and 12 do not give credit. One school gives 5 hours credit, two schools give 6 hours, one gives 8 hours, one gives from 12 to 15 hours and one gives 16 hours.

J. *Thesis requirement*

Of the 45 schools responding to this question, 28 schools reported that a thesis is required and 17 either do not require a thesis or offer the student an option. A tabulation of the results is as follows:

No. of Schools

28	Require thesis
10	Do not require thesis
7	Optional

Of the group of 10 schools which do not require a thesis, 6 schools reported that a seminar which might be called "Research and Writing" is substituted. One school reported that a "substantial report is required" and another school reported "a heavy emphasis in writing in all courses." Two schools do not have any substitute requirements.

The 7 schools which comprise the optional group usually offer the student one or more of the following choices: a thesis, a case study, additional class hours, one or more advanced seminars, or an internship with a written report.

A tabulation of the academic credit hours granted by those which require a thesis is as follows:

No. of Schools	*Semester Hours Credit*
6	0
6	4
2	5
10	6
2	8
1	9

K. *Number of students completing programs*

In response to this question, the 45 schools indicated that a total of 389 students were granted Master's degrees annually. A tabulation of these results is as follows:

6 schools ranging from 20 to 45 students account for 192 students
10 schools ranging from 8 to 15 students account for 111 students
25 schools ranging from 1 to 5 students account for 86 students

41 schools reported   389 students

Detailed Breakdown of Average Number of Graduates

No. of Schools	Average No. of Students
1	40-45
1	40
1	30
1	25
1	22
1	20
3	15
5	10
2	8
9	5
3	4
5	2
2	1
4	No answer

L.	*Institutional Arrangement*	No. of Schools
	Department of Political Science	23
	School of Public Administration	11
	Institute of Public Administration	5
	School of Business and Public Administration	5
	Regional Program (three schools)	1

GROUP II—SCHOOLS OFFERING A MASTER'S DEGREE IN POLITICAL
SCIENCE WITH SOME PUBLIC ADMINISTRATION

The answers to the questionnaires by the schools which fall
into this group were too incomplete for a valid statistical analysis. However, a review of the answers to specific questions
provides a few facts which may be illuminating.

Three schools indicate the existence of a bureau or institute
of public administration. Two schools do not require a thesis
for the Master's degree and one school has an optional requirement. The schools which do not require a thesis do not indi-

cate any substitute requirement. One of these schools does indicate that a thesis requirement is planned.

Of the schools which indicate the number of required hours,
30 hours is by far the most prevalent. In several schools 32 to
36 hours are required. Nine schools indicated that prescribed
"core subjects, plus electives" are required. In these 9 schools,
the "core subjects" represent from 9 to 12 semester hours credit.

In response to the question "What level (or levels) of government service is the primary focus of your program?", 18 schools
indicated all levels, 4 schools indicated federal, 3 indicated
state-local and one indicated state government.

No school in this group indicated an internship requirement
but 5 schools indicated that an internship program was offered
or was an optional requirement. One school indicated that an
internship program is planned and one school gives 3 hours of
academic credit for the internship.

GROUP III—SCHOOLS WHICH DO NOT OFFER GRADUATE STUDY
IN PUBLIC ADMINISTRATION OR POLITICAL SCIENCE

The responses to the questionnaires in this group were not
complete enough for comment. Most of these schools offer an
undergraduate major but did not answer enough questions to
provide any information.

Appendix II.
Conference on
Education and Training for Administrative Careers in Local and State Government
June 12, 13, and 14, 1957

Authors, Chairmen, and Panelists

General Chairman: LLOYD M. SHORT, Chairman of the Department of Political Science and Director of the Public Administration Center, University of Minnesota

Desirable Subjects and Emphases in Pre-Service Curricula

Chairman: STEPHEN K. BAILEY, Professor of Public Affairs, Princeton University

Authors: GEORGE S. BLAIR, Educational and Research Associate, Fels Institute of Local and State Government, and Associate Professor of Political Science, University of Pennsylvania

ROSCOE C. MARTIN, Professor of Political Science, Maxwell Graduate School of Citizenship and Public Affairs, Syracuse University *

WALLACE S. SAYRE, Professor of Public Administration, Department of Public Law and Government, Columbia University *

---

* *Presented papers to the Conference.*

349

Panelists: HAROLD F. ALDERFER, Executive Deputy
Secretary, Department of Public Instruc-
tion, Harrisburg, Pennsylvania; formerly
Professor of Political Science and Execu-
tive Secretary, Institute of Local Govern-
ment, Pennsylvania State University
RICHARD H. McCLEERY, Instructor in
Political Science, Michigan State University
NORMAN D. PALMER, Professor of Politi-
cal Science, University of Pennsylvania
GEORGE A. WARP, Associate Professor of
Political Science and Associate Director of
the Public Administration Center, Univer-
sity of Minnesota

Teaching Methods—Course Instruction

Chairman: JOHN M. GAUS, Professor of Government,
Harvard University

Authors: FREDRICK T. BENT, Educational and
Research Associate, Fels Institute of Local
and State Government, and Assistant Professor of Political Science, University of
Pennsylvania
JOSEPH E. McLEAN, Commissioner of Conservation and Economic Development, State
of New Jersey; formerly professor of Politics, Woodrow Wilson School of Public
and International Affairs, Princeton University *

Panelists: EDWIN A. BOK, Staff Director, Inter-University Case Program, New York City
RICHARD T. FROST, Instructor, Woodrow

* Presented papers to the Conference.

Wilson School of Public and International Affairs, Princeton University

GERALD J. GRADY, Assistant Professor of Government, University of Maine

PHILIP E. JACOB, Professor of Political Science, University of Pennsylvania

DONALD W. SMITHBURG, Associate Professor of Political Science, Illinois Institute of Technology

Teaching Methods—Field Experience

Chairman: GEORGE A. SHIPMAN, Professor of Public Administration and Director of the Institute of Public Affairs, University of Washington

Authors: THOMAS J. DAVY, Educational and Research Associate, Fels Institute of Local and State Government, and Assistant Professor of Political Science, University of Pennsylvania

YORK WILLBERN, Professor of Political Science and Director of the Bureau of Public Administration, University of Alabama *

Panelists: GARY P. BRAZIER, Assistant Professor of Political Science, Western Reserve University

ROBERT J. MOWITZ, Associate Professor of Political Science, Wayne State University

LYNTON K. CALDWELL, Professor of Government, Indiana University

* *Presented papers to the Conference.*

**Equipping the Professionally Trained Functional
Specialist for General Administrative Responsibility**

Chairman: JAMES C. CHARLESWORTH, Professor
of Political Science, University of Pennsylvania

Authors: JAMES G. COKE, Educational and Research
Associate, Fels Institute of Local and State
Government, and Assistant Professor of
Political Science, University of Pennsyl-
vania

JOHN W. LEDERLE, Professor of Political
Science and Director of the Bureau of
Public Administration, University of
Michigan *

Panelists: HAROLD G. REUSCHLEIN, Dean of the
Law School, Villanova University

RUTH E. SMALLEY, Professor of Social
Casework and Vice-Dean, the School of Social Work, University of Pennsylvania

WILLIAM L. C. WHEATON, Professor of
City Planning and Director of the Institute
for Urban Studies, University of Pennsylvania

ROBERT F. WILCOX, Professor of Political Science, San Diego State College

**The Respective Roles of Higher Education and Govern-
mental Employers in Preparing People for Professional
Administrative Careers**

Chairman: JOHN D. MILLETT, President, Miami
University

Authors: THOMAS J. DAVY, Educational and Research Associate, Fels Institute of Local

* Presented papers to the Conference.

and State Government, and Assistant Professor of Political Science, University of Pennsylvania

HENRY REINING, JR., Professor of Public Administration and Dean, School of Public Administration, University of Southern California; President, American Society for Public Administration *

Panelists: JOHN H. FERGUSON, Secretary of Administration and Budget Secretary, Commonwealth of Pennsylvania; Professor of Political Science, Pennsylvania State University

ELMER D. GRAPER, Emeritus Professor of Political Science, and former Director of the Institute of Local Government, University of Pittsburgh; Chairman of the Civil Service Commission of Pennsylvania

ROBERT J. M. MATTESON, Executive Director, American Society for Public Administration

Higher Education and Training for Administrative Careers—Retrospect and Prospect

Chairman: GEORGE A. GRAHAM, Ford Foundation

Author: JOHN A. PERKINS, President, University of Delaware *

Panelists: HARLAN CLEVELAND, Dean, Maxwell Graduate School of Citizenship and Public Affairs, Syracuse University

DONALD C. STONE, Dean of the Graduate School of Public and International Affairs, University of Pittsburgh

* Presented papers to the Conference.

Other Participants

Kenneth Appel, Professor of Psychiatry, University of Pennsylvania

John A. Bailey, Deputy Managing Director, Philadelphia

Sidney Baldwin, Assistant Professor of Public Administration, New York University

Samuel S. Baxter, Commissioner of Water, Philadelphia

Charles Beale, Library Assistant, Fels Institute of Local and State Government, University of Pennsylvania

John Q. Benford, Government Service Consultant, Fels Institute of Local and State Government, University of Pennsylvania

William C. Beyer, Educational and Research Associate, Fels Institute of Local and State Government, and Associate Professor of Political Science, University of Pennsylvania

Don K. Bowen, Assistant Director, American Society for Public Administration

Marvin Bressler, Assistant Professor of Sociology, University of Pennsylvania

William Brody, Administrative Services Director, Department of Public Health, Philadelphia

R. Jean Brownlee, Associate Professor of Political Science, University of Pennsylvania

Henry C. Bush, Assistant Professor of Political Science, Wayne State University

Charles P. Cella, Jr., Supervisor, Government Consulting Service, Fels Institute of Local and State Government, University of Pennsylvania

Albert Coates, Professor of Political Science and Director, Institute of Local Government, University of North Carolina

Miss Katherine Cox, Isabelle Bronk Fellow, Fels Institute of Local and State Government, University of Pennsylvania

John Dolbashian, Technical Assistant, Government Consulting Service, Fels Institute of Local and State Government, University of Pennsylvania

James R. Donoghue, Associate Professor of Political Science, University of Wisconsin

John M. Gillespie, Director, Institute of Public Administration, University of Massachusetts

Ward H. Goodenough, Assistant Professor of Anthropology, University of Pennsylvania

Frederick P. Gruenberg, Treasurer, Samuel S. Fels Fund, Philadelphia

Stanley Guild, Research Assistant, Fels Institute of Local and State Government, University of Pennsylvania

Henry D. Harral, Executive Deputy Secretary, Department of Highways, Pennsylvania; Supervisor of Municipal Assistance Service, Fels Institute of Local and State Government, University of Pennsylvania

Miss Margaret M. Henrich, Librarian, Fels Institute of Local and State Government, University of Pennsylvania

G. Wright Hoffman, Professor of Insurance and Marketing, University of Pennsylvania; Director, Bureau of Business and Public Administration, University of Karachi

Charles A. Hollister, Assistant Director, Bureau of Municipal Affairs, Department of Internal Affairs, Pennsylvania

J. Perry Horlacher, Professor of Political Science, University of Pennsylvania

Walter Isard, Professor of Economics, University of Pennsylvania

C. Arthur Kulp, Dean of the Wharton School, University of Pennsylvania

Rodney P. Lane, Government Service Consultant, Fels Institute of Local and State Government, University of Pennsylvania

Charles F. Leedecker, Executive Secretary, Institute of Local Government, Pennsylvania State University

Norman Lourie, Executive Deputy Secretary, Department of Welfare, Pennsylvania

Morton Lustig, Assistant Supervisor, Government Consulting Service, Fels Institute of Local and State Government, University of Pennsylvania

Stuart A. MacCorkle, Professor of Government and Director, Institute of Public Affairs, University of Texas

John T. McHugh, Government Service Consultant, Fels Institute of Local and State Government, University of Pennsylvania

Hugo V. Mailey, Professor of Political Science, Wilkes College

Raymond F. Male, Executive Assistant to the Governor, New Jersey

Martin A. D. Meyerson, Professor of City Planning, University of Pennsylvania

Miss Elizabeth S. Micheals, Administrative Assistance, Fels Institute of Local and State Government, University of Pennsylvania

William R. Monat, Assistant Professor of Political Science, Wayne State University

G. Sieber Pancoast, Professor of Political Science, Ursinus College

Arnold R. Post, Government Service Consultant, Fels Institute of Local and State Government, University of Pennsylvania

Jonathan E. Rhoads, Provost, University of Pennsylvania

William B. Rogers, Government Service Consultant, Fels Institute of Local and State Government, University of Pennsylvania

Donald T. Sheehan, Director of Public Relations, University of Pennsylvania

Robert Sigafoos, Director of Research, Institute of Local Government, Pennsylvania State University

Sterling D. Spero, Professor of Public Administration, New York University

Ralph D. Tive, Director, Civil Service Commission, Pennsylvania

Dell R. Tredinnick, Government Service Consultant, Fels Institute of Local and State Government, University of Pennsylvania

Donald C. Wagner, Managing Director, Philadelphia

Mark M. Walter, Director, Board of Vocational Rehabilitation, Commonwealth of Pennsylvania

Malcolm L. Webb, Government Service Consultant, Fels Institute of Local and State Government, University of Pennsylvania

Miss Pauline Wert, Director of Training, Commonwealth of Pennsylvania

Robert P. Wray, Deputy Secretary, Department of Public Assistance, Pennsylvania

Appendix III.
Workshops on
The Position and Role of the
Administrative Policy-Making Officer

PROGRAM

Leadership Role of Administrative Policy-Making Officers
Responsibilities of Administrative Policy-Making Officers
Knowledge Needed for the Administrator's Role and Responsibilities
Skills Needed for the Administrator's Role and Responsibilities
Summary and General Discussion

Participants in Workshop No. 1
November 24, 25, 1956
St. Louis, Missouri

Chairman: L. P. COOKINGHAM,* City Manager
Kansas City, Missouri

LYNN ANDREWS	Assistant City Manager, San Antonio, Texas
W. BARTON AVERY	City Manager, Springfield, Missouri
TOM E. CHENOWETH	City Manager, St. Louis Park, Minnesota
CLARENCE H. ELLIOTT	City Manager, Kalamazoo, Michigan
ELDER GUNTER	City Manager, University City, Missouri
PORTER W. HOMER	City Manager, Tucson, Arizona
ED. S. HOWELL	City Manager, Richmond, California
LEONARD G. HOWELL	City Manager, Des Moines, Iowa

* *International City Managers' Association Training Committee.*

BERT W. JOHNSON	City Manager, Evanston, Illinois
MARK E. KEANE	City Manager, Oak Park, Illinois
MATTHIAS E. LUKENS	President, American Society for Public Administration; Assistant Executive Director, Port of New York Authority
*ROBERT B. MORRIS	City Manager, Glencoe, Illinois
*DONALD M. OAKES	City Manager, Grand Rapids, Michigan
DAVID D. ROWLANDS	City Manager, Tacoma, Washington
*CARLETON F. SHARPE	City Manager, Hartford, Connecticut
SAMUEL E. VICKERS	City Manager, Long Beach, California
DONALD C. WAGNER	Managing Director, Philadelphia, Pennsylvania
*JOHN B. WENTZ	Administrative Officer, Beverly Hills, California
RAY WILSON	City Manager, Phoenix, Arizona
ROSS E. WINDOM	City Manager, St. Petersburg, Florida
GRAHAM WATT	Assistant to the City Manager, Kansas City, Missouri
FREDRICK T. BENT	Educational Associate, Fels Institute of Local and State Government, University of Pennsylvania
DON L. BOWEN	Assistant Director, American Society for Public Administration
JEPTHA J. CARRELL	Training Director, International City Managers' Association
THOMAS J. DAVY	Educational Associate, Fels Institute of Local and State Government, University of Pennsylvania
ORIN F. NOLTING	Executive Director, International City Managers' Association
LLOYD M. SHORT	Director, Public Administration Center, University of Minnesota
*EDWIN O. STENE	Professor of Political Science, University of Kansas

* *International City Managers' Association Training Committee.*

*STEPHEN B. SWEENEY   Director, Fels Institute of Local and State Government, University of Pennsylvania

*HUGO WALL   Professor of Political Science, University of Wichita

Participants in Workshop No. 2
March 20 and 21, 1957
Chicago, Illinois

Chairman: DR. LLOYD M. SHORT, Director
Public Administration Center,
University of Minnesota

ROBERT L. ANDERSON   Superintendent of Public Works and Engineer, Winnetka, Illinois

ROBERT T. ANDERSON   Assistant Administrative Officer, County of Los Angeles, California

WAYNE F. ANDERSON   Finance Director and Comptroller, Evanston, Illinois

FRANK BANE   Executive Director, Council of State Governments

SAMUEL S. BAXTER   Commissioner, Water Department, Philadelphia, Pennsylvania

CHARLES BOLTON   Director, Water Department, Cincinnati, Ohio

CARL H. CHATTERS   City Comptroller, Chicago, Illinois

JOHN H. FERGUSON   Secretary of Administration, Commonwealth of Pennsylvania

FRED K. HOEHLER   Consultant to the Mayor, Chicago, Illinois

FRANK M. LANDERS   Director, Budget Division, Department of Administration, State of Michigan

JOSEPH D. LOHMAN   Sheriff, Cook County, Illinois

* *International City Managers' Association Training Committee.*

JOSEPH E. McLEAN	Commissioner, Department of Conservation and Economic Development, State of New Jersey
F. S. OSTERTAG	Assistant City Manager, Corpus Christi, Texas
HAYES A. RICHARDSON	Director of Welfare, Kansas City, Missouri
GEORGE G. SCHMID	Public Service Director, Grand Rapids, Michigan
HARRIS STEVENS	Director of Finance, Oak Park, Illinois
ROBERT WRAY	Deputy Secretary of Public Assistance, Commonwealth of Pennsylvania
EARL O. WRIGHT	Chief, Division of Administration, State Department of Health, Ohio
FREDRICK T. BENT	Educational Associate, Fels Institute of Local and State Government, University of Pennsylvania
DON L. BOWEN	Assistant Director, American Society for Public Administration
THOMAS J. DAVY	Educational Associate, Fels Institute of Local and State Government, University of Pennsylvania
STEPHEN B. SWEENEY	Director, Fels Institute of Local and State Government, University of Pennsylvania

Index